THAT I MAY BE HIS OWN

THAT I MAY BE HIS OWN

AN OVERVIEW OF LUTHER'S CATECHISMS

CHARLES P. ARAND

CONCORDIA PUBLISHING HOUSE · SAINT LOUIS

ACADEMIC PRESS

To My Children
Becky and Benjamin

Library of Congress Cataloging-in-Publication Data

Arand, Charles P.
    That I may be His own : an overview of Luther's catechisms / Charles P. Arand.
        p. cm.
    Includes bibliographical references.
    ISBN 0-570-04262-3
        1. Luther, Martin, 1483–1546. 2. Lutheran Church—Catechisms and creeds. 3. Lutheran Church—Doctrines. I. Title.
BX8068.A1 A733 2000
238'.41—dc21
                                      00-010077

  3 4 5 6 7 8 9 10 11   12 11 10 09 08 07 06 05 04

CONTENTS

Der kleine
Catechismus fur
die gemeine Pfar=
herr vnd Pre=
diger.
Mart. Luther.
Wittemberg.

Abbreviations

Brecht, *Luther*	Martin Brecht, *Martin Luther*, 3 vols., tr. James L. Schaaf (Philadelphia, Minneapolis: Fortress Press, 1985–1993).
BSELK	*Die Bekenntnisschriften der evangelisch-lutherischen Kirche*, ed. Hans Lietzmann et al. (2nd ed. Rev. Göttingen: Verlag Vandenhoeck and Ruprecht, 1952).
Geffcken	Johannes Geffcken, *Der Bildercatechismus des fünfzehnten Jahrhunderts und die catechetischen Hauptstücke in dieser Zeit bis auf Luther* (Leipzig, T. O. Weigel, 1855).
Kolde-Dewell	Dietrich Kolde, *A Fruitful Mirror or Small Handbook for Christians*, tr. Robert B. Dewell, in *Three Reformation Catechisms. Catholic, Anabaptist, Lutheran*, ed. Denis Janz (Lewiston: The Edwin Mellen Press, 1982), 29–130.
LC	Large Catechism. Quotations from the Large Catechism are from *The Book of Concord*, ed. Theodore Tappert (Philadelphia: Fortress Press, 1959).
LPB	*Little Prayerbook*. *LW* 43.
LW	*Luther's Works*. American Edition, Jaroslav Pelikan and Helmut T. Lehmann, gen. eds., 55 vols. (Philadelphia: Muhlenberg and Fortress Press, St. Louis: Concordia Publishing House, 1955–86).
Meyer	Johannes Meyer, *Historischer Kommentar zu Luthers Kleinem Katechismus* (Gütersloh: Bertelsmann Verlag, 1929).
NCE	*New Catholic Encyclopedia*, ed. The Catholic University of America, 15 vols., 3 supplement vols. (New York: McGraw-Hill Book Company, 1967–1988).
PE 2	*Works of Martin Luther*. The Philadelphia Edition, 2 (Philadelphia: Muhlenberg Press, 1943).
PL	*Patrologia latina*. ed. J. P. Migne. 217 vols. Paris, 1844–64.
Peters	Albrecht Peters, *Kommentar zu Luthers Katechismen*, 5 vols., ed. Gottfried Seebaß (Göttingen: Verlag Vandenhoeck and Ruprecht, 1990–1994).
SC	Small Catechism. Quotations from the Small Catechism are from *The Small Catechism: 1986 Translation* (St. Louis: Concordia, 1986).
SF	Short Form of the Ten Commandments, Creed, and Lord's Prayer — *Works of Martin Luther*. The Philadelphia Edition, 2 (Philadelphia: Muhlenberg Press, 1943).
Tappert	*The Book of Concord: The Confessions of the Evangelical Lutheran Church*, edited by Theodore Tappert (Philadelphia: Fortress Press, 1959).
WA	*Dr. Martin Luthers Werke*. Kritische Gesamtausgabe. Schriften (Weimar: Böhlau Verlag, 1883).

WABr   *Dr. Martin Luthers Werke*. Kritische Gesamtausgabe. Briefwechsel, 18 vols. (Weimar: Verlag Hermann Böhlaus Nachfolger, 1930–85).

WATr   *Dr. Martin Luthers Werke Tischreden*. Kritische Gesamtausgabe. Briefwechsel, 18 vols. (Weimar: Verlag Hermann Böhlaus Nachfolger, 1930–85).

Weidenhiller   P. Egino Weidenhiller, *Untersuchungen zur deutschsprachigen katechetischen Literatur des späten Mittelalters nach den Handschriften der Bayerischen Staatsbibliothek* (München: Beck'sche Verlagsbuchhandlung, 1965).

FOREWORD

Like every other confession of faith penned by human hand, Luther's "here I stand" before the children of Germany, his Small Catechism, arose out of a specific historical context. It reflects that context in many ways. The dire spiritual situation of the Saxon peasants moved the reformer to write the sharp words of his preface and to give concrete suggestions for meeting their need to learn the biblical message and to incorporate it into their daily living. The world in which he grew up led Luther to be concerned about care for fields and livestock, and to divide political responsibilities among subjects and rulers instead of citizens and elected officials, to attack witchcraft, and to pray for good weather and good harvests.

Yet more than most texts which direct the biblical Word to specific groups of hearers, the Small Catechism rises easily out of its original historical context and gives voice to human concerns and to God's message for hearers and readers in other cultures. In cultures throughout the world, Christians have adapted it for use in leading children and adults to a deeper understanding of the Gospel of Jesus Christ and to a fuller exercise of life in him.

For Luther intended his Small Catechism as a handbook for Christian living, a primer for making God's children wise about salvation through faith in Christ Jesus and for equipping them for every good work. He designed the Catechism, as Professor Arand's study demonstrates, to begin by bringing its users to repentance through the proclamation of God's Law in the Ten Commandments. The reformer then, of course, turned to the Gospel, as the Creed summarizes God's love as Father, Son, and Holy Spirit, in his work of creation, redemption, and sanctification. Luther continued by treating the "first exercise of faith," prayer, in line with medieval catechetical custom, and then he provided instruction in how the Word of God works in believers' lives, in the means of grace. The design of the Catechism builds upon this sketch of biblical teaching by offering a framework for the practice of the Christian's daily life. That life includes meditation and prayer, so Luther offered suggestions for regular devotional reflection on the Catechism as a summary of biblical passages which contain instruction for the conduct of the callings of the Christian life, in home, at work, in the community, and in the congregation.

At the beginning of the twenty-first century, Lutheran churches throughout the world need to refresh and repeat Luther's insights for their neighbors. For everywhere in the world churches of the Lutheran confession are learning to express anew their own identity as confessors of the Gospel of Jesus Christ. In western and northern Europe, the traditional heartland of Luther's teaching, the churches have lost the trust of their people. In longstanding Lutheran communities in central and eastern Europe, the faithful are learning to reformulate the faith for life in a society that is not only post-Marxist but also imitates the post-modern features of Western neighbors. In North America, the identity of churches no longer shaped by immigrant dreams and defenses must find new expressions. In Lutheran mission churches in Africa, Asia, and Latin America, the confession of the faith of the Augsburg Confession and Luther's catechisms has an important role to play in the life of rapidly growing congregations. Everywhere in the world Lutherans are searching for ways to make their voices heard and to exercise the ecumenical responsibility of bringing our distinctive contributions to the whole church. In this process, the catechisms of Luther will continue to serve as a most helpful tool.

For the structure of the Small Catechism, leading from repentance to faith, from Law to Gospel, and then to the practice of the faith in daily life, commends itself for shaping Christian instruction not only in Lutheran churches but also in the whole household of faith. The contents of the pages of the Catechism present a crisp and living summary of the biblical faith without parallel. The sprightly expressions of Luther's text provide formulations of the biblical message easily learned by heart and repeated in conversation and in prayer.

This volume acquaints its readers with the historical setting in which Luther composed his catechisms. Professor Arand's carefully crafted survey of the context of medieval instruction and piety bring to life the habits of mind which Luther inherited as a member of the church and a student of theology as well as the concerns for the spiritual welfare of his people which moved him to prepare a course of instruction for them. Arand's own investigations of medieval and sixteenth century approaches to instruction in the biblical message and to the cultivation of piety stand here as an enrichment of the research of the last century. This research itself has added much to the ability of our contemporaries to understand and use Luther's handbook for Christian living, and Arand's digest of the research is helpful for applying its insight to our time. In addition, Arand's theological analysis sharpens the reader's skills in such application, with its deep appreciation of the Law/Gospel rhythm that sets the life of repentance in place for those who are introduced to the Christian faith by Luther's Catechism. Like that handbook, this volume will reach beyond the context of its author to assist pastors, parishes, and parents in all corners of the world to bring the Word of God to young children and new believers entrusted to their care.

The Small Catechism is an instrument of the Gospel of Jesus Christ for just such a time as ours. Arand provides significant help for all who wish to use it as a handbook for introducing God's children to the proper understanding and practice of their faith.

— Robert A. Kolb
Concordia Seminary
St. Louis, MO

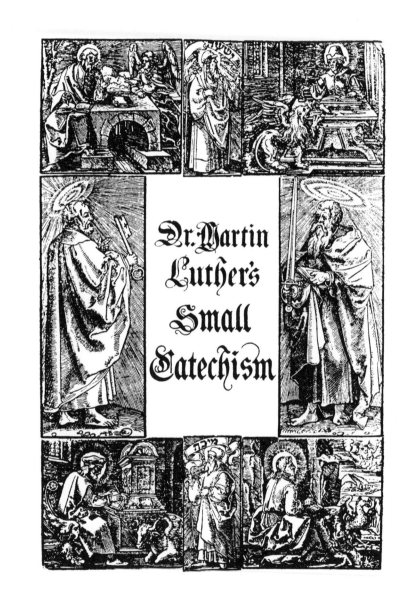

Dr. Martin Luther's Small Catechism

ACKNOWLEDGEMENTS

Upon arriving at the seminary, my teaching responsibilities included courses on the Lutheran Confessions. At that time, I wanted to acquaint myself thoroughly with the documents themselves, to which end I decided to embark upon a systematic study of them. I planned to take five years in order to familiarize myself with both the primary sources and secondary literature of each document.

I chose to begin with Luther's catechisms, partly because I had thoroughly enjoyed teaching them in the parish. Moreover, having just arrived from the parish, these texts would keep me in touch with an important component of pastoral work. I also chose them partly because they were among the briefer of the Lutheran confessional documents. That was ten years ago. It took two years simply to work through all of the material available on the First Commandment alone. If that were not enough, the appearance in print of Albrecht Peters's masterwork served as a further stimulus to my work, particularly in picking up certain points that Peters had not.

Along the way, I have received much encouragement and assistance in order to bring this work to print. My colleague Robert Kolb, in particular, has been very supportive, especially when I felt overwhelmed with the magnitude of the task. Another colleague, Paul Robinson, has been especially helpful in pointing out resources for identifying the continuity (and hence catholicity) of Luther's catechism with the church's catechetical work throughout the Middle Ages. Many of my other colleagues, James Voelz, Paul Raabe, Robert Rosin, J. A. O. Preus, and Andy Bartelt have shown remarkable patience with my obsession for and endless discussion of the catechism. I thank them all for not only their forbearance, but also their encouragement.

There were also a number of student assistants without whom I could not have completed this work. Early in the task, John Karle performed a yeoman's task in tracking down many of the original sources and doing much of the basic bibliographical work. More recently, graduate students Tom Eggers and Jaim Gann have greatly assisted me through their editorial work, especially the tedious task of making sure that all of the footnotes were in order. Similarly, Al Collver has given much assistance in obtaining good copies of woodcuts from the catechism for this book.

Finally, I want to thank my wife Betty and my children, Benjamin and Becky, for their patience as I labored to bring this project to conclusion. At times, no doubt they were convinced that I was in another world, especially when I was seemingly unresponsive to their questions and conversations. As is probably the case in most such projects, this book took longer than expected to write. Thus, I also thank them for the time that they ungrudgingly granted me.

A Book for the Ages

The Reformation began as a debate among theologians, academicians, and churchmen when Luther posted his 95 Theses for discussion in 1517. But by the mid-1520s, and especially following a visitation of the churches in 1528, it became painfully evident that the Reformation had not taken hold at the grassroots of the population as once hoped. If it was to succeed, it needed to develop evangelical institutional supports such as church orders, liturgies, hymnals, and catechisms to replace the old ones that had been cast aside in the early heady days of the Reformation. The latter half of the 1520s witnessed a flurry of activity on all these fronts, particularly in the production of catechisms that culminated in 1529 when Luther published his Small and Large Catechisms. More than any other document, the Small Catechism would secure Luther's revolution.[1] It would "immediately become and permanently remain the single most typical and influential statement of the Protestant faith."[2] Just as it is difficult to imagine the Anglican Reformation without the *Book of Common Prayer* or the Calvinistic Reformation without the *Institutes on the Christian Religion*, so it is impossible to imagine the Lutheran Reformation without Luther's Small Catechism.

Following its publication, the Small Catechism became the most widely used pedagogical, theological, and confessional text among Lutherans for the next 450 years.[3] Wherever Lutherans undertook the training of the young in the faith, they used this text. Whenever they shipped the message overseas, they equipped missionaries and catechists with this text. Already by the end of the sixteenth century Lutherans had translated it into nearly every language on the continent. By the end of the next century, it had found its way to nearly every continent of the world and had begun to take root in the New World.[4] Over the next 200 years, the Small Catechism provided a common text for linking Lutherans together despite the wide geographical dispersion of Lutherans and despite the subsequent history of Lutheran disunity.

Throughout these years, the catechism was the one theological text of the church, besides the Bible, that was read, learned, and prayed by rank-and-file church members. Its text has been read from the lectern and its contents preached from the pulpit. Its explanations were used in the school classroom or in *Kinderlehre* connected to the Sunday service. As a result, the Small Catechism cultivated a Lutheran pattern of thought, served as the basis for a common grammar, and provided a pattern of piety for countless people around the world down to the present day. Martin Marty, reflecting on the impact of his own catechization in the 1930s admitted, "I can testify that the little book was a constant companion, its every page subjected to memory.... Several decades of graduate theology have not succeeded in supplanting in my mind a view of the structure of the universe that the faith, which Luther's book with its 'Chief Parts' provided."[5] In other words, it has stamped the minds of children and parents with the deepest concepts of the faith itself. For that reason, it often became the day-to-day working theology of people and pastors alike.

It seems though, that in the waning days of the twentieth century, the catechism is losing the role that it has played during the past four centuries. Increasingly, the adults who enter the church today have little to no Christian memory—even from childhood.[6] If they as parents have not been trained in the catechisms, the church cannot expect that the children of these adults will be formed in the faith at home. In the church, pastors themselves are using the catechism less and less as the primary text for catechetical instruction—especially for adults. Outlines of Christian doctrine or surveys of biblical theology have supplanted the catechism. James Nestingen has described our situation on the eve of a new millennium well: "It [the Small Catechism] is no longer the working paradigm, encompassing the witness of Scripture in the language of daily experience to serve preaching and reflection on the church's faith and mission."[7]

At the same time, however, there are small signs that the climate may be ripe for recovering and rediscovering the catechism's value for the church. In the wider culture one hears the cry "to teach the basics—simply, directly, consistently, energetically."[8] This applies also to the church, for those who are entering through its doors are not only biblically illiterate, but they live in a universe of religious options. As a result, many have become eclectic and syncretistic in their spiritual lives. They regard religion primarily as a subjective internal experience rather than a faith that has anything to do with the objective content of doctrine. But this is precisely where the catechism becomes important. It integrates theology and life. It fastens people's attention on the basics of both so that they are not distracted by peripheral concerns. Thus by getting back to basics, as it were, the church has the opportunity to rediscover and recover something of the original purpose of the catechism.

LITERATURE ON THE CATECHISM

Given the nature of the catechism along with its history of use, one can expect there to be an equally rich body of literature on the catechism. In general, the literature can be divided into several categories: popular introductions, instructional manuals, doctrinal compendiums, historiographical works, and theological commentaries.

The type of commentary on the Small Catechism that has the longest pedigree, reaching back to the days of the Reformation itself, are those instructional manuals that provided explanations (in the form of questions and answers) on Luther's own words. They would also provide many Scriptural passages to deepen, illumine, and support Luther's texts. Some of these began to appear already during Luther's lifetime as, for example, the Catechism of Justus Menius (1532) and the Small and Large Catechisms by Johannes Spannenberg (1549).[9] One of the most influential of this genre was written by Johann Conrad Dietrich: *Institutiones Catecheticae* (1613) and its *Epitome* (1616). The latter became the basis for the catechism prepared by C. F. W. Walther and used in The Lutheran Church—Missouri Synod for several generations.

Often these works not only provided comments on Luther's text but amplified it with discussions of other topics not covered by Luther, until they expanded to become compendiums or manuals of Christian doctrine suitable for university training.[10] At times then, their length and complexity lost sight of the simplicity of Luther's text and became difficult for children. By the nineteenth century, Wilhelm Loehe encouraged instead that:

> One should rather make the catechism itself the object of instruction. It is a true reflection of the Word of God, a Bible for the laity, and a delight to theologians. It is the periphery which the teacher, surrounded by his pupils, should learn to point to, repeat, and understand. It is no small thing to have an understanding of the words of the Small Catechism.... We should not add anything to it or take anything from it but hold to its words.[11]

This view recognizes that the Small Catechism does not address all of the theological topics of dogmatics. Instead, it sounds certain key themes that permeate all of Lutheran thought and thus provides the starting point for further theological reflection.

A number of the books published in the twentieth century have attempted to introduce people anew to the vitality and relevance of Luther's thought in the Small Catechism. One of the best works in the field that opens the mind of the catechism is Robert Kolb's *Teaching God's Children His Teaching*.[12] Although intended to assist lay catechists, it provides a good, brief, and substantial introduction to the theological thought-world of the catechism. Another good work is James Nestingen's popular *Free to Be*,[13] which was originally intended to lead high school students into the thought and application of the catechism. A slightly older work that integrates the Large Catechism's thought with contemporary challenges is Martin Marty's *The Hidden Discipline*.[14] It is particularly helpful for showing how the forgiveness of sins is the center from which the entire catechism radiates.

A more scholarly group of works includes those that explore either the history of the catechism itself or examines the reception of the catechisms within history. Johann Michael Reu's *Luther's Small Catechism* continues to be a classic as it examines the historical development of Luther's text together with its subsequent reception. The material by Otto Albrecht in the Weimar Edition of *Luthers Werke* also remains a valuable historical and bibliographical resource. For a briefer and more current introduction, see Christoph Weisman, *Eine Kleine Biblia*, who compares Luther's catechism with a catechism written by Johannes Brenz.[15] Hans-Jürgen Fraas' *Katechismustradition: Luthers kleiner Katechismus in Kirche und Schule*[16] provides a helpful overview of the reception and use of the catechism within the European church over the past several centuries. Arthur C. Repp's book, *Luther's Catechism Comes to America*, provides the most complete treatment on the spread and use of Luther's catechisms in America up through the first half of the nineteenth century.

The final group includes scholarly commentaries on Luther's catechisms that provide a close and extensive analysis of Luther's text. A number of very fine works have been produced here, but unfortunately, none in English. An older but still valuable work was written by Theodosius Harnack as part of the confessional revival over one hundred years ago, *Erklärung des Kleinen Katechismus Dr. Martin Luthers*.[17] Perhaps the most detailed historical commentary on Luther's catechism in light of Luther's writings is Johannes Meyers' *Historischer Kommentar zu Luthers Kleinem Katechismus*[18] that was published upon the 400th anniversary of the Small Catechism. It takes a close look at the etymology and development of

Luther's wording. A work that examines the Small Catechism in the light of biblical research and intended for a slightly more popular audience is Herbert Girgensohn's, *Teaching Luther's Catechism*,[19] which was translated over thirty years ago. More recently, Albrecht Peters' five-volume masterwork, *Kommentar zu Luthers Katechismen*,[20] provides the most thorough exposition of the catechism to date, especially in light of contemporary biblical scholarship and the theological tradition of the church. It is the standard for our generation.

Goal of this Book

That I May Be His Own is written in the conviction that there is more to the catechism than what first meets the eye. As Timothy Wengert has reminded us, the Small Catechism is "something far richer and more complex than anything many of us had ever imagined."[21] With that in mind, *That I May Be His Own* is written first and foremost in order to reacquaint the reader with the inexhaustible riches that the catechism offers. It seeks to benefit the reader personally by leading him or her into the catechism's genius, thought pattern, and perspective on God and the world. Thus it hopes to show how the catechism renews minds and cultivates the *habitus* of thinking the things of God, that is, helps us to think theologically.

It is also written as a resource for the catechist (pastor, teacher, or parent) who seeks to convey the catechism through conversation with those whom they are mentoring in the Christian faith. This will be not so much by providing how-to steps as by enriching the mind of the catechist. It assumes that many pastors are either developing their own curriculums or devising their own lesson plans; a single curriculum, "one size fits all," is often not helpful today. Thus, this book hopes to provide instead the essential themes and leitmotifs that pastors or catechists needs to bear in mind as they develop their own courses. But before catechists take it upon themselves to alter the catechism of the church, either formally or materially, they are asked to do so by first considering why Luther did what he did with his structure and explanations.

Along the way, this book will take into account and try to bring out several aspects of Luther's catechism that affect our understanding of its entire content.

First, this book hopes to highlight the catholicity of Luther's catechisms. Often, in an attempt to highlight Luther's Reformation insights, his continuity with the past is overlooked. While other books have looked for this continuity in the magisterial theologians of the medieval church, *That*

I May Be His Own will instead examine selected pre-Reformation cate-chisms and catechetical literature. These writings supply the backdrop for the components and, at times, even the wording of Luther's catechisms. Luther grew up in the catechetical tradition of his church and as a priest was no doubt quite familiar with that tradition.[22] Like Luther's catechisms, they were written for a popular audience and demonstrate how the theology of the church found its way into the lives of the people sitting in the pews. Some of these catechisms were not written by "great theologians" like Luther, but were probably as influential in shaping the theology and piety of the church as were many of the magisterial theologians of the church. It also allows us to see what Luther's own catechisms owed to the church's cate-chetical tradition and how they emerge as the fruit of that tradition.

Second, this book will identify and develop the distinctive evangelical motifs of Luther's catechisms. It will do so by looking at the entire frame-work of the Small and Large Catechisms. In order that we do not lose sight of the forest on account of the trees, and thereby obscure the overall picture of what Lutheran faith and life look like, this book proposes a holistic read-ing of the text rather than an atomistic treatment of the catechisms' chief parts. Often, the individual chief parts may be taught over such extensive periods of time (the Ten Commandments the first year, the Creed the sec-ond year etc.) that catechists and catechumens fail to see their lives within the total context of God's work. This book especially seeks to explore how the first three chief parts relate to one another, interact with one another, and interpret one another. Toward that end, it hopes to examine and reflect upon a) the structure of the catechism; b) the leading motifs and themes in the catechism; and c) the theological expressions of the catechism.

Third, this book hopes to unpack what might be called the fullness of the catechisms' words.[23] In this it will provide a close reading of the cate-chisms' language, always recognizing that the content of these words can-not be exhausted by a single commentary or any single interpretation. Luther provides a seamless integration of doctrine and life. In his day, doc-trine had a dynamic and hermeneutical character that shaped and illumined life itself. *That I May Be His Own* is thus written with the conviction that catechetical instruction has historically served to teach people how to make sense of their lives in the light of God's work, and Luther's *Enchiridion* per-sonifies that goal. Unfolding the fullness of the words within the overall framework of the catechism is not without its difficulties because the cate-chism is a multi-faceted document with many features that must be taken into account.

The catechisms are historical documents rooted in and bound by their *Sitz im Leben*. Luther was, if anything, an occasional theologian, that is to say, he wrote much of his theology in response to specific pastoral questions or theological issues of his day. Hence the many pastoral challenges facing the church during the 1520s can and do shed light on many of the elements and characteristic features of the catechism. Most importantly, many of the specifics in the catechism arose out of the reformer's experience with the visitations and reflects the pastoral crisis raised by the theological controversies with the Antinomians and Sacramentarians. In a more general way, the catechisms provide an evangelical alternative to the theology of the late Middle Ages, a theology that often filtered down to shape the religious life of the village parish and its parishioners.

The catechisms forge a very interesting relationship between theology and pedagogy, particularly with regard to those aspects that influence the formulations or presentations of the material as well as the very content of the catechisms themselves. For example, one could argue that Luther weaves "fear and love" through all of the commandments for pedagogical reasons in order to aid the memory. On the other hand, one can also argue that there is a theological reason for doing so. Similarly, the Small Catechism does not say everything that could be said on various topics, such as the Trinity. This raises a number of crucial questions. Does Luther present the Trinity as briefly and simply as he does purely out of pedagogical concerns, namely, that he does not want to overwhelm the catechumen? Or do his presentations of the Trinity betray a more subtle and profound understanding of the Trinity and of how to approach this mystery?

While the catechisms arose as instructional tools, they eventually became confessional and theological testimonies of the church. In a sense, this was a natural process inasmuch as they set forth the *publica doctrina* of the church for the laity. As a result, they acquired the status of doctrinal authorities and standards within the church in addition to their pedagogical function. Generations of confirmands have publicly promised to abide by the Small Catechism as a summary of the church's confession. On the other hand, their use as doctrinal standards may at times have obscured some of the other functions that they originally served by accenting the doctrinal statements rather than their formative function. In any event, the catechism also needs to be read as the church's text and as part of the ongoing dialogue of the church with her heritage.

THE PLAN AND DESIGN

That I May Be His Own will appear as a two-volume work. The first book presents an historical and theological overview of Luther's catechisms and could be used in a university or seminary as a stand-alone volume for an introductory course on the catechism. It will also serve as a prolegomenon for the second book, which will provide a more in-depth historical and theological reading on the catechism's chief parts. In particular, it will concentrate on what was for Luther the heart of the catechism itself: the Ten Commandments, Creed, and Lord's Prayer, as well as his treatment of the Sacraments. It is hoped that publishing the work in two volumes will not only expedite their appearance in print, but also make the total work more versatile and less intimidating for today's busy reader.

This volume has a modest goal—but with potentially far-reaching consequences for how people think of the catechism and how the church carries out its catechetical task. It will argue that the idea of "catechism" should be defined less in terms of its form (a book of questions and answers) and more in terms of its contents (a collection of texts, notably, the Ten Commandments, Creed, and Lord's Prayer). Thus Luther's Small Catechism as presented in this work is, in reality, Luther's short explanation of the catechism! Similarly, his so-called Large Catechism is really Luther's longer explanation of the catechism. This will allow us to expand our understanding of the catechism and thus see a more versatile role for it as a handbook for Christian living.

Chapter 1 will show that the texts of the catechism impart to Luther's Small Catechism a catholicity so that the Small Catechism is not so much Luther's as it is the entire church's. More specifically, it locates the SC squarely within the tradition of western Christianity. Chapter 2 will show that church rarely limited itself to a single medium in order to convey the catechism to its people. Instead, it adapted itself to various situations and utilized a variety of forms in order to convey the catechism. This highlights the versatility of the catechism in general and Luther's catechism in particular. Chapter 3 will look at Luther's methodological and pedagogical blueprint for using the texts of the catechism so that they might become lifelong companions for the Christian. Chapter 4 explores how Luther arranged and organized the texts of the catechism so as to construct a Lutheran framework for Christian living, a framework that also signals key Reformation themes.

Most importantly, it is hoped that this book will generate a renewed appreciation and love for Luther's catechisms so as to stimulate further devotional reflection and intensive study of the catechisms themselves.... *That I May Be His Own* is written in the conviction that the catechism is not something we grow out of but something we grow into. In the words of Leopold von Ranke: the Small Catechism "is as childlike as it is profound, as comprehensive as it is inscrutable, simple, and sublime. Blessed is he who nourishes his soul with it."[24]

NOTES

1   One might consider Luther's translation of the Bible. But the fact is that only 5-30 percent of the populace was literate and hence capable of reading the Bible. The catechism was the document which provided entrée to the Bible for the majority of people.

2   Robert I. Bradley, *The Roman Catechism in the Catechetical Tradition of the Church: The Structure of the Roman Catechism as Illustrative of the "Classic Catechesis"* (Lanham, Md.: University Press of America, 1990), 92–93.

3   See Johann Michael Reu on the spread of the catechism in *Dr. Martin Luther's Small Catechism: A History of its Origin, its Distribution and its Use, A Jubilee Offering* (Chicago: Wartburg, 1929).

4   See the chapters, "The Triumph of Luther's Small Catechism Throughout Europe in the Sixteenth Century," 155–72, "The Small Catechism in the United States," 294–339, and "Luther's Small Catechism throughout the World" in Johann Michael Reu, *Luther's Small Catechism.*

5   "Preface" to Arthur C. Repp, Sr.'s work, *Luther's Catechism Comes to America: Theological Effects on the Issues of the Small Catechism Prepared In or For America Prior to 1850*, Alta Monograph Series, No. 18 (Metuchen, N.J.: Scarecrow Press, Inc. and the American Theological Library Association, 1982).

6   Virgil Thompson, "The Promise of Catechesis," *Lutheran Quarterly* 4 (1990): 259–60.

7   James Nestingen, "Preaching the Catechism," *Word and World* 10 (1990): 33.

8   Margaret A. Krych, "The Future of the Catechisms in Teaching," *Currents in Theology and Mission* 21 (1994): 334.

9   For copies of these, see Johann Michael Reu's magisterial work, *Quellen des Geschichte.*

10 It is of interest that the subtitle of the catechism used within the Missouri Synod describes the book as a "Manual of Christian Doctrine."

11 *Three Books About the Church* (tr. and ed. with an introduction by James L. Schaaf; Philadelphia: Fortress, 1969), 171–72.

12 Hutchinson, Minn.: Crown Publishing, 1992.

13 James A. Nestingen, *Free to Be: A Handbook to Luther's Small Catechism* (Minneapolis: Augsburg, 1975).

14 Martin E. Marty, *The Hidden Discipline: A Commentary on the Christian Life of Forgiveness in the Light of Luther's Large Catechism* (St. Louis: Concordia, 1962).

Another work of a more general nature is G. H. Gerberding, *The Lutheran Catechist* (Philadelphia: Lutheran Publication Society, 1910).

15   Christoph Weismann, *Eine kleine Biblia: Die Katechismen von Luther und Brenz, Einführung und Texte* (Stuttgart: Calver Verlag, 1985).

16   Göttingen: Vandenhoeck & Ruprecht, 1971.

17   Erlangen: A. Deichert, 1882.

18   Gütersloh: C. Bertelsmann, 1929.

19   2 vols. (Philadelphia: Muhlenberg, 1959).

20   Göttingen: Vandenhoeck & Ruprecht, 1991.

21   See Timothy Wengert, "Forming the Faith," in *Formation in the Faith: Catechesis for Tomorrow*, Symposium Papers, Number 7 (St. Louis: Concordia Seminary Publications, 1997), 45.

22   Gottfried Krodel, "Luther's Work on the Catechism in the Context of Late Medieval Catechetical Literature," *Concordia Journal* 25 (October 1999): 364–404.

23   Robert Wilken, *Remembering the Christian Past* (Grand Rapids: Eerdmans, 1995), 7–8.

24   Quoted in Harold J. Grimm, *Luther and Education, Luther and Culture* (ed. George W. Forell; Decorah, Iowa: Luther College Press, 1960), 142.

1

WHAT MAKES A CATECHISM?
THE CLASSIC TEXTS OF THE SMALL CATECHISM

The term "catechism" conjures up memories for many adults of a little question and answer textbook once used in seventh and eighth grade in order to prepare for the rite of passage known as confirmation.[1] Such an understanding of the Small Catechism is too constrictive. For Luther, a catechism was both more basic and more far-reaching. In the catechism, the church has gathered the fundamental components of Scripture that go to the heart of defining what it means to be a Christian. It identifies those elements that constitute the very identity of a Christian. This is who we are. Thus, near the end of his life Luther could write Katie to quell her fears and say, "You, dear Katie, read John and the *Small Catechism*, about which you once said: Everything in this book has been said about me" (*LW* 50: 302). And so on its title page Luther describes the Small Catechism as an *Enchiridion*, that is, a handbook, manual, or guide on being a Christian.[2] Put another way, one might describe it as a *Vademecum*, that is, "a spiritual companion on a man's journey from cradle to grave; the Christian's book of daily prayer and meditation."[3]

The reason for Luther's deeper and more penetrating view of the catechism's formative function lies in his understanding of what constitutes a catechism.[4] In the preface to the Large Catechism, he states that a catechism's "contents represent the minimum of knowledge required of a Christian. Whoever does not possess it should not be reckoned among Christians nor admitted to the sacrament, just as a craftsman who does not know the rules and practices of his craft is rejected and considered incompetent" (LC Short Preface, 2). This suggests that "just as a craftsman's knowledge is not merely intellectual but defines his very existence, so too knowledge of the catechism defines the life of the Christian. It gives substance and direction to the faith."[5] It changes the way people think and act. Put another way, the catechism deals with the formation of a Christian *habitus* of the mind and heart, which "look[s] at life and live[s] not from our perspective—that's philosophy—but from God's perspective—that's theology."[6]

Ordinarily, but not always, the church conveyed the basic knowledge of what it means to be a Christian at the point of a person's entrance into the church, namely, Baptism. In his Foreword to the *German Mass*, Luther writes:

> Catechism means the instruction in which the heathen who want to be Christians are taught and guided in what they should believe, know, do, and leave undone, according to the Christian faith. That is why the candidates who had been admitted for such instruction and learned the Creed before their Baptism used to be called *catechumenos*. (*LW* 53:64)[7]

Luther recognized that catechesis provided the counterpart to Baptism for the making of disciples. If Baptism carries us into the church by transferring us from the kingdom of Satan into Christ's kingdom,[8] catechesis imparts the mind of Christ so that we put to death the old ways of thinking and bring to life new patterns of thought.[9] Taken together, both sides of the Great Commission, "baptize and teach," were carried out by the church. In the early church, the catechetical instruction preceded Baptism (when adult Baptism was still common), and during the Middle Ages through the Reformation it took place after Baptism (since infant Baptism had become the norm). In both cases, to receive instruction was to confess oneself a Christian.

Luther's view of the catechism as changing the way we think, as well as its tie to Baptism, is rooted in the Scriptures. The New Testament is replete with examples that our new status brought by Christ must lead to new patterns of thought and with it to new forms of living. So Jesus exhorted Peter to turn his back on Satan and learn to "think the things of God" (Matthew 16:22). In the preceding verses, this involves the confession of the Gospel, namely, that Jesus is the Christ (v. 16). In the subsequent verses, it means living out the ramifications of this confession, namely, "pick up your cross and follow me" (v. 23).

Elsewhere, Paul stresses the same thing when he says, "Do not conform any longer to the pattern of this world, but be transformed by the renewing of your mind" (Romans 12:2). Drawing on the imagery of Baptism, in Colossians 3:2, Paul makes the connection directly to Baptism: "raised with Christ, set your minds on the things that are above, not on earth, for you have died, and your life is hid with Christ in God." Philippians 2 exhorts people to have the same mind of Christ, who "did not hang onto divinity, but took the form of a servant." Here Paul stresses that we must first think and believe like Christians before we act and live like Christians. Thinking the things of God and living from God's perspective ultimately means that we learn how God relates to us in order to cultivate a habit of the mind and heart that is lived from faith to faith.

THE HEART AND CORE OF A CATECHISM

The term "catechism"[10] cannot be defined simply as any elementary instruction in the faith without resulting in a uselessly broad definition in which everything in the church potentially becomes catechetical. So what is it that a Christian needs to know? From very early in its history, the church identified certain topics as essential.[11] By the late Middle Ages when those topics had multiplied extensively, authors distinguished between kinds of knowledge: those parts that are perennially necessary to know for salvation, and those that belong to particular needs and situations.[12] With regard to the former, every Christian needed to know the triad of Creed, Lord's Prayer, and some kind of moral norm like the Ten Commandments.

The faith expressed in the Creed laid the foundation for the Christian life. It outlined the central acts of God upon which the Christian life is based. As the second section of the catechism, the Lord's Prayer was ranked equal in importance with the Creed. It contained everything that a Christian should seek from God. Finally, the Ten Commandments served as the moral norm for the Christian life. Because these three parts defined the core of a catechism, Luther could state that the papal church had the true catechism (WA 26:147, 15–38; *LW* 40:23f.). Also, when Luther speaks about preaching on the catechism (LC Short Preface 25) this is what he means. Thus the publication of his December 1528 sermons is simply titled, "Ten Sermons on the Catechism" (*LW* 51:137–93; WA 30:I, 57–122).

Those basic texts have proven to be perennially relevant and contemporary expressions of Christian existence. They define what it is that makes a catechism a catechism more than any particular mode of presentation or setting. In fact, by identifying the catechism with this syllabus (Decalogue, Creed, Lord's Prayer) one may consider under the genre of "catechism" all the various methods of catechizing (preaching, teaching, question and answer), modes of presenting the catechism (posters, pictures, booklets), settings for teaching the catechism, (church, school, home), texts of varied lengths (small and large catechisms), different audiences (clergy, parents, children), multiple uses (preparation for Baptism, confession, and the Lord's Supper, basis for meditation), and different ends (reformation, evangelism, assimilation). Even, in Luther's works we can apply the term "catechism" to writings as diverse as Luther's Short Form (1520), his *Little Prayer Book* (1522), the Small Catechism, and the Large Catechism.[13]

From his earliest thinking on the subject, Luther regarded the Ten Commandments, Creed, and Lord's Prayer as the heart of a catechism. In connection with his *German Mass*, Luther proposed that the church also needs, in addition to a worship service in the vernacular, "a short catechism on the Creed, the Ten Commandments, and the Our Father" (*LW* 53:64). He then explains why: "These three plainly, briefly, contain exactly everything that a Christian needs to know" (*LW* 53:64–65). In his December 1528 sermons, he calls these texts the "elements and fundamentals of Christian knowledge and life" (*LW* 51:135). He notes also in the Large Catechism that these three parts "constitute the heritage of Christendom from ancient times" (LC Short Preface 6).

Several years later, Luther elaborated on what he meant. "And all of this we have received from the beginning of Christendom. For there we see and grasp the way in which the Creed, the Our Father, and the Ten Commandments were put together as a short summary and doctrine for the young and for those in need of instruction. From early on this is what was called a 'catechism.'"[14] At the same time, Luther recognized that the church gave these chief parts different emphases during different periods of its history and used them for different purposes.

CREED AND LORD'S PRAYER

In the third and fourth centuries, the Creed and Lord's Prayer played important roles in the pre-Baptismal instruction of catechumens.[15] Within the context of the Baptismal vow, the Creed and Lord's Prayer served as the texts that expressed the new spiritual existence of the convert. The Creed, as it unfolded the Baptismal formula, was part of the *traditio* and *redditio symboli*—the formal presentation of the Creed to the catechumen and its subsequent recitation by the Baptismal candidate just prior to Easter.

The imparting of the Creed in Rome also included the *traditio orationis dominicae* (formal presentation of the Lord's Prayer).[16] In Augustine's day, the Creed would be given to the catechumens two weeks before Easter and would be accompanied with exhortations to learn and assimilate it, along with a phrase by phrase explanation of its content. A week later, eight days before Easter, the catechumen would recite it back to the bishop at which time Augustine provided another sermon on it.[17] That same day, he would present them with another of the church's treasures, the Lord's Prayer, along with an explanation. The catechumen would recite it then on Easter Eve.[18]

For the early church fathers, the Creed provided a brief compendium of Scripture. The Creed would illuminate the Scriptures while the Scriptures would prove the truth of the Creed.[19] They used a number of metaphors to bring out this relationship. In the case of Cyril, the phrases of the Creed charted out the main lines of the catechetical edifice while the biblical stories shaped its interior. Caesarius of Arles also used the analogy of a structure: "The Creed is like an exceedingly beautiful building which is well begun; it has a very firm foundation, and an immortal summit, for it has God as its beginning and eternal life at the end."[20] Augustine saw the Creed as a compendium of the core elements of the biblical faith[21] that allowed catechumens to step back and scan the horizon of Scripture in a single glimpse. In a sense, it provided a map to read the biblical terrain.[22] As such, the creed linked the catechumen to a community of fellow searchers and travelers. Peter Chrysologus told his catechumens how the Creed opens up the wealth of faith to them. "As a spring gushes out of a small opening and broadens out with its copious flowing waters, just so does the doctrine in the compressed language of the Creed open up the widest paths of belief. And just as a root set deep into the earth sends its shoots far into the air, so does faith rooted deep in the heart spring up to the utmost height of belief."[23]

If the Creed provided a summary of the heart of Scripture, the Lord's Prayer was an appropriate companion. The Lord's Prayer provided access to common participation in the liturgical service for participation also meant learning how to pray. Augustine explains that the proximity of the Creed and Lord's Prayer links *orthodoxia* ("right belief") with *eusebeia* ("right worship"). "You have been taught the creed first, so that you may know what to believe, and afterwards the prayer, so that you may know whom to call upon. The creed contains what you are to believe; the prayer, what you are to ask for."[24]

In general, many of the fathers focused on the Lord's Prayer as the best of prayers and as an incentive to pray because it was given by Christ himself. Peter of Chrysologus brings this out nicely. "Christ taught us to pray briefly. Why will he not give himself to those who entreat him, since he gave himself to those who did not ask him? Or what delay in answering will he show who by formulating prayers has thus anticipated his suppliants' desire?"[25] Others, such as Gregory of Nyssa went on to speak of the Lord's Prayer as part of the spiritual equipment of the Christian. In particular, as prayer unites us with God himself, so it separates us from the devil. "For the effect of prayer is union with God, and if someone is with God, he is separated from the enemy."[26] Gregory then described the many blessings that prayer seeks and the evils from which it protects the Christian.

The Creed and Lord's Prayer continued to play important catechetical roles in the Middle Ages, but with several significant differences. By the sixth century, the pre-Baptismal instruction offered to adult catechumens had all but disappeared and been replaced with infant Baptism in most areas.[27] There is no evidence that the church of the Middle Ages replaced the adult catechumenate with a corresponding ecclesiastical structure for the post-Baptismal catechesis of children. Instructional classes for children were often recommended in church legislations, but rarely convened.[28] In the late Middle Ages, elementary education might be provided for some at monastic and cathedral schools (for boys), chancery schools, or local parish schools (which girls also occasionally attended). Because these schools used the Psalms and other religious materials to teach grammar, they also received some religious formation in the process. But schools were never the primary means for the religious instruction of the laity.[29] There were in the end too few schools to have a profound impact. Instead, the usages and rites of the ancient catechumenate were carried over into the rite of infant Baptism.

Sponsors and clergy acted as surrogates for the infant in the *traditio* and *redditio* of the Creed and Lord's Prayer.[30] In these liturgies they would speak for the infant what the adult catechumen had once said on his or her own behalf. With this, the responsibility for catechizing children fell to the parents and godparents.[31] From the eighth century, synods decreed that parents and godparents were obliged to know by heart the Our Father and the Creed as the basic statements of Christian life.[32] By the twelfth century, liturgies for the Baptismal rite included strictures to godparents in which they were given the responsibility for catechizing the children in these two fundamental elements of Christianity at home.[33] Canons during this time also required godparents for Baptism to be examined as to whether they could recite the Creed and Lord's Prayer.[34]

The decline of the catechumenal system also coincided with the decline of the classical system of education, which in turn made the catechetical endeavor all the more difficult. The church attempted to turn things around in the eighth century during which time ecclesiastical legislations outlined a minimal goal to be obtained (sometimes evidently in circumstances of great difficulty), namely, "the universal memorization of the Creed and the Our Father, together with a basic understanding of Christian morality."[35]

The Council of Clovesho (747) instructed bishops to teach the essentials of the faith, the doctrine of the Trinity and the Creed, and to ensure that godparents knew these truths. When the Carolingian reforms were launched with the publication of the *Admonitio Generalis* in 789, they enjoined not only parents and godparents, but also bishops and priests to take an active role in teaching the basics of the Christian faith and to prohibit heathen customs.[36] This newly-defined pedagogical function of the priesthood became a dominant feature of all succeeding legislation. The canons that emerged from the ecclesiastical reform councils in 813 emphasized that the most effective way to instruct the laity was through preaching. What is striking about these canons is that they place little emphasis on biblical interpretation in preaching and instead stress "the subject matter of catechesis: the interpretation of the Creed and Lord's Prayer, morality and its eschatological sanctions, and explanation of the liturgy."[37]

Thus what continued to be taught throughout the Middle Ages was the basis of the Christian faith and life as it had been identified from the church's tradition. Synodal statutes urged priests to stress the Creed and Lord's Prayer in their sermons, "since these provided the key to salvation."[38] Catechesis focused on the Creed and the Lord's Prayer as sufficient for the formation of lay Christians. This itself was a major achievement for this period.[39] These two texts could be found in the liturgy, heard from the pulpit, and listed in confessional manuals. Both were seen as weapons in the battle to subdue sin.

In the Middle Ages, the Creed continued to play a role in which it defined the basic identity of a Christian. In addition to defining the spiritual identity of a believer it also acquired the role of defining the political identity of a Christian citizen.[40] Catechetically, the Creed was often simply read to the laity without explanation. When expositions were provided, the creed might be used as a framework or outline within which the narrative of biblical stories could be fleshed out. At other times, the Creed was paraphrased in a slightly expanded manner. For example, Gerson added three significant points in his *Brief Introduction to the Faith*, as in connection with the Second Article: "I believe that our Savior Jesus Christ was conceived by the work of the blessed Holy Spirit in the womb of the glorious Virgin Mary without the work of man and that the glorious Virgin gave birth without pain and that she remained a virgin pure and entire perpetually, that is to say, before childbirth, at the time of childbirth, and after childbirth." In a similar way, he expanded upon Christ's descent into hell: "I believe that our Savior, Jesus Christ, after he had suffered death and passion descended into hell and delivered the souls of the blessed patriarchs and prophets and all the other just who had done their penances and who left their trespasses in the faith and in the hope of the redemption."[41]

The Lord's Prayer continued to play an important role throughout the Middle Ages. In sermons, its petitions would be expounded phrase by phrase for the parishioners. In this connection, preachers often emphasized the Lord's Prayer as a weapon for spiritual warfare. Like the Creed, it became a symbol of orthodoxy, standing against, for example, the Waldensian preachers who emphasized that the Lord's Prayer was merely a model for prayer and that prayer need not be limited only to these words.[42] The Lord's Prayer also found a permanent place in the confessional manuals of the late Middle Ages, although often not a prominent place. Here it often became merely one part of the Rosary, placed on the same level as the Hail Mary. Within those manuals, recitation of the Lord's Prayer became a means to entreat Mary to obtain forgiveness, a means for obtaining indulgences, and a means for obtaining release from purgatory for the souls of loved ones. Along with the Creed, knowledge of the Lord's Prayer by heart was required for admission to Easter communion. Both the Creed and Lord's Prayer were texts used within the confessional in order to uncover sins. Major sins against the Creed included not knowing it by heart, doubting the doctrine of the Creed, and debating the truth of the Creed. The Lord's Prayer was also listed as an item that parishioners ought to know.

As Martin Luther revitalized the catechesis of the church, he showed that he was no radical. Since Luther considered himself a catholic Christian, it is only natural that he would incorporate the Creed and the Lord's Prayer into his catechism. In doing so he confessed that he stood squarely within the catholic tradition of the church and has not in fact left the church.

At the same time, Luther adapts these texts to the goals of the Reformation. To that end he strips them of the encrusted layers of other materials that had obscured them and restores them to a place of prominence and central importance within the Christian life. He expounds them in a way that renders them capable of carrying the message of the Reformation. The Creed now provides a framework within which the Christian can interpret his or her entire life as a life lived from the gifts of the triune God from conception to the resurrection. In this context, the Creed ceases primarily to involve historical knowledge and focuses on a trusting, existential faith. Within the Lord's Prayer, Luther found a foundation and model for Christian prayer, one by which all prayers could be judged. It provides a framework for understanding the Christian life as life under the cross.

DECALOGUE

The Ten Commandments became an important catechetical component fairly late in the church's tradition. In the early church, the doctrine of the two ways (the way of life and the way of death), as laid out in the Didache and Apostolic Constitutions of the second and third centuries, provided the basis of most moral teaching.[43] The Decalogue may have underlay this teaching but it did not function as the normative text of Christian morality. Augustine may have been the first to promote the Decalogue's use as such a standard, perhaps as a result of his conflict with the Manicheans. He focused on the two-fold command of love for God and for neighbor as a summary of the Decalogue, which he pointed out is the foundation of Christian morality.[44] Augustine remained an exception to the rule, however, since most theologians, preachers, and catechists did not follow his lead until well into the Middle Ages.

For the most part, the church in the early Middle Ages adopted an ambivalent attitude toward the Decalogue. The reason for this ambivalence may lie in the hostility between the Church and Synagogue, namely, the tension between the church's roots and its future. On the one hand, Christians saw themselves as recipients of a new covenant that had been sealed with the ultimate sacrifice of Jesus' death, and now a new and better law, namely, the Sermon on the Mount, guided them. In other words, Christianity had superseded Judaism and the New Testament had superseded the Old Testament. On the other hand, the church had rejected Marcion's proposal to abandon the Old Testament, an act that would have completely severed Christianity from its roots in Judaism. While rejecting Marcion, the church had affirmed that the Old Testament was an integral part of the revealed truth of Christianity. Christians seemed to solve the tension by affirming that the Decalogue was "not cancelled, but rather amplified and extended by Jesus."[45]

Nevertheless, instead of following Augustine and using the Decalogue, the church of the early Middle Ages followed the example of Pope Gregory the Great (d. 604), who regarded the Decalogue as essentially inferior to the precepts of the Gospel. Because Christians were seeking a life of perfection in line with the New Testament, they needed a spiritual framework within which they could measure their motivation and behavior. They may have concluded that the Decalogue only dealt with external actions, whereas the Gospel dealt with matters related to the heart. Gregory's *Moralia* became the basis for Christian ethical instruction for centuries.[46]

Culling ethical imperatives and prohibitions almost exclusively from the Gospels, the Epistles, and patristic theology, Gregory created "a patch-work of moral teaching organized into seven virtues (love, hope, faith, prudence, temperance, courage, and justice)[47] and seven vices or 'deadly sins' (pride, envy, wrath, avarice, gluttony, sloth, and lechery)."[48] This system had the advantage of emphasizing social ethics in an age of hostility and provided a set of categories that people could recognize as un-Christian. In addition, the vices provided a connection to the Baptismal renunciation in which the catechumen renounces Satan and all his works, which were exemplified in these vices. The weakness of this system was that it did not emphasize obligations to God, was not Scriptural in origin, and implied for the average person that holiness was "the business of special categories of Christians like 'religious men and women.'"[49]

The Decalogue started coming into its own and making headway against the Seven Sins around the Middle of the twelfth century. Robert Bast suggests that the renaissance in biblical studies that emanated from Paris and Chartres expanded the study of the biblical texts beyond Paul's Epistles and the Psalter. A new emphasis on the literal sense of Scripture and a new focus on books that had been neglected, especially the Prophets and the historical books of the Old Testament, also contributed to new interest in the Ten Commandments. Hugh of St. Victor's *Institutiones in decalogum legis domincate* "stand at the beginning of a growing movement to accord the Ten Commandments an active role in the shaping of the moral life."[50] He refers to the Decalogue as the "perfect path and narrow way" which Christians must travel. Peter Lombard, who heard Hugh's lectures in Paris, included a brief exposition of the Decalogue in his famous *Sentences*.

By the thirteenth century, synodical decrees appeared mandating instruction in the Decalogue. During this period, the church began to connect the Ten Commandments with the practice of confession. The Fourth Lateran Council of 1215 had established an institutional alliance between examination and confession when it mandated that all the faithful should go to confession at least once a year on pain of excommunication.[51] This was the first church-wide law regarding private confession.[52] As children reached the age of discretion, a more in-depth instruction was given as part of the preparation for confession that in turn purified one for a worthy reception of communion.[53] With communion offered at Easter, the high-point of the church year, Lent became the season for exhorting people to partake in the annual confession and communion. Lenten sermons were "supposed to concentrate on explaining sins and the Ten Commandments," as in Eichstätt where rectors were encouraged to take up "at least once in the year the matter of the Ten Commandments and follow it with the appropriate corrections of vices."[54]

Shortly after the Lateran decree, regional synods began to decree that the Decalogue should have a fixed place in the confession of sins. After the Synod of Trier in 1227, the Decalogue was introduced as a moral norm in most parishes and consistently urged.[55] Subsequent synods also urged its use (Clermont, 1268; Lambeth, 1281; Utrecht 1284 and 1310).

Still, the framework of vices and virtues did not give way readily to the Decalogue. The diffusion of the Decalogue as "a generally accepted system of Christian ethics" was inhibited throughout the thirteenth and fourteenth centuries. For the most part, the Ten Commandments played "a modest role, the Sins a dominant one."[56] This phenomenon is due to several factors. First, the sacrament of penance preserved the role of the Seven Deadly Sins. Most of the confessional manuals of the fourteenth century continued to focus on them. Second, there were practical reasons: the Seven Sins were more manageable, flexible, and familiar to most people. They also fit in with the septenary system of classification, a system that was designed to aid the memory. Finally, their prominence during the penitential season of Lent cast a shadow over the entire year.

One of the difficulties of the Ten Commandments was that people found them to be a mouthful and not easy to remember.[57] Bellarmine mentioned that it is difficult to remember anything more than seven in number. Secondly, there were theoretical issues. Why should Christians use the Ten Commandments if the New Testament is superior? Theologians eventually came up with two answers: Thomas Aquinas rooted the Ten Commandments in natural law; Gabriel Biel rooted them in the authority of revelation.[58]

But by the end of the fourteenth century and all through the fifteenth century, "the Ten Commandments became so prominent as to virtually exclude all other parts of the confessional catechism."[59] Reformers of the fifteenth century expressed the conviction that chaos was conquering order, that all authority was under assault, and that the bonds of security were snapping. In such times people needed a new symbol around which to rally, and the Ten Commandments provided such a symbol. The sense of urgency that drove late medieval catechesis finds expression in the catechetical program developed by Jean Gerson. Around 1400, he launched a personal crusade to reinvigorate elementary catechesis.[60] Gerson was instrumental for making the final shift from the Vices to the Ten Com-

mandments and providing a synthesis of the two that laid the foundation
for the use of the Ten Commandments in the sixteenth century.[61]

Perhaps the best example of the Decalogue's new prominence, however, can be found in the *Beichtbüchlein* of Johannes Wolff, who referred
every part of his work to the Ten Commandments, for which reason he
acquired the title, "Doctor of the Ten Commandments of God."[62] Parts
One and Two of his work bring the teaching of the Ten Commandments
into the practice of confession, the first for children and inexperienced pen-
itents, the second for those who are more advanced. Part three shows how
all of the traditional categories for classifying sins and virtues can be sub-
sumed under the Decalogue. In the final section, Wolff explains what one
could expect from frequent Decalogue catechesis, giving voice to the theoretical assumptions behind the catechetical movement.

The Ten Commandments offered several advantages over the Seven
Sins as a framework for Christian ethics. First, they were Scriptural in a way
that the Vices (being derived from Greek philosophy) were not. "It was
Law—God's own Law, etched by his finger into tablets of stone, delivered
on Sinai amidst the frightful clamor of thunder and lightning, backed by
the promise of eternal blessedness for those who kept it and swift, dreadful
punishment for its transgressors."[63] Behavior is thus seen as obedience to
divine commands. Second, the commandments spelled out one's obligations to God in a way that the Vices did not. The latter at best dealt with
conduct over and against one's neighbor. The First Commandment, however, provided a foundation for the entire system in a way that the first vice
could not for the Vices. Third, the commandments provided guidelines with
regard to specific activities, whereas the Seven Sins dealt more with the feelings or disposition of a person, rather than the working out of those feelings
in practice. Finally, John Bossy also points out that the content of the Fourth
Commandment was an obligation not much noticed under the system of
Vices. The promise attached to it gave it even greater prominence.[64]

Just as he did with the Creed and Lord's Prayer, Luther readily received
and incorporated the Ten Commandments into his catechism. In fact, he
not only incorporated them but also used the abbreviated memory text of
the Middle Ages and the traditional numbering which were familiar to the
people of his day. He expounded the Ten Commandments in tracts and
writings fifteen times between 1518 and 1528.[65] Luther's treatment of the
Ten Commandments, however, shifted in light of his Reformation insights.
First, he stressed the Ten Commandments as the best description of God's
will for the Christian life over and against the humanly devised traditions

and works of the Roman church. In this light, special achievements no longer have value before God. Second, faith becomes the key to all good works, including the fulfillment of the Ten Commandments. This emphasis resulted in a revaluation of the every day works of the Decalogue. He emphasized that the Ten Commandments describe the contours of human life as God created it. Over and against the antinomians and libertines, who argued that the law must no longer be preached to the Christian who now "walks by the Spirit," Luther stressed that the human being, as a creature and sinner, has an ongoing need for the Ten Commandments. These conclusions moved to the forefront in the debate with John Agricola over the matter of repentance.[66] This explains in part why Luther devotes nearly one half of the entire large Catechism to a discussion of the Ten Commandments.

BAPTISM AND THE LORD'S SUPPER

In addition to the three parts that Luther called "the heritage of Christendom," he envisioned catechetical instruction on a second group of texts. In the Large Catechism, Luther adds, "When these three parts are understood, we ought also to know what to say about the sacraments, which Christ himself instituted, Baptism and the holy Body and Blood of Christ." (LC Short Preface 20) These topics gradually found their way into Luther's catechetical works during the decade of the 1520s.

Already in his *Formula Missae* (1523), Luther made the connection that there should be no mass without communicants. At the same time, only those who gave no offense in lifestyle, who were fully aware of what the Lord's Supper was, and who genuinely desired it were to be admitted. An appropriate exam should take place about once each year. In order to assist pastors in the task, Luther appended in 1523 "Five Questions Concerning the Lord's Supper" (WA 11:79–80) to his Short Form of 1520.[67] These questions were taken from his sermon on the Sacrament of the Altar of the same year. Two years later, the compiler of the first Wittenberg catechism, entitled *Eyn buchlin fur die leyen und kinder* (1525), added a description of Baptism from Mark 16 and the Words of Institution to the three traditional texts.[68] Finally, in the *German Mass* (1526) Luther used the language of five chief parts in connection with the word "catechism" for the first time.[69]

By including Baptism and the Lord's Supper in catechetical instruction, Luther revived a practice of the early church that supplemented prebaptismal catechesis with instruction on a fourth topic, namely, the sacraments. Two different traditions about the timing of this instruction developed within the early church, traditions that reflected different pedagogical methods. In the case of Chrysostom and Theodore of Mopsuestia, it occurred just prior to the Easter Vigil, so that the catechumen might better anticipate the event. In the case of Cyril of Jerusalem and Ambrose it took place following Baptism at the vigil, namely, during Easter week. Cyril believed that once the catechumens experienced the sacrament they would be more receptive to instruction. Apparently, his pedagogical principle was that experience should precede explanation, and that this ordering best served the mysteries. Often the liturgical rite itself provided the outline for instruction on the sacraments. Among the more famous examples of such instruction are the mystagogical lectures of Cyril in Jerusalem, Ambrose, and Theodore of Mopsuestia.[70] Augustine's practice was to begin the neophytes' instruction in the mystagogy on Easter morning.[71]

During the Middle Ages, instruction on the sacraments fell away as a regularly featured part of catechesis—an omission that Luther lamented and criticized in the Large Catechism (LC IV, 1). The sacraments were rarely topics for preaching until the Fourth Lateran Council in 1215, which required annual communion at Easter. But even then, preaching on the sacraments consisted primarily of exhorting people, especially during Lent, to go to confession and to partake of the Lord's Supper at Easter. Manuals written for priests largely gave instruction on how to perform the sacraments properly. Many confessional manuals in the late Middle Ages simply listed the seven sacraments with perhaps a few brief comments.[72] It was enough for people to know which rites were sacraments. These manuals might also list ways in which the sacraments helped a person against sin or how a person sins against the sacraments (e.g., Wolff's *Beichtbüchlein*). However, expositions of the nature and benefits of the sacraments were not commonplace.[73] Of all the sacraments, confession probably received the most attention. Baptism received the least attention. Even though later medieval commentaries on the Mass were "big" books, the average priest would not have possessed them.

Luther's treatment of the sacraments in the catechisms stands in sharp contrast to the relative neglect they received in the Middle Ages. With his *Babylonian Captivity of the Church* Luther launched a sustained and powerful attack on the sacramental system of the medieval church. While reducing the number of sacraments to two, Luther brought out their Gospel character. Where Baptism had been a relatively neglected sacrament in the Middle Ages, having been pushed to the periphery of the Christian life by the Sacrament of Penance, Luther moved Baptism to the center as a miniature picture of the Christian's entire life. Luther "took on Jerome's hackneyed view of Baptism and Penance (the first and second planks after the shipwreck of sin) and turned it on its head. Baptism never sinks, because Baptism is the ship itself."[74] Confession did not replace Baptism, instead, it became the way in which a Christian lives out his or her Baptism. Although the Mass (especially the adoration of the host) had been the central religious event of church life in villages, around which all other pilgrimages and devotions, revolved, laypersons received it very infrequently (perhaps two or three times a year). Again, Luther refocused attention on the sacrament itself as bringing the Gospel into people's lives.

AUXILIARY MATERIALS

While the topics and texts of the Decalogue, Creed, Lord's Prayer, Baptism and Lord's Supper defined the essence of the catechism, instruction was not confined exclusively to them. Often other topics and materials were appended to these core texts. Unlike the enduring relevance of the core texts, however, these materials were often expanded or reduced from time to time depending on the needs and situations. In the case of the confessional manuals in the Middle Ages, additional materials assisted in an ever increasingly minute examination of the penitent. These materials included catalogues of sins (the seven deadly sins, alien sins, crying sins, sins against the Holy Spirit) and listings of good works (six or seven works of bodily and spiritual mercy, the sevenfold gifts of the Spirit, the twelve fruits of the Spirit, eight beatitudes, and seven virtues). In the case of devotional writings, additional items and prayers might serve to obtain merits for salvation or solicit indulgences from the saints. Thus, the Hail Mary and other prayers to the saints were frequently included in addition to the Lord's Prayer. The accumulation of these materials often had the effect, however, of overshadowing the chief texts.

One of the first changes Luther made in the early stages of his catechetical writings was to restore the primary texts of the catechism to a place of prominence by stripping them of the mass of auxiliary material that had been appended to them. At the same time, Luther's own Small Catechism was not immune to a certain amount of expansion itself in the years following its publication. From its initial printing, new materials were appended in nearly every subsequent edition. In some instances, entrepreneurial printers took it upon themselves to add other items for marketing purposes so that they could bring to market a "new and revised" edition. These materials included various Psalms, prayers, different woodcuts, and portions of the liturgy. In a few instances, Luther himself played an active role in the addition of materials, such as a Brief Form for Confession, Daily Prayers, the Table of Duties, and the Marriage and Baptismal booklets.[75] When he does insert new items, Luther again shows that he was no radical and does not compose these materials *ex nihilo*. Instead, like other portions of the catechism, he uses the best of what he has inherited, but gives it a distinctive evangelical stamp.

CONFESSION

Confession, along with the Mass, had provided a central focus for religious life and practice in most villages during the Middle Ages. The other sacraments paled into insignificance by comparison. Confession and the Eucharist, however, were inextricably intertwined. People were required to receive communion once a year on pain of exclusion from the church and the denial of a Christian burial. But there could be no communion without confession, which served to purify a person and make that person worthy for receiving communion.

Against this backdrop of confession with its requirements for the complete enumeration of sins, many lay people would have dreaded the requirement of making confession—even once a year. In the Large Catechism Luther reflects that concern when he describes it as an "intolerable burden," "sheer anguish and a hellish torture since people had to make confession even though nothing was more hateful to them" (LC V.a 1–2). Following Luther's publication of the "Babylonian Captivity of the Church," the continuation of private confession was up for grabs. But by the end of the 1520s, the problem had shifted away from the burdensome nature of the confessional toward the tendency of dispensing with it altogether, in the name of a newly found evangelical freedom (LC V, 5–6). This debate was brought to a head in the debate between Melanchthon and Agricola in the latter half of the 1520s over the place of the law in repentance.[76]

Although the mandate for the practice of private confession is not found in the Bible nor was it widely practiced until its introduction by Irish monks in the eleventh century, Luther still found it to be a valuable opportunity for pastoral care. The section of confession did not appear in the first edition of either the Small or Large Catechisms. At some point in 1529 it found its way into the Large Catechism. In the Small Catechism a short form for confession was added in the June 13 edition. Two years later, in the High Wittenberg edition of 1531, Luther inserted three questions on confession and revised the form for confessing sins to the pastor. The inclusion of confession in both catechisms brought to a close a decade long debate among the evangelicals over its continued place within the Lutheran church.[77] It shows that in the end, the Lutheran reformers didn't abandon the practice of private confession like the Calvinists in favor of only a general confession. Instead they reformed it and incorporated it into their pastoral program.

DAILY PRAYERS

Luther had experienced the value of growing up with the discipline of daily prayer and, after becoming a monk, the extensive medieval monastic system of prayer, which shaped his days. Such formal discipline cultivated a habit of mind that is turned to God throughout the day and throughout a lifetime.[78] Now he needed to help the laity cultivate a prayer life as well. Such devotional advice and prayers had already been provided in the "Booklet for Laity and Children in 1525."[79] With his house prayers, "Luther transferred the prayer exercises (in an elementary form) that he had learned in his 'monastic family' into the sphere of the 'worldly' family and thus stimulated a lay piety."[80] This contained a certain amount of irony. The monastic movement of the early church originally had begun as a lay movement that retreated from the world in protest against the church conforming itself to the world. Now as Luther moves "the monastic prayer life into the sphere of the Christian (lay) family," that lay movement received a new impulse in a different direction. Rather than withdrawing from the world, the family now becomes an outpost for the church in the world![81]

Tracing their exact textual history within Luther's monastic prayer life is difficult, but it seems that Luther used material from the Roman Breviary and fifteenth-century catechetical writings in composing these sections. The inclusion of these prayers in the Small Catechism gave them a permanent place within Lutheran lives and provides an important link to the catholic prayer life of the church. Luther's house prayers are, according to origin, form, and contents, ecumenical prayers, which could find a place in every Christian prayerbook.

The morning and evening prayers bear striking resemblance to one another which suggests a common origin and a common author. Yet they may still be more a compilation than an original composition. For example, the introductory words of Luther's morning prayer ("I thank you, my heavenly Father ... that you have kept me through the night....") may trace their roots to a morning prayer in the *Rosetum* (Rose Garden) of Jean Mombaer,[82] a text that could be recognized as a first step to Luther's morning prayer. Its compilatory character takes us back even further into the ninth century. E. Sander has pointed out comparisons of this morning prayer with some that arose in the Carolingian period and were still around in the sixteenth century, slightly modified with a corresponding prayer for the evening.[83] The inheritance of the theme goes even further back to a Greek text by an Egyptian Monk named Makarios (died 390).[84] The endings of both prayers also trace their origins to the monastic prayer life and the Roman breviary. Luther seemed to form them from elements of Compline, which he had prayed daily as a monk and would have known by heart.[85] They clearly echo several Psalms, namely, 31:5; 91:5; and 34:7, that were mediated to Luther through the evening service of Compline. Frieder Schulz also conjectures that the concluding sentence of evening prayer was probably transferred to the morning prayer.

As with the morning and evening prayers, Luther took the dinner prayers from the Latin church's tradition, translated them into German, and incorporated them into his catechism. This applies both to the form as well as to the content of the prayers. With regard to structure, Schulz points out that it bears a strong resemblance to the Latin Collect,[86] in that it presupposes "that the praying table fellowship has come first with the Psalm and Lord's Prayer to the Word."[87] These prayers were written for the table liturgies of the monastic community, perhaps in the form of a dialogue with one speaking the Psalm verse and the rest speaking the prayer.

In both prayers Luther also retained the Latin superscriptions, *Benedicte* and *Gratias* (which serve as further evidence that he took them over from the monastic table prayers), where the invitation to the head is: *Benedicte*, i.e., Speak the table blessing. In the German setting, both prayers also stand in the Catholic songbook *Gotteslob*. These prayers can trace their roots far back into the history of the church, particularly, the Latin Church. Already the *Gelasianum* of the eighth century bears the superscription, "Prayers before Food" and "Prayers after *Cibos*" for two brief table collects.[88]

TABLE OF CHRISTIAN CALLINGS

The introductory sentence of the Table of Christian Callings reads: "A Chart of Some Bible Passages for the Household: Through these verses all kinds of *holy orders* [italics added] and estates may be admonished, as through lessons particularly pertinent to their office and duty."[89] The Table of Christian Callings does not have any direct or immediate connection with the Middle Ages, and yet the idea of listing obligations for different situations in life does have a lengthy history. The New Testament provides several "tables" or "listings" upon which Luther based his own list of responsibilities: Colossians 3:18–4:1; Ephesians 5:22–6:9; 1 Timothy 2:3–15; 6:1–2; Titus 2:1–10; 1 Peter 2:13–3:7. The Middle Ages themselves did not as a rule provide suggested listings in its confessional manuals or catechetical writings.

As early as A.D. 1000, society had been divided into clergy (those who pray), warriors (those who fight), and commoners (those who work).[90] Since at least the thirteenth century, catechists had used these categories in order to enjoin obedience to the traditional heads of the household, the church, and the body politic.[91] In general, these three groupings would be divided into the sacred (clergy) and the secular (commoners and warriors) with the former regarded as a superior mode of living. Government leaders were emphasized the least until the late fifteenth century.[92] Moreover, "the supreme authority of spiritual fatherhood was easier to assert when played off only against the household."[93]

The one writing on the eve of the Reformation that comes closest to offering something akin to a table of duties is Jean Gerson's *Tractate Concerning the Way of Life for All the Faithful*. This tract by the highly esteemed Parisian chancellor was printed in 1513 in Wittenberg. Thus Luther may well have been aware of it. In this tract, Gerson too outlines the triad of the ecclesiastical estate, military estate, and civilian estate. He provided a concise ethic in twenty-three "considerations" or "rules." He began with the obligations of the nobles and then concluded, as Luther does, with an exhortation to all Christians. In his instructions and considerations, he cited indiscriminately the Scriptures and church fathers. As for others in the Middle Ages, the spiritual estate is elevated above the simple estate. Like Luther, he addressed superiors first and then the subordinates.[94]

Luther already began working out a table or listing in his *Little Prayer Book* of 1522. There he pointed his readers toward Paul's Letter to Titus in order to give instruction for living a Christian life (*LW* 43, 42). In the first chapter Luther found guidelines for "what kind of a person a bishop or pastor should be," in the second for "persons in all situations of life—the young and the old, women and men, masters and servants," in the third Paul exhorts "honor and obedience to governmental authorities" (*LW* 43:42). He concludes with an exhortation to shun those who are stubborn and are heretics. Just prior to this work on the catechisms, Luther addressed the issue again in his *Great Confession* of 1528 in connection with the Second Article. He appears to have assembled his Table of Duties during his work on the Marriage Booklet in 1528. He felt strongly that they belonged to the catechism proper as can be seen from his introduction to "On the Ordination of the Worthy Sir Licentiate Stephan Klingebeil" of 1528:

Within our little community, we have the right catechism, that is, the Lord's Prayer, the Creed, the Ten Commandments; confession, Baptism, prayer, the cross, life, death, and the Sacrament of the Altar. In addition, it treats marriage, the secular authorities, father and mother, wife and child, man and son, servant and maid. In summary, I have brought all the walks of life in the world to good conscience and order, so that everyone knows how they should live and serve God in their station.... (WA 26:530, 28)[95]

Luther's Table of Christian Callings would have a profound impact on Lutheran history through expansion, copies, sermons and an entire genre of literature.

MARRIAGE AND BAPTISMAL BOOKLETS

Luther also included in the Small Catechism two further appendices of a liturgical nature: a marriage service (with introduction) and a Baptismal service (with introduction).[96] Both were written as remedies to the pitiful inadequacies of most of the clergy which were made painfully clear by the parish visitations. Thus he prepared this *Order of Marriage for Common Pastors* and published it in the early spring of 1529, even before the Small Catechism emerged from the presses. Luther subsequently inserted it into the May 16 edition after Part V. The Baptismal booklet was added a month later in the June 16 edition. These were intended to guide pastors' administration of these rites as well as to assist people's participation in the worship life of the congregation.

Unlike other services, the tradition had not firmly fixed the contours of the marriage service. As Martin Brecht points out, Luther worked "on the basis of the earlier church ordinance found in the Brandenburg missal which was prescribed for Wittenberg."[97] "For Luther, weddings and marriage were a 'secular business,' to be sure, but they had to do with a 'godly estate,' and also with a great venture." The act of marriage took place outside the church in front of the church doors. This included the "marriage questions, the exchange of rings, and the announcement of marriage." After the actual marriage, the pastor and the wedding party then proceeded into the sanctuary itself. Once in front of the altar, the pastor read several pertinent Bible passages about marriage. This was followed with a formulary that mentioned the cross imposed "on the married estate with its pain of childbirth and bitter toil, but then continued with the promise contained within God's command to procreate." The final prayer of the service referred to God's ordinance of marriage and prayed for perseverance in it.[98]

Unlike the marriage ceremony, the Baptismal liturgy that Luther inherited traces the course of its origin, development, and decay back to an early Roman Baptismal liturgy in the days of the adult catechumenate. That earlier pattern was conflated and fragmented from the time of Gregory the Great.[99] Luther published his first edition of the Baptismal booklet in 1523 (*LW* 53:95–105; WA 12:42–48) in order to address the pressing need of providing an order in which the laity could intelligently participate. This itself had been necessitated by Luther's insistence that the intercession of the church was the basis for the faith of the child. In general, it followed the Roman rite, except that the exorcism had been abbreviated, the Creed moved from its location before the Lord's Prayer and placed in the questions, and the collect replaced by the so-called "flood" prayer. It initiated a new evangelical practice of Baptism, but was eventually criticized even by Nicholas Hausmann who wanted a "purification" of the Latin rite.[100] As a result, Luther revised the order and made several important changes in the 1526 edition.[101] In particular, Luther omitted many of the human ceremonies and usages that clouded the essentials of the sacrament (*LW* 53:106–9; WA 19:537–41).[102]

OTHER MATERIALS

Already in the first few editions a number of other materials were added. For example, in the June 16 edition, a German litany with music, three collects, and twenty Illustrations were added. Entrepreneurial printers would add even more. Thus after 1531, the catechism would occasionally include a variety of other supplementary materials. At times Psalm 111 was added (which was sung at the Lord's Supper); the Te Deum, the Magnificat, the Prayer against the Turk (Lord Keep Us Steadfast in Thy Word). In the years following Luther's death, several other parts would be added, which he did not write, for example, a section on the Office of the Keys[103] and the Christian Questions and Answers.[104] These latter two would find an enduring and influential place in the catechism—at least within the Saxon tradition.

SUMMARY

Although it has been common to speak of the Small Catechism as Luther's Small Catechism, it is also appropriate to simply refer to it as the Small Catechism or the church's Small Catechism. In other words, it belongs to the entire church. Every portion of it bespeaks its catholicity. It contains, and in turn is defined by, those components of Scripture that the church has at all times and in all places identified as formative texts for shaping a Christian identity and shaping a Christian life.

NOTES

1   Indeed, many were taught such a definition. For example, the second question in the catechism prepared for use in The Lutheran Church–Missouri Synod reads, "What is a catechism? A catechism is a book of instruction in the form of questions and answers." *A Short Explanation of Dr. Martin Luther's Small Catechism: A Handbook of Christian Doctrine* (St. Louis: Concordia, 1943), 39.

2   The word "Enchiridion" has double meanings, that of either a small manual or handbook that one might hold in the hand or that of a small weapon like a dagger. Augustine seems to follow the former when he writes, "Now you ask of me a small handbook, that is one that can be carried in the hand, not one to load your shelves." It contains the most necessary things for a person regarding the chief end of life. St. Augustine, *The Enchiridion on Faith, Hope, and Love* (ed. Henry Paolucci; South Bend, Ind.: Gateway Editions, 1961), 5. Erasmus of Rotterdam goes with the latter meaning of treating the Enchiridion as a spiritual weapon that the Christian needs throughout life—a theme that he pursues throughout his little book, whose original title was *Enchiridion militis Christiani. The Enchiridion of Erasmus* (tr. and ed. Raymond Himelick; Bloomington: Indiana University Press, 1963). First published in 1503, it went through many editions. In a number of ways, Luther's catechism epitomizes both definitions. Every Christian is sworn to battle the world, the flesh, and the Devil. Those who could not handle the whole *gladium spiritus* in its Vulgate version needed a "kind of all-occasions weapon, something portable, practical, and concrete enough to give real meaning to the Scriptural metaphor" (13). Hence, a dagger was a small blade, not too cumbersome to keep handy or too ineffectual to do any good. "If people thought it necessary to arm themselves physically against the danger of highwaymen, was it not even more essential to arm the mind and spirit to cope with the real difficulties of everyday Christian living?" (13–14).

3   Gottfried Krodel, "Luther's Work on the Catechism in the Context of Late Medieval Catechetical Literature," *Concordia Journal* 25 (October 1999): 364–404.

4   See Hans Jürgen-Fraas, Wolfgang Grünberg, Gerhard Bellinger, and Peter Hauptmann, "Katechismus," in *Theologische Realenzyklopädie* (ed. Gerhard Krause & Gerhard Müller; Berlin: de Gruyter, 1988), XVII:710ff.

5   Mary Jane Haemig, "Preaching the Catechism: A Transformational Enterprise," *Dialog* 36 (1997):101. Haemig provides a good discussion of what kind of transformation the catechism is intended to effect.

6   Robert Rosin, "Christians and Culture: Finding Place in Clio's Mansions," in *Christ and Culture: The Church in a Post-Christian America*, Symposium Papers, Number 4 (St. Louis: Concordia Seminary Monograph Series, 1996), 85.

7   See Wilhelm Maurer, *Historical Commentary on the Augsburg Confession* (tr. George Anderson; Philadelphia: Fortress, 1986), 210, footnote 586. See also, *LW* 47:52–53 (WA 30.3:367.19–20); *LW* 34:91 (WBr 5 no. 1572.39ff); and *LW* 49:307 (WBr 5; nos. 1602.49–50, 1590.70ff). In the latter, he writes, "As a consequence, the young people, both boys and girls, grow up so well instructed in the Catechism and the Scriptures that I am deeply moved when I see that young boys and girls can pray, believe, and speak more of God and Christ than they ever could in the monasteries, foundations, and schools of bygone days, or even in our day."

8   See the introduction to Luther's Baptismal Booklet (*Taufbüchlein*) on this point. There, Luther puts this transfer of lordship into the starkest of terms as he

describes Baptism as taking action against the devil and driving him away from the child. See Timothy Wengert's *A Contemporary Translation of Luther's Small Catechism: Study Edition* (Philadelphia: Augsburg Fortress, 1994), 67–68.

9 See Mary Jane Heimig, "Preaching the Catechism: A Transformational Enterprise," *Dialog* 36 (1997):100–104; and Charles P. Arand, "Does Catechesis in the LCMS Aim for the *Ars Vivendi Fide*?" *Concordia Journal* 22 (January 1996): 57–65.

10 2 Clement 17:1 uses the word to designate pre-Baptismal instruction. The Latin *catechizare* appears in Tertullian, Ambrose, and Augustine for the teaching of Christianity to neophytes when preparing them for participation in the sacrament of Baptism. William Harmless points out that the verb *catechizare* had a broader range of meaning in the early church than today. "Latin authors—from Tertullian and Victorinus to Jerome and Augustine—tended to lump together under the single word *catechizare* what we tend to distinguish: evangelizing and catechizing." *Augustine and the Catechumenate* (Collegeville, Minn.: Liturgical, 1995), 108.

11 Augustine is the first to use the noun *catechismus* as a designation for the basic topics of Christian instruction. Augustine, "Faith and Works," trans. Sister Marie Liguori, in *Saint Augustine, Treatises on Marriage and Other Subjects*, in *The Fathers of the Church*, Volume 27 (New York: Fathers of the Church, 1955), 221–82. See also Charlton T. Lewis and Charles Short, *A Latin Dictionary* (Oxford: Clarendon, 1975), ad loc.

12 P. Egino Weidenhiller. *Untersuchungen der deutschsprachigen katechetischen Literatur des späten Mittelalters* (München: C. H. Beck'sche Verlagsbuchhandlung), 16.

13 These components also identify other writings, like the Heidelberg Catechism and the recent Catechism of the Catholic Church, as catechisms. See Joseph Cardinal Ratzinger and Christoph Schönborn, in *Introduction to the Catechism of the Catholic Church* (San Francisco: Ignatius, 1994), 16.

14 Martin Luther, "An Open Letter to Those in Frankfurt on the Main, 1533," tr. Jon D. Vieker, *Concordia Journal* (October 1990): 343.

15 Leonel L. Mitchell. "The Development of Catechesis in the Third and Fourth Centuries: From Hippolytus to Augustine," in John H. Westerhoff III and O. C. Edwards, Jr., *A Faithful Church: Issues in the History of Catechesis* (Wilton, Conn.: Morehouse-Barlow, 1981), 76.

16 Josef Andreas Jungman, *Handing on the Faith: A Manual of Catechetics* (London: Burns & Oates, 1959), 5.

17 In the case of St. Cyril of Jerusalem, the Creed was probably presented to the catechumens at the end of the fifth week. The remaining two weeks before Holy Week were used for expounding it.

18 The Lord's Prayer would be taught sometimes before Easter (Augustine and Theodore) sometimes after (Ambrose and Cyril).

19 Cyril, for example, states, "But in learning the Faith and in professing it, acquire and keep that only which is now delivered to you by the Church, and which has been built up strongly out of all the Scriptures. For since all cannot read the Scriptures, some being hindered by lack of learning and others by lack of leisure, we comprise the entire doctrine of the Faith in a few lines in order that the soul may not perish from ignorance. This summary I wish you both to commit to memory and to study with all diligence among yourselves." Cyril of Jerusalem,

Catechetical Orations 5:12, PG 33, col. 520. He continues, "Within these verses are contained all instruction in the faith." Cyril of Jerusalem, *The Works of St. Cyril of Jerusalem: Procatechesis and Catecheses 1–12, and Catechesis 13–18 and Mystagogical Lectures, The Fathers of the Church*, Vols. 61 and 64 (tr. Leo P. McCauley and Anthony A. Stephenson; Washington: Catholic University of America, 1968).

20   *Saint Caesarius of Arles: Sermons or Admonitions on Various Topics*, in *Fathers of the Church* (tr. Sister Mary Magadeleine Mueller; New York: Fathers of the Church, 1956), 55.

21   See Augustine's treatment of the Creed in Harmless, *Augustine and the Catechumenate*, 274–86.

22   Harmless, *Augustine and the Catechumenate*, 278. Augustine states, "The words you have heard, scattered all across the Sacred Scriptures, are here gathered up and reduced to a tight unity. With the burden of our sluggish memory thus eased, every one should be able effectively to say and do what he believes." Robert I. Bradley, *The Roman Catechism in the Catechetical Tradition of the Church: The Structure of the Roman Catechism as Illustrative of the "Classic Catechesis"* (Lanham, Md.: University Press of America, 1990), 31.

23   "Saint Peter Chrysologus: Selected Sermons and Saint Valerian Homilies," *Fathers of the Church* (tr. George E. Ganss; New York: Fathers of the Church, 1953), 111.

24   Harmless, *Augustine and the Catechumenate*, 287.

25   "Saint Peter Chrysologus," 115.

26   *St. Gregory of Nyssa: The Lord's Prayer*, in *Ancient Christian Writers* (tr. Hilda C. Graef; Westminster: Newman, 1954), 24.

27   To be sure, large portions of Germany had only recently converted to Christianity, but as a rule these involved mass conversions and Baptisms with little to no instruction. But there are no written accounts given to the barbarians, or treatises on catechesis from this period. See Peter Göbl, *Geschichte der Katechese im Abendlande vom Verfalle des Katechumenats bis zum Ende des Mittelalters* (Kempten: Verlag der Joseph Kösl'schen Buchhandlung: 1880), which remains a standard on the subject. See the Catechism of Weißenburg, which provided materials for priests to catechize the laity, c. 798–820. Wilhelm Braune and Karl Helm, *Althochdeutsches Lesebuch*, 15th ed. (ed. Ernst A. Ebbinghaus; Tübingen: Niemeyer Verlag, 1969), 34–37.

28   Richard Poore and Robert Grosseteste suggested that parish priests hold instruction classes for children. H. Leith Spencer, *English Preaching in the Middle Ages* (Oxford: Clarendon, 1993), 211.

29   *Dictionary of the Middle Ages* (ed. Joseph R. Strayer; New York: Charles Scribner's Sons, 1988), 10:301. In his Table Talk, Luther does praise the "little schools" that taught the Creed and the Lord's Prayer and thus preserved the church through the Middle Ages: "Little boys have learned at least the Lord's Prayer and the Creed in the schools, and the church has been remarkably preserved through such small schools." *LW* 54:452.

30   Milton McC. Gatch, "Basic Christian Education from the Decline of Catechesis to the Rise of the Catechisms," in John H. Westerhoff III and O. C. Edwards, Jr., *A Faithful Church: Issues in the History of Catechesis* (Wilton, Conn.: Morehouse-Barlow, 1981), 88.

31   A work attributed to St. Eligius (d. 659) shows him insisting on parental responsibility in handing on the truths of the faith. "Know by memory the Symbol and

the Lord's Prayer, and teach them to your children. Instruct and admonish the children, whom you have received as newborn from the Baptismal fount, to live ever in the fear of God. Know that you have taken an oath on their behalf" (PL 87:527) quoted in *NCE* 3:209. A treatise from the ninth century attributed to a Christian woman, Dodana, entitled *Liber Manualis* illustrates the way a home catechesis might have been carried out at its best (*PL* 106:109–18).

32 P. Egino Weidenhiller, *Untersuchungen der deutschsprachigen katechetischen Literatur des späten Mittelalters* (München: C. H. Beck'sche Verlagsbuchhandlung), 13–14.

33 See Berthold of Ratisbon quoted in M. Reu, *Dr. Martin Luther's Small Catechism: A History of Its Origin, Its Distribution and Its Use* (Chicago: Wartburg, 1929), 1.

34 Berard L. Marthaler, *The Catechism Yesterday and Today: The Evolution of a Genre* (Collegeville, Minn.: Liturgical, 1995), 10. For another example that states that men and women should not be sponsors unless they know the basics, see M. Gatch, 87–88. Luther, too, notes the practice when he suggests that adults who can not recite the catechism should "not be accepted as sponsors at Baptism" (SC Pref. 11). This practice continued well into the sixteenth century. See Robert Kolb, "The Layman's Bible: The Use of Luther's Catechisms in the German Late Reformation," in *Luther's Catechisms—450 Years: Essays Commemorating the Small and Large Catechisms of Dr. Martin Luther* (ed. David Scaer and Robert D. Preus; Fort Wayne, Ind.: Concordia Theological Seminary Press, 1979), 16–26.

35 *NCE* 3:210.

36 Rosamond McKitterick, *The Frankish Church and the Carolingian Reforms, 789–895* (London: Royal Historical Society, 1977), 6.

37 Milton McC. Gatch, "Carolingian Preaching," in *Preaching and Theology in Anglo-Saxon England: Aelfric and Wulfstan* (Toronto: University of Toronto, 1977), 37.

38 Thomas L. Amos, "Preaching and the Sermon in the Carolingian World," *De Ore Domini: Preacher and the Word in the Middle Ages* (Kalamazoo: Medieval Institute Publications, 1989), 45.

39 Gatch, "Basic Christian Education from the Decline of Catechesis to the Rise of the Catechisms," 90.

40 In the early church, the Creed was also called a *symbolum*, that is, a password by which a faithful Christian is recognized or the mirror in which you see yourself. This role of the creed arose as a result of a legal action taken by the Roman Emperor Theodosius who in 380 decreed that the Roman Empire was to be a Christian empire. In this connection, "Christian" was defined in terms of the Creed. Thus in order to become a citizen in good standing within the empire, one had to confess belief in the triune God. Here the Creed spelled out the knowledge, the obedience, and the affirmation of which qualified a person for citizenship and church membership. Thus Baptism and the Creed marked the transition from pagan to Christian and from barbarian to Roman. This legal or constitutional role of the Creed in the socio-political realm carried over into the medieval kingdoms and remained an important factor up through the year 1000. Harmless, *Augustine and the Catechumenate*, 283. See J. N. D. Kelly, *Early Christian Creeds*, 3rd ed. (London: Longman Group Limited, 1979), 52–61, for a discussion of the origin and meaning of the word *symbolum*.

41 Jean Gerson, *Brief Introduction to the Christian Faith*, tr. by Paul Robinson from *Je croy en la benoiste et sainte Trinité, Oeuvres Complètes*, Vol. VII: L'Oeuvre francaise (ed. P. Glorieux; Paris: Desclée & Cie, 1966), 206–209.

42   I am indebted to Prof. Paul Robinson for these insights. He is currently finishing a Ph.D. dissertation at the University of Chicago on Medieval catechetical preaching on the Lord's Prayer.

43   See Weinrich's analysis of this "Two Ways" in William C. Weinrich, "Early Christian Catechetics: An Historical and Theological Construction," in *Luther's Catechisms—450 Years: Essays Commemorating the Small and Large Catechisms of Dr. Martin Luther*, (ed. David P. Scaer and Robert D. Preus; Fort Wayne, Ind.: Concordia Theological Seminary Press, 1979), 65–73.

44   As early as 397, Augustine had shown in *Serm.* 9.7 and 13 that he regarded the Decalogue as the norm and framework for Christian morality. See P. Rentschka, *Die Dekalogkatechese des h. Augustinus: ein Beitrag zur Geschichte des Dekalogs* (Kempten, 1905), 106. Augustine "is the first writer of catechetics to point out that the Decalogue, as summed up in the two great commandments of love of God and love of our Neighbor, is the foundation of Christian morality." "Introduction," *St. Augustine: The First Catechetical Instruction* [*De Catechizandis Rudibus*] (tr. and annotated by Joseph P. Christopher; Westminster, Md.: Newman Bookshop, 1946), 5–6. See also Robert I. Bradley, *The Roman Catechism in the Catechetical Tradition of the Church: The Structure of the Roman Catechism as Illustrative of the "Classic Catechesis"* (Lanham, Md.: University Press of America, 1990) and *NCE* 3:226.

45   See Robert James Bast, *Honor Your Fathers: Catechisms and the Emergence of a Patriarchal Ideology in Germany, 1400–1600* (Leiden: Brill, 1997), 33. See especially the chapter, "The Ten Commandments and the 'Crisis Dynamic'," 32–45.

46   Bast, "The Ten Commandments and the 'Crisis Dynamic'," 34.

47   The first three came from Paul and were known as the chief theological virtues implanted in people at Baptism. The second four came from Greek philosophy and were known as the cardinal virtues that were held in common by all, Christian and non-Christian alike.

48   Bast, "The Ten Commandments and the 'Crisis Dynamic'," 34. They were called deadly because each of them, if practiced persistently, could damn the soul by destroying its capacity to love. They were generally listed in a descending hierarchy of importance in accord with their ability to destroy love. See Bernard Hamilton, *Religion in the Medieval West* (London: Bernard Hamilton, 1986), 132–41 for a handy summary and description.

49   John Bossy, "Moral Arithmetic: Seven Sins into Ten Commandments," in *Conscience and Casuistry in Early Modern Europe* (ed. Edmund Leites; Cambridge: Cambridge University Press, 1988), 215. He traces the transition from catechizing on the Vices to the Ten Commandments and how each was expounded individually or together.

50   Bast, "The Ten Commandments and the 'Crisis Dynamic'," 35.

51   See W. David Myers, *Poor, Sinning Folk* (Ithaca, N.Y.: Cornell University Press, 1996), 27–60, for an account of the practical ways in which the practice of confession was implemented in the daily lives of the average parishioner. He also helpfully points out how the rise of the practice of adoration of the sacrament created concern about worthiness to receive it.

52   Previously local synods would occasionally decree the need to attend confession and communion two to four times a year. In that connection, the Lateran Council was actually a lowering of the standard when it mandated once a year.

53 See P. Egino Weidenhiller, *Untersuchungen zur deutschsprachigen katechetischen Literatur des späten Mittelalters* (München: C. H. Beck'sche Verlagsbuchhandlung, 1965), 12. Weidenhiller has a good discussion of the contents of medieval catechisms on pages 16–24. The particular value of this work lies in the fact that it examines distinctively German catechism materials.

54 Myers, *Poor, Sinning Folk*, 39.

55 Harmut Jetter, *Erneuerung des Katechismusunterrichts. Theologische und pädagogische Grundfragen zu Luthers Kleinem Katechismus in der Gegenwart* (Heidelberg: Quelle & Meyer, 1965), 9.

56 Bossy, "Moral Arithmetic: Seven Sins into Ten Commandments," 218.

57 Bossy, "Moral Arithmetic: Seven Sins into Ten Commandments," 220.

58 Bossy, "Moral Arithmetic: Seven Sins into Ten Commandments," 220–22.

59 Lewis W. Spitz, "Further Lines of Inquiry for the Study of 'Reformation and Pedagogy'," in *The Pursuit of Holiness in Late Medieval and Renaissance Religion* (ed. Charles Trinkaus with Heiko A. Oberman; Leiden: E. J. Brill, 1974), 295. "The impression that the pre-Lutheran and much contemporary Catholic confessional and catechetical instructional materials make is that of a Christianity which, as J. Toussaert puts it, was 80 percent morals, 15 percent dogma, and 5 percent sacraments," Spitz, 300.

60 His teaching marked a new departure for Christian catechesis by treating the commandments as the rock of Christian ethics, establishing a tradition of effective vernacular exposition, and integrating these things into a larger theological position and scheme of catholic piety, including the practice of confession.

61 See Bossy, "Moral Arithmetic: Seven Sins into Ten Commandments," 224.

62 *Beichtbüchlein des Magisters Johannes Wolff (Lupi)* (ed. F. W. Battenberg; Gießen: Verlag von Alfred Topelmann, 1907), 112–17. Bast reports how after the death of their pastor, the parishioners of St. Peterskappel set up a remarkable monument to him. On the wall of the chapel they erected a memorial sculpture that consisted of two parts. The first is an epitaph depicting Wolff himself staring down at the viewer. One hand counts off the fingers in an unmistakable reference to his system for drilling the commandments from the pulpit. Carved around him is the honorific title "Doctor of the Ten Commandments of God," 27.

63 Bast, "The Ten Commandments and the 'Crisis Dynamic'," 43.

64 Bossy, "Moral Arithmetic: Seven Sins into Ten Commandments," 232f.

65 *Decem praecepta Wittenbergensi praedicata populo*, WA 1:398–521 (1518, based on sermons preached 1516–17); *Eine kurze Erklärung der zehn Gebote*, WA 1:250–56 (1518); *Instructio pro confessione peccatorum*, WA 1:258–65 (1518); *Eine kurz underwysung, wie man beichten sol*, WA 2:59–64 (1519); *Von den guten Werken*, WA 6:202–76, (1520); *Eyn kurz form der zehen gepott. Eyn kurz form der glaub. Eyn kurz form des Vaterunsers*, WA 7:204f (1520); *The Abrogation of the Mass* (WA 8:457–554, (1521–22); *Judgement on Monastic Vows*, WA 8:573–669 (1521–22); *Betbüchlein*, WA 10II:377–88 (1522); *Sermon Exodus 20:12*, WA 11:30–48 (1523); *Predigten über das 2. Buch Mose*, WA 16:422–528 (1525); *Unterricht der Visitatoren an die Pfarrherren ym Kurfurstenthum zu Sachsen* (prologue by Luther, text by Melanchthon) WA 26:207f (1527); *Katechismuspredigten* (three series: May 18–23; Sept. 14–21; Nov. 30-Dec. 7, 1528), WA 30:1–85; *Auslegung D. Martin Luthers über etliche Capitel des fuenfften Buchs Mosi, Gepredigt zu Wittenberg* (1529),WA 28:509–762; Small Catechism and Large Catechism.

66   See Timothy J. Wengert, *Law and Gospel: Philip Melancththon's Debate with John Agricola of Eisleben over Poenitentia* (Grand Rapids: Baker Books, 1998).

67   "A Brief Explanation of the Ten Commandments, the Creed, and the Lord's Prayer," *Works of Martin Luther, The Board of Publication, U.L.C.*, vol. II (Philadelphia: Muhlenberg Press, 1943), 354–55. This was originally intended to help people prepare for confession. Its expanded role suggests that it is also helped them to prepare for the Lord's Supper.

68   This text was compiled anonymously, most likely, speculates Timothy Wengert, by Stephan Roth, a student and catechist in Wittenberg and later city secretary in Zwickau. It included excerpts from Luther's *Little Prayer Book* (*LW* 43:11–38) and other sources in Luther's writings. See Wengert, *Law and Gospel*, 34.

69   Luther never actually used the phrase "six chief parts." In the Small Catechism, he does not introduce the topic of confession with the usual words, "How the Head of the House Should Teach..."; and so Luther came to speak of the "five parts covering the whole of Christian doctrine" (LC Short Preface, 24).

70   Cyril of Jerusalem. *Mystagogical Cateches*, V, 11–18, "The Lord's Prayer." *In The Works of St. Cyril of Jerusalem: Procatechesis and Cateches 1–12*, and *Catechesis 13–18* and *Mystagogical Lectures* (tr. Leo P. McCauley and Anthony A. Stephenson; Washington: Catholic University of America Press, 1968); *The Fathers of the Church*, Vols. 61 and 64; Theodore of Mopsuestia, *Catechetical Homilies: Commentary of Theodore of Mopsuestia on the Lord's Prayer, and on the Sacraments of Baptism and the Eucharist* (Cambridge: W. Heffer and Sons, Ltd., 1933). *Woodbrook Studies*, Vol. VI 11–16.

71   See Harmless, *Augustine and the Catechumenate*, 313–17.

72   Krodel, "Luther's Work on the Catechism," 365–72.

73   See Weidenhiller, *Untersuchungen*, 21–22. Jean Gerson represents an exception to this rule. In his *Brief Explanation of Christian Doctrine* he highlights the distinctive gift of each of the seven sacraments for the Christian life.

74   Timothy J. Wengert, "Lutheran Children: Baptism and the Fourth Commandment," *Dialog: A Journal of Theology* 37 (Summer 1998): 186.

75   The Preface, the Brief Form of Confession, as well as the *Baptismal Booklet* and *Marriage Booklet*, have not always been incorporated into subsequent editions of the Small Catechism as used within Lutheran churches. Already in 1580 Jacob Andreae intended to omit them from the *Book of Concord* on the grounds that they belong in the realm of church order rather than of doctrine. The Elector of Brandenburg and the Lower Saxon provincial churches, however, wanted the Small Catechism "unmutilated." The Electors of Saxony and of the Palatinate were dubious about including the two Booklets because of the negative attitude of the South Germans toward the exorcisms at Holy Baptism. The matter was never completely settled. "Technically, the Dresden edition of 1580 was to be published with the two Booklets in a separate printing, with their place indicated by printing the foliations 169–73 on the last leaf containing the Small Catechism so that they could be included or omitted at the discretion the competent political authority." Arthur Carl Piepkorn, "Suggested Principles for a Hermeneutics of the Lutheran Symbols," *Concordia Theological Monthly* 29 (January 1958): 10–11. Piepkorn also provides the data for a number of the earliest editions of the *Book of Concord*.

76   See an excellent treatment of this subject in Wengert, *Law and Gospel*.

77 Luther still found it necessary to defend the inclusion of confession within the catechism as late as 1533 in an "Open Letter to those in Frankfurt on the Main, 1533," tr. Jon D. Vieker, *Concordia Journal* 16 (October 1990): 333–51.

78 Robert A. Kolb, *Teaching God's Children His Teaching: A Guide for the Study of Luther's Catechism* (Hutchinson, Minn.: Crown Publishing, 1992), 7–1.

79 This is one of the most important forerunners of the SC. Timothy Wengert discovered the only remaining copy. See "Wittenberg's Earliest Catechism," *Lutheran Quarterly* 7 (1993): 247–60. The dinner prayers are the same in *A Booklet for the Laity and Children* and the Small Catechism. The morning and evening prayers differed, though a similar pattern is suggested.

80 Peters V: 203.

81 Peters V: 194.

82 Peters V: 195.

83 Peters V: 196.

84 Peters V: 196f.

85 Schulz points out that these verses were used in Dormitorium for praying the Completorium Ordo Romanus XVIII, 10: "*ubi dormiunt in dormitorio*" (Andrieu, *Les Ordines Romani*, Bd 3, 206). Ps 31:6 appeared in the Responsorium breve. The Oration "visita quaesumus" contained angels...." Also the hymn of the Komplet occupied itself with the evil foe. See Peters, V: 192f.

86 Peters V: 200.

87 Peters V: 200.

88 The "pattern for Luther's prayer before Dinner appears first in the Missale of Bobbio from the eighth century," Peters, V: 201.

89 Wengert, *A Contemporary Translation*, 57.

90 Bradley, 34.

91 See Wilhelm Maurer, *Luthers Lehre von den drei Hierarchien und ihr mittelalterlicher Hintergrund* (München, 1970). Bast, "The Ten Commandments and the 'Crisis Dynamic'," 44. Kolde insists that the Fourth Commandment applies "not only to our natural parents, but also to spiritual and earthly authorities, Denis Janz, *Three Reformation Catechisms: Catholic, Anabaptist, Lutheran* (New York: Edwin Mellen Press, 1982), 55. In his small catechism Wolff focuses on parents and refers to the others in passing. In his larger treatment, he deals first with parents, then spiritual authorities, and then earthly authorities.

92 Kolde devotes nearly an equal amount of space to parents and priests, and only a slightly less amount of space to earthly authorities (focuses on denying rights of rulers or fostering treason). Wolff, on the other hand, devotes the majority of space to spiritual authorities.

93 Bast, "The Ten Commandments and the 'Crisis Dynamic'," 147.

94 Peters V:101–104 provides a number of parallels.

95 Peters, V: 95–96.

96 For translations of these introductions, see Wengert, *A Contemporary Translation of Luther's Small Catechism: Study Edition* (Philadelphia: Augsburg Fortress, 1994), 61–63, 67–69.

97 Brecht, *Luther*, II: 258.

98 Brecht, *Luther*, II: 258.

99 For its development, see J. D. C. Fisher, *Christian Initiation: Baptism in the Medieval West* (London: Society for Promoting Christian Knowledge, 1965).

100 Brecht, *Luther*, II: 122.

101 See Bryan Spinks, "Luther's *Taufbüchlein*," *Liturgical Review* (November 1975): 17–20 and (May 1996): 13–21.

102 The exsufflation was omitted, the second of the two opening prayers, the giving of salt, the first of two exorcisms, and the prayer after the exorcism, the salutation before the Gospel, etc.

103 No such part is found in any of the editions during Luther's lifetime, nor does it appear that the materials originated with him, Reu, *Dr. Martin Luther's Small Catechism*, 39. Its best known form was derived from Osiander's and Sleupner's *Nürnberg Sermons for Children* (1533).

104 "Christian Questions for Those Who Want to Receive the Lord's Supper." They appear for the first time in a separate Erfurt edition of 1549. In *Luther's Small Catechism* we find them for the first time in an undated Wittenberg edition (1551–1566). It appears that Lange of Erfurt (died in 1548) was their author. See Reu, *Dr. Martin Luther's Small Catechism*, 44–45

2

The Versatile Catechism

For more than one and one-half millennia the church used the Ten Commandments, Creed, and Lord's Prayer as its basic instructional syllabus. Throughout that time, these texts demonstrated their value as perennially relevant expressions of Christian existence, texts that renewed the minds of those who imbibed them.

Although the church identified these components as definitive for the Christian life, it did not identify or use a single medium or setting for bringing these texts into the lives of the people. Where a certain uniformity characterized these texts, diversity and variety characterized the delivery systems used for conveying those texts to the people. Here the church found it necessary to adapt itself to the exigencies of its day and the needs of its people, and this meant that it could not restrict its presentation of the catechism to one format or setting.

Not until the sixteenth century did the term "catechism" become indelibly linked with one particular genre. Prior to that, the Decalogue, Creed, and Lord's Prayer appeared in many forms: sermons, liturgies, confessional manuals, prayer books, wooden tablets, and instructional books. Although it might be somewhat anachronistic to apply the title "catechism" as a technical term to many of these forms of presentation prior to the sixteenth century, it is not inappropriate to regard them as catechetical literature for the reason that they contained the texts of the catechism.

This inherited tradition of catechetical literature (sermons, confessional manuals, prayer books, and instructional books) flowed like tributaries of a river into Luther's own catechisms. These various forms have several important implications for our understanding of Luther's catechism and its use. First, and perhaps most importantly, they highlight the versatility of the catechism within the church, a versatility that might be likened to a theological Swiss Army Knife. The texts of the catechism were useful in many different situations and for many different purposes. During the sixteenth century, and for centuries afterward, the Small Catechism served as an instructional text, a prayer book, a guide to pastoral care, a theological norm, and a confessional manual. Second, these different forms bring out the various opportunities that the church had to reinforce the catechism through frequent and varied contact with the catechism. As people in advertising know, if you want to get a message out, you need at least four or five different means for delivering the message before people finally "get it." If the texts of the catechism were useful in a variety of settings and for various purposes, these forms in turn served to stamp the catechism on the minds and hearts of the people. Third, these various forms make clear the importance of learning the catechism and make the point that they should permeate all aspects of Christian existence. Finally, the incorporation of the texts of the catechism into these various forms expresses the unity of theology and practice which enabled Luther to used the catechism as a way of exercising pastoral care.

The Reformation did introduce one new element to the traditional media for conveying the catechism—the printing press. The reformers had inherited a wide range of instruments and used all of these media for getting their message out, but the reformers took them to a new level through the sheer quantity and numbers in which these were printed. The printing press allowed them to turn these formats into instruments of mass communication, especially in the vernacular. Thus the printing press allowed them to "broadcast" their program "to a much larger and more geographically diverse audience than had ever been possible before."[1] According to Mark Edwards, the Reformers engaged in the first large-scale "media campaign" to "shape and channel a mass movement"[2] during the 1520s. While the printing press made possible the wide dissemination of Luther's writings, it especially applies to the catechisms, which were, after all, intended for a popular audience.

THE CATECHISM AS SERMON

The most common medium for familiarizing people with the texts of the catechism throughout the history of the church has been the sermon. This was so for two reasons. First, preaching goes to the heart of Christianity. In part this is due to the nature of Christianity which from the beginning has been a religion centered on the verbal proclamation of the Gospel. The Word incarnate in flesh becomes the Word incarnate in words through proclamation. For most of the church's history, little to no distinction was drawn between teaching and preaching. Second, sermons were suited for a society and culture in which oral communication was the most effective means to reach large numbers of people. In fact, it could be argued that the dominant medium for catechetical instruction from the early church through the Middle Ages and even down to the seventeenth century was in fact the sermon.[3] In some instances these sermons were recorded in order to provide a sermon resource for other priests. Because many were not recorded, sermons are easily overlooked as a catechetical medium.

In the third and fourth centuries, catechesis took place as oral instruction[4] within the structure of the catechumenate in preparation for Baptism. Such instruction took the form of sermons or lectures delivered by the bishops during various stages in the catechumenate.[5] As Harmless notes, however, the catechumens did not always receive special instruction. Instead, they attended the liturgies of the Word together with the faithful and gleaned whatever they could from ordinary sermons. During the course of that preaching, the fathers would also preach a special sequence of sermons during Lent on the Creed, Lord's Prayer, or the sacraments.[6] From this golden age, several important series of sermons have been preserved. These were delivered at different points in the catechumenate depending upon the bishop. Augustine's *On Catechizing the Uninstructed* (*De Catechizandis Rudibus*)[7] was aimed at providing pedagogical guidance for evangelizing the *accedentes*. Ambrose's *First Book of Abraham* was delivered to the catechumens themselves. Cyril of Jerusalem's eighteen lectures[8] as well as Theodore's ten were given to the *competentes* or *illuminandi*. Augustine also addressed the catechumens in his *Enchiridion on Faith, Hope, and Love*.[9]

In the Middle Ages, sermons continued to be the chief means by which catechetical instruction took place. Although regular preaching to the laity was rare in the early Middle Ages, by the twelfth century it had increased (due in part to the growth of theology in new universities and due in part to the need for an antidote to the sometimes heretical sermons of wandering preachers).[10] Interestingly, this catechetical preaching was not simply one among several types of sermons, but was in fact the dominant form of the sermon delivered to the people. According to Jean Longère, preaching in the Middle Ages could be defined as "ordinary instruction given to the community of the faith."[11] It differed from catechesis proper only in that it did not always deal with matters of doctrine, but also embraced the affective dimensions of existence. In fact, most medieval preaching in the vernacular was more catechetical than liturgical, that is, it was based on the texts of the Creed and Lord's Prayer rather than on a system of pericopes. This is not to say, however, that even this kind of preaching was all that common.

One of the significant changes that did occur from the early church to the medieval church involved the teaching office. While in the early church the teaching (preaching) office was the exclusive preserve of bishops, it was gradually delegated to presbyters who could serve the church on the outskirts of civilization. The Clovesho canons of 747 represent one of the attempts to equip the clergy for their task prior to the Carolingian period. These canons focused on the importance of preaching within the church, particularly the need for a doctrinal or catechetical and moral teaching rather than exegetical commentary.[12] The Carolingian reforms of the ninth century expressed deep concern for the church's teaching office, which was carried out through preaching. The legislators of the canons of the reform councils in 813 seem to have in mind the catechetical instruction of people in remote areas.[13] Presbyters were to recite the formulas within hearing of the people during the homily, a practice that would eventually develop into a new office in the vernacular called *Prone*.[14] In the late Middle Ages, Archbishop John Peckham and the Lambeth Council of 1281 promulgated the *Ignorantia sacerdotum* (the ignorance of priests), which obligated "priests to explain homiletically to their parishioners four times a year the basic topics of the catechism."[15]

A number of examples of sermons and preaching manuals have been preserved from the early Middle Ages. Although generalizations are always hazardous, one can generally divide the catechetical sermons that have been preserved into two types. First, there were those that might be called catechetical treatises that were designed to be read from the pulpit by priests (especially those serving in rural areas). Generally these included a listing of the catechism's texts with perhaps a few brief comments on them. They often reflect the low expectations the church had for catechetical instruction in which people needed to know the texts, but not their meaning.

One of the earliest and most important extant catechetical texts of this type from around the Carolingian period is the so-called Catechism of Weißenburg (ca. between 798 and 820). This work probably served as a preaching manual of sorts for priests in order to help them teach important topics in the faith to the laity. It contained a German translation of the Lord's Prayer with an appended explanation, followed by the deadly sins, which are patterned after Galatians 5:19–21. Then follow the Apostles' Creed, the Athanasian Creed (without explanation), and the Gloria in Excelsis.[16]

In the fifteenth century, Jean Gerson stands out as one of the most important figures for reinvigorating catechetical instruction within the church. His first treatise, *Doctrinal for Simple Folk*, was intended for "illiterate laypeople" and was to be read to them, according to his recommendation, perhaps two or three chapters per Sunday, by the parish priest.[17] It contained numerous points of Christian teaching with brief explanations. A decade later, he composed the three treatises that became the most well-known of his catechetical writings: *The Mirror of the Soul*, *The Examination of the Conscience*, and *The Art of Dying Well*. These were compiled in his work *Opusculum tripartitum*. In the introduction, Gerson identifies four audiences. The first are unlettered and simple curates whose task is to hear confessions. The second group consists of unlearned laity. The third group includes children and young people who need to be instructed in the basic Christian teachings. The final group embraces those who care for the sick. *Mirror of the Soul* provided a sermon resource that priests could read from the pulpit in order to catechize their people in the Ten Commandments. Gerson has in view those who don't often hear sermons. Ordinarily, a sermon was not common with the Mass and those who lived in rural areas probably did not have the advantage of having regular preaching services.

The second type of catechetical sermons were written by a preacher and provided more detailed and expanded explanations. These sermons were disseminated in manuscript or in print and served a clerical audience. David d'Abray goes so far as to describe such manuscript copies as the closest thing the Middle Ages had to a mass medium.[18] Examples include Alan of Lille, a twelfth-century preacher who has left behind a treatise and a lengthy sermon on the Lord's Prayer that was probably delivered to his fellow Cistercians. In the fifteenth century, Thomas Ebendorfer of Haselbach provides another example of detailed catechetical preaching on the Lord's Prayer. On the eve of the Reformation, Johann Geiler von Kaiserberg, cathedral preacher in Strasbourg, preached on the Lord's Prayer nearly every day from March to June 1508. "The number of distinctions lodged under each petition and the subtlety of his reasoning make it incredible that any but the most learned hearer could have followed him."[19] Perhaps the best known catechetical sermons from the high Middle Ages are a series of short instructions attributed to Thomas Aquinas in the vernacular in Naples during Lent of 1273.[20]

Preaching also proved to be the primary means for catechizing both young and old among Lutherans throughout the sixteenth century.[21] Indeed, Luther's own reformation might best be characterized as a preaching revival, but in a way that had not been seen before. The pulpit and the printing press came together to create a powerful and effective one-two punch. First, Luther's printed sermons proved to be some of the most popular and effective tools in his repertoire.[22] Others would read them aloud to people, giving them an even wider audience than the original sermon would have had. The Large Catechism, for example, appeared in 29 editions prior to 1546. Between his death and the turn of the century, twenty-five new editions appeared in German, five in Low German, and three in Latin. Many of these were adapted to the needs of various pastors. Second, if the printing press helped in the spread of the sermon, the sermon in turn aided the popularity of the printed word among the populace. The reason for this is that in sermons truths would have be connected with folk wisdom, abstract concepts conveyed with concrete metaphors, and a feel for the vernacular language and its use would have to be developed.

As early as 1522, Wittenberg reestablished the tradition of preaching on the catechism four times a year.[23] Ten years later, the Wittenberg Church Order (1532) reaffirmed intensive catechetization four times a year with one of those being in Lent. These were to be conducted at Vespers on Monday, Tuesday, Thursday, and Friday.[24] This practice continued throughout much of the sixteenth century.

Catechesis was not, however, confined to these quarterly sermon series. In the German Mass, Luther proposes a more continual catechesis throughout the year by suggesting that on Monday and Tuesday morning there should be a German lesson on the Ten Commandments, Creed, Lord's Prayer, Baptism, and Lord's Supper in order to "preserve and deepen the understanding of the catechism" (*LW* 53:68). Luther brings out the importance of such teaching as one of the most important parts of the divine service. He observed that a person can hear sermons for two or three years without understanding them if they have not been catechized (*LW* 53:67). Why? As Mary Jane Haemig notes, "Catechetical preaching provides listeners with a gospel (or rather a law-gospel) hermeneutic with which to approach scripture."[25] Two years later, the Instructions for the Visitors again called for regular catechetical sermons (*LW* 40:308).[26]

Luther's catechisms themselves are the product of nearly thirteen years of preaching on the classic texts of the catechism. Early in his career, between July 2, 1516 and February 24, 1517, Luther preached on the Ten Commandments.[27] In October of 1516, he preached on the Lord's Prayer and published a brief German and Latin exposition of it.[28] He again preached on it during Lent of 1517 after he had concluded his series on the commandments.[29] Luther preached on the Ten Commandments, Creed, and Lord's Prayer during Lent in 1522 and again during Lent in 1523. When Bugenhagen was called away in 1528 to reform the churches in

Braunschweig, Luther filled in for him and preached three series of sermons on the catechism: May 18–29, September 14–25, and November 30–December 19. Preaching four afternoons a week, he covered the entire catechism during each series. Luther's Holy Week Sermons of 1529 formed the basis for many of Luther's remarks on Confession and the Lord's Supper in the Large Catechism, which he was still writing at this time.[30]

Luther's catechisms owe their language, expressions, and thought to these sermons more than to any other form in which the basic texts were presented. As Brecht observes, Luther's striking formulations in the Small Catechism arose out of "his magnificently simple and understandable sermons."[31] Luther himself acknowledged that he did not preach for Bugenhagen or Melanchthon, but for his "little Hans and Elsa" (WATR 3, no. 3421). At the same time, the Small and Large Catechisms served as a basis for the preaching of sermons on the part of pastors.[32] In some instances the Small Catechism itself provided the basis and the material for sermons. More importantly, it is worth noting that Luther gave the Large Catechism the title *German Catechism*. This referred to the catechetical instruction that was carried out in the context of worship in the German language—in contrast to the Latin service (which even in Luther's time was the regular liturgy in Wittenberg).[33] In other words, to preach on the main parts of the catechism in German was to hold a "German Catechism." The Large Catechism served as a model and sourcebook for pastors of this kind of preaching (WA 30:I, 454f, 477).

The widespread use of sermons as a medium for teaching the catechism reveals that Luther and the other Reformers did not work with a sharp distinction between proclamation and instruction. All proclamation was instruction and all instruction was proclamation. What the catechism and preaching share in common is what Jordahn has called a "moment of proclamation."[34] The catechism provides more than cognitive knowledge. Its instruction confronts the hearer with the very voice of God. The goal of sermon and catechism were one and the same: Christ and faith. Each confronts the person with Christ.

Instruction, particularly catechetical instruction, never takes place in a vacuum. As it forms a Christian consciousness, it also places a person on the front line of the battle between God and Satan. Catechetical instruction and doctrinal sermons were "for Luther not a matter of informing the interested, but of defending those under attack. The stakes were high: God's Word rouses Satan's ire."[35] A sermon was both teaching and exhortation, but teaching was more important than exhortation.[36]

THE CATECHISM AS A CONFESSIONAL MANUAL

Next to the sermon, the practice of confession emerged in the Middle Ages as the most common setting in which to acquaint people with the texts (and their explanations) of the catechism. The preparation and practice of confession became the matrix for the church's catechetical work. But catechizing as preparation for confession had one significant difference from catechizing as preparation for Baptism in the early church. The latter had a broader purpose of equipping people for the Christian life. The former had as a primary goal not the spiritual edification of the catechumen as much as the smooth functioning of the sacrament of confession. People needed to know what and how to confess. Out of the matrix of confession arose a wealth of texts, often called "confessional books" (*Beichtbüchlein*) to assist both the priest and the penitent. These were prepared to guide "the daily work of the priest at that most important point of contact with his parishioners, the sacrament of penance—the confessional."[37] Since these manuals were to serve as aids to self-examination, they were often referred to as "confessional mirrors" (*Beichtspiegel*), e.g., "The Mirror of the Sinner" or "The Mirror of Christian Faith," etc. Many of these confessional manuals tend to be characterized by the quest for perfect confession and the endless cataloging of sins. These confessional manuals functioned as "the catechisms of the late medieval church."[38]

According to Johannes Geffcken, by the end of the fifteenth century, three types of manuals had emerged: the learned manual for those who wished to further their education, the simple manual geared toward concrete practice, and vernacular manuals designed for popular use. Initially they were available only in manuscript form (often in Latin, occasionally in German) and thus were directed to the priests and only indirectly to the penitent.[39] After the invention of printing, the laity began to use booklets or manuals similar to the penitentials used by the confessors. These manuals would also contain materials of a devotional character and overlap with the genera of prayerbooks or devotional manuals.

Two of the most common confessional manuals included the *Beichtbüchlein* (1478) by Johannes Wolff[40] and *Mirror of a Christian Man* by Dietrich Kolde. Wolff's is especially interesting. It is divided into three parts: Part I is instruction for beginners, children, and others on how to confess when they go to confession for the first time. Part II provides instruction for older children, the learned, and the uneducated but understanding people on how to confess. Part III contains miscellaneous materials connected

to confession. He calls the preacher the "Doctor of God's Ten Commandments." The first printed German lay catechism, and subsequently one of
most popular of the late-medieval manuals, was *The Mirror of a Christian
Man*, first written in 1470 by Dietrich Kolde.[41] In these works, the Creed and
Lord's Prayer received relatively little attention and when they did it was
from the standpoint of obeying or not obeying them. The treatment of the
Decalogue tended to overshadow or even bury the other parts.

In his own role as father confessor, Luther also prepared several writings to aid people in confession just prior to the Easter confession of 1518.
In his *Instructions on Confession*, 1518 (*Instructio pro confessione peccatorum*;
WA 1:257–65),[42] he briefly expounds the Ten Commandments (*Decem pre-
cepta*) and provides a catalog of ways in which we break each of the commandments and keep each of the commandments. The same procedure is
followed in *A Short Explanation of the Ten Commandments, Their Fulfillment
and Transgression* (*Eine kurze Erklärung der zehn Gebote*, 1518 [WA 1:247–
56]).[43] These early works were written in the traditional mold.

At about this time, Luther launched a full-scale assault on the confessional with his treatise, *The Sacrament of Penance*, 1519 (*LW* 35:3–22). After
demolishing both the theology and practice of the confessional, Luther
needed to supply guidance for an evangelical understanding and practice of
confession. On January 4–5, Spalatin pressed Luther for some advice on
how confession should be made. Luther drafted a proposal for an evangelical *Beichtspiegel* that found its way into print at the end of January as *Ein
kurtz Underweysung, wie man beichten sol* (*Brief Explanation on How One
Should Confess* [WA 2:59–65]). Unhappy with how it appeared in print,
Luther reworked it and published it sometime after March 25 as *Confitendi
ratio* (A Discussion of How Confession Should be Made [WA 6:157–69; *LW*
39:27–47]).[44] Spalatin prepared a German translation that appeared in May.

Luther followed up his recommendations with a new confessional
manual in the Spring of 1520 entitled A Short Form of the Ten Commandments, A Short Form of the Faith, A Short Form of the Our Father
(WML 2:351–84; WA 7:204–14).[45] The entire work was published in the
form of a simple confessional mirror written to assist the penitent in confession.[46] As with previous confessional manuals, Luther continued the
practice of providing a catalog of ways in which the commandments are
obeyed or disobeyed as a guide for self-examination prior to confession.
His phrasing of the Creed shows its link back to the Baptismal liturgy as
each paragraph of his explanation of the Creed begins with either "I
renounce" or "I believe." Several distinctive features stand out in this work.

First, Luther provides in his preface a rationale for his arrangement of the texts. Second, Luther eliminated all of the secondary materials that had been found in earlier manuals[47] and incorporated only the three classic catechetical texts, the Ten Commandments, Creed, and Lord's Prayer.[48] Luther identified these texts as a summary of all Scripture and all that a person needs for salvation.[49] Although the name "catechism" is not applied by Luther to the book, Ferdinand Cohrs suggests that it could be called the first evangelical catechism[50] or as Krodel puts it, as Luther's first, "embryonic" catechism.[51]

Between 1520 and 1529, a shift in emphasis among Lutherans moved away from stressing the catechism as a confessional manual toward emphasizing the confessional as a catechetical opportunity, especially to teach people prior to their receiving the Lord's Supper. An examination on the basics of Christian doctrine prior to Communion became the custom in Wittenberg after 1524 and laid the foundation for the religious education of adults as well as children and youth. This carries through into the Small Catechism and Large Catechism where the confessional intent is not as evident (although by no means excluded) as the pedagogical intent. In other words, Luther emphasized the confessional as important not only for instruction on how and what to confess, but for instruction on all the basics.

In a sermon from 1529, Luther addressed himself particularly to the young people and exhorted them to "learn the Ten Commandments, the Creed, and the Lord's Prayer at home, so that they can recite them to the deacons, who will then admit the young people to Communion" (WA 29:219.10ff).[52] Through constant use in preparation for Communion, the parts of the catechism became stamped on individual minds and, more significantly, into the daily life of each person.[53] Luther stressed that the Lord's Supper was instituted for those who were not Christian in name only, but in fact and truth. Using the confessional as a catechetical opportunity provided a means for helping people to become functional Christians.

After 1520, Luther did not prepare another form of confession for the laity until 1529, at which time he prepared "A Short Order of Confession before the Priest for the Common Man" (LW 53:116–18; WA 30:I, 343–45). This work soon found its way into the 1529 edition of the Small Catechism. It was subsequently replaced in the Small Catechism in 1531 with a more detailed order, "How one Should Teach the Simple to Confess" (LW 53:119–21; WA 30:I, 383–87). The addition of these forms suggests that the catechism was considered less as a confessional manual as a whole than the subject of confession being an opportunity for catechetical instruction.

It is on account of this instructional opportunity that Luther defended his inclusion of this section in 1533 in "An Open Letter to Those in Frankfurt on the Main." Here Luther used the word "confession" in a dual sense. First, Luther argued that he maintained such a practice so that people may be instructed in Law and Gospel, sin and absolution. Second, he observed, "For such Confession does not go on only for their recounting of sins, but also one should listen to them concerning whether or not they understand the Lord's Prayer, the Creed, the Ten Commandments and whatever else the Catechism gives them. For we have come to know quite well how little the common crowd and the youth learn from the sermon, unless they are individually questioned or examined. Where better would one want to do this and where is it more needed than for those who should go to the Sacrament?"[54]

Luther continued, "In this way, those in need of instruction are to be examined and by their answers show that they know the parts of the Catechism, that they recognize the sin they again have done, and are willing to learn more and desire to do better. If they will not do this, they may not come to the Sacrament."[55] Again, the Sacrament of the Altar will not and cannot be given to anyone "unless he is first examined regarding what he has learned from the Catechism."[56]

THE CATECHISM AS PRAYER BOOK

Next to his sermons, Luther's devotional literature must be counted among his most popular and influential writings. In this literature, he picks up the tradition of medieval prayer books which had been written for the laity and had been used in the church for centuries. In the early church the Psalter or selected Psalms served as devotional materials for the laity. In the years prior to the invention of the printing press, dating back to the ninth century, prayer books with a variety of devotional materials were handsomely bound and illuminated by hand. They could be used for the personal edification of those lay people of noble birth who could afford them.[57] Written in a small format, they could easily be carried by a person at all times.

With the advent of the printing press, such prayer books became more widely available. Printers vied with one another for publishing new editions with new materials. In addition to confessional manuals, these devotional books provided yet another way to place the texts of the catechism into the hands of the people. Their contents often paralleled those found in the confessional manuals, but were supplemented with orders of salvation and many prayers. For that reason, these prayer books represented a broader genre than confessional manuals. Their importance lay in the fact that they shaped lay piety at the grass roots level.

These books were not prayer books in the sense of containing nothing but collections of prayers. Instead, they also contained meditational and instructional materials for a lay person's spiritual edification. One of the more popular books in Germany was the *Hortulus animae*. Published in 1498 in Strassburg, it contained an office of prayers to the Virgin Mary, prayers on the passion of Christ, the seven penitential psalms, a litany, morning and evening prayers, prayers to angels, apostles, evangelists, martyrs, confessors, teachers, virgins and holy widows, a prayer for each of the main festivals of the year, instruction for going to confession and the sacrament, a reminder of death, and prayers for the hour of death, including the prayers to St. Bridget. Many such prayer books "were regarded as essential for any layman who wished to save his soul," and often promised forgiveness, and indulgences from the pains of purgatory, as well as other rewards such as protection in childbirth and at the time of death for those who used them.[58] It is little wonder that Luther found them objectionable and in need of "a basic and thorough reformation if not total extermination" (*LW* 43:11–12).

In the early years of the Reformation, Luther quickly realized that it would do little good to fulminate against the false and extravagant claims of these prayer books. Instead, he worked to replace them with evangelical counterparts that would communicate evangelical piety in terms that any layman would readily accept and understand. Upon returning from the Wartburg in 1522, Luther took the material from his 1520 Short Form and, and with a few modifications, made it the backbone of his *Little Prayer Book (Betbüchlein)*[59] which became one of the first evangelical versions of the medieval prayer books and confessional manuals.

With the three texts of the catechism (Ten Commandments, Creed, and the Lord's Prayer) forming the core of the prayer book, Luther reduced the complex catalogues of sins to the Ten Commandments. The Creed replaced the "elaborate steps to gain salvation listed in the old prayer books" (*LW* 43:7). The Lord's Prayer replaced "the traditional miscellaneous collection of prayers with their fantastic promises of protection and reward" (*LW* 43:7). To use Luther's words, "I am convinced that when a Christian rightly prays the Lord's Prayer ... his praying is more than adequate" (*LW* 43:12). In addition to these primary texts, Luther included several other elements as well. For example, he retained the traditional Hail Mary, but with an evangelical interpretation. Beyond that, new and additional materials were added seemingly with each new printing until it

expanded to nearly 208 pages in 1529.[60] The *Little Prayer Book* was a tremendous success with over thirty-five known editions during Luther's lifetime. With the appearance of Luther's Small Catechism, the *Little Prayer
Book* began to decline in popularity as the Small Catechism assumed the
role that the earlier work had played.

Just as Luther envisioned using the practice of confession as an opportunity to instill the catechism, he also utilized the genre of prayer books as
an opportunity for meditating on the catechism for both pastors and people. This conviction carried through to his catechisms of 1529. In the preface to the Large Catechism, he suggests that since pastors were now free
from the babbling associated with the seven canonical hours, they might
meditate on the catechism or the prayer booklet. He then holds himself up
as an example for such daily mediation upon the chief parts of the catechism. The Small Catechism clearly acquired the character of a prayer
book through the addition of Luther's morning and evening prayers, dinner prayers, and instructions for using the catechism in connection with
those daily prayers. Again, it must be kept in mind that Luther sees prayer
as including meditation on the texts of God's word, texts that in turn bring
a person to God.

Luther continued to regard the catechism as a prayer book throughout
his life. Six years after the first publication of the Small Catechism, his friend
Peter the Barber requested some help in how to pray. In *A Simple Way to
Pray*, 1535 (WA 38:358–75; *LW* 43:187–211), Luther responded by outlin-
ing some suggestions for prayer based upon the structure and content of the
Small Catechism.[61] It reveals how Luther used the Small Catechism as a lifelong resource for prayer. In it, Luther recounts how when he himself feels
joyless in prayer he takes the Psalter into his room and whispers to himself
word for word the texts of the catechism and meditates on each portion as a
way of rekindling the joy of prayer in his heart. He takes for Peter each petition of the Lord's Prayer and provides a brief meditation that is keyed to the
text of the catechism as well as the needs of the day. The Lord's Prayer, in
particular, can serve to prompt and guide a Christian's thoughts. For the
other parts of the catechism, Luther proposes a fourfold way of meditating
on each item as instruction, as thanksgiving, as confession, and as petition
which renders them for use as "a school text, song book, penitential book
and prayerbook" (*LW* 43:209).

In a later edition, Luther extended and applied the same method to the
Creed. Luther's method allows for a great deal of flexibility. A person need
not meditate on every portion every time one prays. Instead, it may be

enough to concentrate on one commandment or a single petition and move on to the next one at a later time. In this way, the Spirit can use these texts "as flint and steel to kindle a flame in the heart" (*LW* 43:209).

THE CATECHISM AS AN ELEMENTARY HANDBOOK FOR CHRISTIAN INSTRUCTION

Finally, as concern increased during the late Middle Ages about the need for ecclesiastical reform and the need for instruction in the basics of the Christian faith, printed texts were prepared increasingly for catechizing the laity. Some of these were written in verse to aid memorization. One influential treatise composed in French verse (A.D. 1260), the *Manuel des péchés*, included explanations of the articles of the Creed, the Ten Commandments, the sacraments, the seven deadly sins, and instruction on how to make a good confession.[62] One of the first books of instruction to which the term "catechism" is applied appears in the fourteenth century with the publication of *The Lay Folks Catechism* of 1357.[63] Written at the direction of Archbishop John Thoresby of York, it was intended to combat the widespread ignorance of clergy and to promote reform.[64] One of the most prominent and influential catechisms addressed to laity in the fifteenth century was Jean Gerson's *ABC's of Simple Folk*.[65] The development of these primers in the fifteenth century provided for the continued transmission of the core elements of the church's heritage.

The term "catechism" as a title for these primers did not come into extensive use until the mid- to late-1520s when a flood of catechetical literature hit the market. Between 1522 and 1529, sixty-two printings of thirteen different instructional booklets emerged from Wittenberg presses alone. The total number throughout Germany numbered at least 176. Most of these were published between 1524 and 1529. Luther's own catechisms may be seen as a response to three events: one pastor's single-minded effort and persistent requests for a catechism; an answer to the need revealed among the parishes in the Visitations of 1528; and a response to a controversy between two of Luther's co-workers.

THE REQUEST OF A PASTOR

In 1523, Nicholas Hausmann, "a pastor in Zwickau and a comrade-in-arms with the Wittenberg theologians," requested the elector to initiate a visitation of the churches in Saxony.[66] Elector Frederick delayed. At the end of 1524, Hausmann again turned to Wittenberg and reiterated the need for a visitation.

At this time, he apparently also requested that a catechism be prepared for the "common folk," for Luther responded on February 2, 1525 (WABr 3:431) that he had instructed Justus Jonas and Johann Agricola to prepare just such a "catechism for children" (*catechismus puerorum*). A month later, on March 26, Luther reiterated to Hausmann that a catechism had been requested from its authors (WABr 3:462). After waiting several more months, Hausmann again turned to the court of Electoral Saxony and on May 2 asked, "What kind of lessons should be held for the unlettered small children?" (WABr 3:462).[67] He repeated his desire on August 23, 1525 to Stephen Roth, assistant at the Wittenberg city church, "O that it [the catechism] would be supplied and quickly published."[68] While Luther had initially assigned the task of writing a catechism to Jonas and Agricola in 1525, their joint work on the project ended when Agricola returned to Eisleben to become rector of the newly-established Latin School.

In the meantime, during the fall of 1525, *A Booklet for the Laity and Children* appeared in Wittenberg. Timothy Wengert identifies this booklet as the first attempt to use Luther's own words to catechize Wittenberg's young people and thus it stands in a direct line with Luther's own catechisms of 1529.[69] Its contents included the texts of the Ten Commandments, the Apostles' Creed, the Lord's Prayer, a text from Mark 16 for Baptism, and the Words of Institution. Cohrs notes that the first part of this booklet contains "the five chief parts almost word-for-word, just as we know them from Luther's Enchiridion." Also, for the first time, Baptism and the Lord's Supper appear as components of the catechism, along with the Ten Commandments, Creed, and Lord's Prayer. Here also are contained for the first time the biblical texts [for the sacraments] that became sanctioned through Luther's Enchiridion.[70] It concludes with the words "End of the Lay Bible." It follows with Luther's introduction to the *Little Prayer Book* (1522) on the relation between the first three chief parts (*LW* 43:13) as well as Luther's explanation of the Creed (*LW* 43:24–29). Then follows a morning prayer, meal prayers, and an evening prayer. The work concluded with a brief meditation on the Lord's Prayer, excerpted from Luther's *An Exposition of the Lord's Prayer* (*LW* 42:78–81), and a meditation on confession by the compiler.

A year later, in his preface to the *German Mass*, Luther called again for the production of a simple catechism and proposed an outline of what it might look like. He insisted on the need for a simple, straightforward catechism on the three chief parts in a question and answer format.[71] Meanwhile, he proposed that his *Little Prayer Book*, first published in 1522, and revised in 1525, could serve as a source for catechesis (*LW* 53:64–67). He also invited others to write one themselves. Luther proceeded to sketch out a plan for a fuller religious life in Wittenberg in which catechization could take place.

CHURCH VISITATIONS

Another event contributed to the urgency of developing a catechism. The collapse of the old church structures in the wake of the Reformation had several unintended consequences. The nobility plundered the assets and property of monasteries. Church property began to fall into ruin. The laity had stopped paying their church obligations and were unwilling to give even a small portion for the support of pastors. As a result, while large sums had earlier been spent on clergy, pastors now went unpaid and often lived at subsistence levels. In addition to the decay of institutional supports, the Reformation unintentionally left a swath of religious indifference in its wake. "The peasants learned nothing, knew nothing, prayed not at all, did nothing except abuse religious freedom, and did not go to confession or commune."[72] On top of this, congregations remained agitated and unsettled following the Peasant's Revolt of 1524–1525.[73]

As a result of these events, calls for visitations of the churches to assess the condition of parishes and to assist in the introduction of the Reformation were increasingly heard. Already in 1523, Nicholas Hausmann had called for a visitation in order to help pastors preach the Gospel. On October 31, 1525 and again on November 22, 1526 Luther joined Hausmann in urging that visitations be carried out, particularly with a view toward making sure that pastors received a regular income. These early calls were delayed first by Elector Frederick's death and then by other events.[74] Later, they were delayed by the prince's hesitancy about the possibility of having to support the church out of his own treasury.

An initial visitation was carried out under Spalatin, in the first half of 1526, in order to examine the pastors' theological aptitude. Beginning in 1527, and for the next year and a half, teams of theologians, jurists, and court counselors crisscrossed the territories of Saxony in an extensive visitation of the churches. They started with the region around Weida, then moved to Saale and then to Jena. The early rounds of visitations in 1526 showed the need to improve and revise previous methods and procedures for conducting the visitations and educating the pastors. Melanchthon began preparation of a series of articles in August 1527 in order to lay a foundation for addressing the inadequate theological education of the clergy. Initially slated for publication by the turn of the year, they were delayed due to a shortage of paper and did not appear until March 22, 1528 under the title, *Instructions for the Visitors of Parish Pastors in Electoral Saxony* (*LW* 40:263–321; WA 26:195–240). The first full visitations to utilize these instructions took place from October 22, 1528 to Easter 1529, in the electoral district around Wittenberg. Luther himself served as one of the visitors up until January, at which time he had to attend to affairs at the university. He went out again with the visitors around Torgau in 1530.

Participation in the visitations profoundly affected both Luther and Melanchthon. They discovered that the stereotype of the sixteenth-century peasant was all too true. The peasants were a "harsh, crude folk who far preferred fairs and hard drinking to church services."[75] The visitation records revealed the deplorable state of affairs within the congregations. For example, they reported of a parish at Ducher where 110 families lived but often not more than three persons attended the worship services. But what bothered Luther most was not that the German peasants were a "crowd of drunken louts with the sexual mores of a herd of rabbits," but that they were ignorant of the basics of Christianity.[76] At Werche, the peasants could not recite the Lord's Prayer, the Ten Commandments, the Creed. At Zinna the peasants refused to learn the Lord's Prayer because of its length. But the state of ignorance was hardly confined to the laity. The records also report of a pastor in Elsnig who himself could barely pray the Lord's Prayer or recite the Creed.[77]

No doubt these experiences prompted Luther to move with all haste to write a catechism. In January, 1529, he wrote to a pastor in Braunschweig, "I am working on a catechism for the simple country folk"[78] (*rudibus paganis*) (WABr 5:5, 22). With these experiences still fresh in his mind, Luther expressed his dismay and outrage in the prefaces of his two catechisms. "[N]ow that the Gospel has been restored, [the people] have mastered the fine art of abusing liberty" (SC Preface 3). In the new preface to the Large Catechism of 1530 Luther reiterated this complaint, regarding "this rotten, pernicious, shameful, carnal liberty" (LC New Preface, 3).[79]

THEOLOGICAL CONFLICT

In connection with the visitations, a new theological conflict erupted in Electoral Saxony over the place of the Law and repentance in the Christian life, which impacted the composition of Luther's catechisms. The two protagonists were Melanchthon and Agricola, both of whom carried out the controversy through their catechetical writings.[80] While serving as Rector at the girls school in Eisleben, Agricola had raised an objection to the place of the Law in Melanchthon's *Instructions for Visitors* in August 1528. In these instructions, Melanchthon had expressed a concern about morality and church practices and thus gave a prominent place to the role of the commandments and the preaching of the Law in order to bridle the flesh and terrify consciences.[81] Melanchthon had maintained that knowledge of the Law was absolutely necessary for repentance because sinners cannot discover nor experience the Gospel in their hearts without it.[82] Agricola maintained, however, that repentance was a consequence of the preaching of the Gospel. Consequently, the realities of the Law, judgment, and the wrath of God receded into the background. In his first catechetical work, *Elementa Pietati congesta*,[83] Agricola maintained that the law shows us our sins, and tames or restrains our lusts, but the Law does not kill.[84] True knowledge of sin instead proceeds from faith. In Melanchthon, where there is no fear there is no faith. Agricola emphasized a fear of God over against a fear of punishment. Agricola charged that on the question of *poenitentia*, Melanchthon mistakenly taught that the terrors of the conscience over sin arise from a fear of divine judgment and eternal punishment. To the contrary, it must arise from the love of righteousness. God must be feared on account of himself, not on account of punishment.

Agricola subsequently revised and simplified his Latin catechism, *Elementa Pietati congesta* into a new catechism, *One Hundred and Thirty Common Questions*.[85] Where Melanchthon saw the Christian life as moving from *mortificatio* to *vivificatio*, from Law to Gospel, from terror to comfort, Agricola begins with a discussion of *Gottseligkeit*, that is, word and faith. First the Gospel reveals God's goodness; then we recognize our sins and repent. The Law can do nothing more than force people to do things through the fear of punishment. It cannot produce contrition. Question 18 states: "The law says, 'You must love God more than yourself or die.' The gospel says, 'I announce to you that God loved you first and beforehand and wants to bestow this love on you, because you love yourself so much. He also wants to give you the Holy Spirit, so that because of his goodness you can hate and abandon yourself, your life, property, and honor'."[86] Only through the Gospel do we come to hate ourselves and follow him. Agricola decried Melanchthon's position as a wisdom of the world. The foolishness of the Gospel is that God wins the world over not through force but through love and the gift of his Son. "Christians do out of love and desire everything God demands of them. For they are sealed with the spontaneous Spirit of

Christ."[87] He argued that the law of Moses was really no different from the morals that one could learn from the ancient Greeks or Romans.

THE APPEARANCE OF THE
SMALL CATECHISM IN PRINT

Luther's catechisms had their roots in these three events: Hausmann's request, the visitations, and the antinomian controversy. Especially when considered within the context of the controversy with Agricola, the catechism must be seen as arising immediately out of the challenge posed by Agricola's *One Hundred and Thirty Common Questions* and, at the same time, as providing the most important correction to Agricola's catechetical approach. With the publication of Luther's catechism, a turning point was reached in evangelical catechisms. Agricola's best-selling works sank into obscurity. His *One Hundred and Thirty Common Questions* eventually came under Luther's ban. So after 1529, "Luther's catechisms ruled the marketplace, finally becoming in 1580 a part of the confessions of the Lutheran Church."[88]

When Luther's catechism first appeared in January 1529, each section appeared on large sheets of paper, to be sold like newspapers and hung up in churches, schools, and homes.[89] When the Small Catechism was published in book form, it was published as a small book, approximately 2¾ inches by 3⅝ inches. As Mark Edwards notes, the Reformation perfected the use of such small books or pamphlets.[90] Frequently in quarto format— that is, made up of sheets folded twice to make four leaves or eight pages— and without a hard cover, these pamphlets were handy, relatively cheap, readily concealed and transported, and accordingly well suited for delivering their message to a large popular audience. They could be easily transported. Contemporaries called such a pamphlet a *libellus* or *Büchlein*, a little book.

The Small Catechism appeared often. It was printed in thirty German editions before Luther's death in 1546. By the end of the sixteenth century, at least 125 more editions appeared in one form or another. In addition to the German, the Small Catechism was printed in thirty editions for use in the schools to teach the language as well as the faith. One Greek translation and several Greek and Latin translations were produced in a total of fifteen editions. Six German/Latin and one German/Latin/Greek edition appeared on the market between 1550 and 1600. A polyglot edition in German, Latin, Greek, and Hebrew appeared in 1572 and went through twelve editions by 1599. Two dozen Low German printings also appeared along with thirteen Low German/Latin editions prepared by Georg Major.[91] The catechism became the subject of numerous expositions.[92] The sheer numbers in which it was printed, combined with Luther's authority, made the Small Catechism the standard or norm for all other catechisms.

OTHER OUTLETS
FOR DISSEMINATING THE CATECHISM

While Luther used three of the primary forms (sermons, prayer books, and confessional manuals) inherited from the Middle Ages in order to bring the catechism to people in the pew, he and the other reformers did not limit themselves to those forms. Instead, they borrowed others and created still new ones. Two of the more important means included the liturgy itself as well as congregational hymns and hymnbooks. The former provided the setting especially for sermons on the catechism, whereas the latter constituted something of a new feature inasmuch as congregational singing had not been a prominent feature of worship services in the Middle Ages.

THE CATECHISM IN THE LITURGY

From nearly the beginning, Luther's catechetical endeavors were intimately related to the liturgical life of the church. In fact, Bruno Jordahn contends that if we would understand Luther's catechisms properly, "we must start from the point that the catechism had primarily a liturgical function."[93] This is true in two ways.

First, Luther saw the beginning of catechetical instruction as an initiation to worship."[94] In some ways, it formed the backbone of the liturgy. In the *German Mass*, Luther linked the "need for liturgical renewal with the mandate for a worshipping congregation well-trained in catechism." The catechism cultivated, as it were, a "liturgy of the mind" that was related to the liturgy of word and sacrament. Luther maintained in his *German Mass* that a person could listen to a sermon for several years and not get much out of it unless he or she had first been taught the catechism.

Second, the catechism settled in as an established part of the service itself. In addition to being expounded through sermons, it became customary to read or recite the catechism on a regular basis in connection with the lectionary of the day.[95] At times it would be expounded in the liturgy itself. A variety of Sunday services would be offered from early morning Matins through the celebration of the Mass to Vespers held in late afternoon. In each of these, the catechism was incorporated in a variety of ways.

SUNDAY MATINS AND VESPERS

Two services which provided an opportunity for preaching and expounding the catechism came with Sunday Matins and Vespers. In 1533, the revised church order for Wittenberg included the requirement that early morning Matins on Sunday should be devoted to sermons on the catechism.[96] This service was suited especially for servants who could not take part in the Mass on account of their housework.[97] The service order was kept relatively simple: A Hymn (usually on the Ten Commandments),Sermon, Hymn, Prayers. Vespers provided another opportunity for catechesis on Sunday afternoons. The *Instructions for the Visitors* of 1528 had already urged that on Sunday afternoons there "be constant repetition, through preaching and exposition, of the Ten Commandments, the articles of the Creed, and the Lord's Prayer" (*LW* 40:308). Such a service could serve "children and other simple and unschooled folk" (*LW* 40:308). The procedure was that the children first recited a portion of the catechism. Then followed a short sermon which explained what had just been recited. Then the children were examined. In addition, it recommends that in addition to the three chief parts, that one also diligently preach about marriage and the sacraments of Baptism and of the altar.

THE SUNDAY MASS (SERVICE WITH HOLY COMMUNION)

The *German Mass,* as envisioned and developed by Luther, did not focus much on preaching to the congregation, but did incorporate catechetical elements in a variety of ways. Due to the separation of confession and absolution from the main service, the Ten Commandments found a place in the preparation for confession, which also provided an opportunity for instruction.[98] With respect to the Creed, it seems that Luther envisioned people not only reciting the Creed but singing an exposition of it with the hymn, "We All Believe in One True God." Luther not only had the people pray the Lord's Prayer, but provided them with a brief explanation of its contents which he substituted for the *sursum corda* in the preface.[99] He introduced it with the words, "After the sermon shall follow a public paraphrase of the Lord's Prayer and admonition for those who want to partake of the sacrament, in this or a better fashion" (*LW* 53:78, 79). Luther continues, "In this way ... the Lord's Prayer together with a short exposition would be current among the people" (*LW* 53:80). At this point the congregation proceeded to pray the Lord's Prayer together. With regard to Baptism and the Lord's Supper, Luther gave great prominence to the Words of Institution and also prefaced them with catechetical exhortations so that people would give their full attention to the words (for an example, see *LW* 53:80).

WEEKDAY SERVICES

The Reformers developed weekday preaching services, perhaps as evangelical counterparts for the daily mass in the medieval church. Already in 1523, Luther discussed the general shape of a worship service in his treatise *Concerning the Order of Public Worship* (*LW* 53:7–14; WA 12:35–37). He recommended that weekday services were to be held early in the morning and in the evening, the equivalent of the earlier Matins and Vespers services.[100] The Old Testament was read in the morning and the New Testament in the evening or the reverse. In these services the centrality of the Word emerges. The Mass was no longer offered daily, as he put it, for "the Word is important and not the Mass" (*LW* 53:13). In his *German Mass*, Luther notes, "on Monday and Tuesday mornings, we have a German lesson on the Ten Commandments, the Creed, the Lord's Prayer, Baptism, and sacrament, so that these two days preserve and deepen the understanding of the catechism" (*LW* 53:68). On Wednesday, he assigned a German lesson on the Gospel of Matthew, then for Thursday and Friday mornings he assigned the epistles and the rest of the New Testament. Throughout the sixteenth century, "in order that mature Christians might retain a comprehensive knowledge of doctrine and understanding for the interrelation of doctrines, the church regulations for the cities called for one or two weekday services devoted to preaching on the catechism."[101]

Four times a year, over a two-week period, the catechism received even greater attention through a special sermon series. The 1533 revised church order for the city of Wittenberg prescribed that the entire catechism be preached in eight *Wochenpredigten* services in each quarter of the year.[102] The Sunday prior to the start of each series the pastor should admonish the people that it is their responsibility and duty to bring their children and servants (see, for example, Luther's admonition to parents in his Third Catechism Series of 1528 [*LW* 51:137–93; WA 30:I, 57–122]). Each series consisted of eight sermons spanning a two-week period and were preached on Monday, Tuesday, Thursday, and Friday. The Wittenberg church order set aside the afternoon vespers for such purposes.[103]

Ordinarily, the church orders stressed that the form of these services should be kept simple. Before the sermon there should be a psalm, antiphon, four readings, "as is customary." Then the boys should sing the hymn, "These Are the Holy Ten Commandments." After the sermon the hymn can be sung, "Man, Will You Live Eternally," with the choir singing the final verse. The service then concludes with the *Magnificat*, a Latin antiphon, Versicle, Collect, and the *Benedicamus*.[104]

THE CATECHISM IN HYMNS AND CHORALES

Luther's explanation of the catechism also found its way into the hymnody of Lutheran worship services and hymnals.[105] Indeed, hymnody provided the reformers with one of the more effective means by which to teach the catechism and spread the message of the Reformation by word of mouth. In some respects, hymns provided the lay person the primary means of verbal participation in the liturgy. Putting the catechism to verse had the advantage of not only putting the Gospel into the ears of its hearers (like the sermons), but of also putting the catechism on the lips of the congregational members, thereby helping them to remember its texts and contents. Finally, hymns addressed both the cognitive and affective dimensions of the Christian. With respect to the former, Lutheran hymns not only expressed the response of faith sung within a liturgical context, they were also theological songs that declared the substance of the faith. With respect to the latter, hymnic catechesis both created and interpreted Christian experience.[106] Their incorporation into the hymnbook enabled the catechisms to find a perennial presence in the religious life of a Lutheran congregation for centuries.

Hymns provided another advantage to learning the catechism as well. As an accompaniment to learning the catechism, their rhymes and melodies functioned as mnemonic aids for remembering its contents.[107] Luther saw an intimate integration of music and text that each supports and reinforces the other. When the words were translated from Latin to German, the music had to be changed to fit the new rhythm and cadence of the words.[108] "I hate to see the Latin notes set over German words. I told the publisher what the German manner of singing is. This is what I want to introduce here" (*LW* 53:54). Music provided a link between education and worship. Music reinforced the teachings in the catechism and enabled the congregation's affirmation with their own voices.[109]

To some extent, the development of catechetical hymnody coincided with the increased production of catechisms during the 1520s. As early as 1523, Luther wrote to Spalatin about his plan to produce German psalms and hymns for the people so that God's Word might flourish among the people by means of song (*LW* 53:221). In 1524, the first evangelical hymnal was published, the so called *Achtliederbuch* (Book of Eight Hymns), which contained four hymns by Luther. The most important of the early collections was the *Geistliches Gesangbüchlein* (Spiritual Hymn Booklet) published in Wittenberg. In 1529, the year that Luther published the catechisms, he also issued a new hymnbook, the *Geistliche lieder auffs new gebessert zu Wittemberg D. Mart. Luther* (Wittenberg, 1529). It contains a section of catechetical hymns following the hymns designated for the seasons of the church year. Luther introduces that section of "specifically catechism-hymns" with the words:[110]

> Now follow spiritual songs in which the Catechism is covered, since we certainly must commend Christian doctrine in every way, by preaching, reading, singing, etc., so that young and unlearned people may be formed by it, and thus in this way it will always remain pure and passed on to our descendents. So may God grant us his grace and his blessing through Jesus Christ. Amen.[111]

Robin Leaver notes that the catechetical function of hymns was so fundamental to Lutheran theology and practice that until the late eighteenth century, every Lutheran hymnal would have a substantial section of specific "Catechism Hymns."[112]

The hymns that Luther himself composed for the first three chief parts of the catechism include: "Here is the Tenfold Sure Command," 1524 (Ten Commandments);[113] "We All Believe in One True God," 1524 (Creed);[114] "Our Father, Thou in Heaven Above," 1539 (Lord's Prayer).[115] Hymns for the last three chief parts include: "To Jordan When Our Lord Had Gone," 1541 (Baptism);[116] "From Depths of Woe I Cry to You," 1523 (Confession); "From Trouble Deep I Cry to You" (1539);[117] and "O Lord, We Praise Thee," 1524 (Lord's Supper); On the commandments: "Lord Keep Us Steadfast in Your Word" (1542).[118] These hymns articulated and explained Luther's theological concept of catechetical teaching within the context of the distinction between Law and Gospel.[119] Brecht contends that Luther's hymns mark him as one of the most "significant religious poets" of his age. "Poetry, for him, was to be employed almost exclusively to serve the task of proclamation."[120] Through these hymns, the catechism could shape both the doctrine and piety of the laity.

CONCLUSION

As the reformers addressed the daily needs of parish life, they took with utmost seriousness the task of catechizing the laity and clergy alike. To that end, they utilized every available means possible in order that the catechism might permeate the entire life of the congregation. In the process, they managed to re-evangelize the people of their day that they might become functional Christians and not Christians in name only. That is to say, through the catechism they laid a lasting foundation for shaping both the faith and piety of the people. But they understood the catechism more in terms of its contents than in terms of one particular genre, as became the case in later Lutheranism.

NOTES

1   Mark U. Edwards, Jr., *Printing, Propaganda, and Martin Luther* (Berkeley: University of California Press, 1994), 7.

2   Edwards, *Printing, Propaganda, and Martin Luther*, 1. See also Arthur Geoffrey Dickens, "The Printers and Luther," in *The German Nation and Martin Luther* (New York: Harper & Row, 1974), 102–15.

3   See Werner Jetter's article, "*Katechismuspredigt,*" in *Theologische Realenzyklopädie*, vol 17 (ed. Gerhard Krause and Gerhard Müller; Berlin: de Gruyter, 1988), 744–86.

4   The original root of the term catechesis designated an oral instruction. Etymologically the Latin verb *catechizare* (meaning "to instruct") is derived from the Greek verb (*katexeo*) and means "to teach," or "to inform by word of mouth." It became applied to the act of informing and instructing by oral repetition where children in school were instructed and then "sung out" their answers to the questions asked by the teacher. In the NT it is used in Luke 1:4; Acts 18:25; and Gal. 6:6. In the sense of instructing catechumens it appears first in the so-called Second Epistle to the Corinthians (17:1), written around the year 150. The first Latin writer to use *catechizare* in the meaning of "to instruct orally" in the Christian faith was Tertullian; e.g., *De Cor. Mil.* 9: "quem Petrus catechizat." See also St. Augustine, *The First Catechetical Instruction* [*De Catechizandis Rudibus*], (tr. Joseph P. Christopher; Westminster, Md.: Newman Bookshop, 1946), 93–94.

5   Generally, the catechumenate was divided into four stages. Those interested in learning about the faith and desiring to be enrolled in the catechumenate were known as the *accedentes* (those approaching the faith). Once they entered the catechumenate proper, they were known as the *catechumenos*. After petitioning for Baptism (usually at the beginning of Lent) and receiving the Creed, they entered a period of intense instruction and examination and were known as the *competentes* (competent ones) or *electi* (chosen ones). Upon receiving the Creed they were known as the *illuminandi* (enlightened ones). Following Baptism, they were known as neophytes.

6   Harmless, *Augustine and the Catechumenate*, 31–32.

7   Augustine, *First Catechetical Instruction* (*De Catechizandis Rudibus*), tr. Joseph P. Christopher. Ancient Christian Writers. (Westminster, Md.: Newman Press, 1946).

8   See *The Works of St. Cyril of Jerusalem: Procatechesis and Catecheses* 1–12, and *Catechesis* 13–18 and *Mystagogical Lectures, The Fathers of the Church*, Vols. 61 and 64 (tr. Leo P. McCauley and Anthony A. Stephenson; Washington: Catholic Univer-

sity of America Press, 1968). See also *Egeria's Travels* (ed. John Wilkinson; London: S.P.C.K., 1971) in which this process is described by a pilgrim to Jerusalem.

9   See William Harmless, *Augustine and the Catechumenate*, for an excellent account of Augustine's sermons in terms of content and style. He also discusses and describes the works of several other early church fathers.

10 Joseph R. Strayer, ed., *Dictionary of the Middle Ages* (New York: Charles Scribner's Sons), 10:300–1.

11 Quoted in Paul Robinson, "'For the Salvation of Simple Christian People': Preaching the Faith in the Middle Ages," unpublished paper delivered at the Theological Symposium, "Formation in the Faith: Catechesis for Tomorrow," held at Concordia Seminary, St. Louis, May 6–7, 1997.

12 Milton McC. Gatch, "Carolingian Preaching," in *Preaching and Theology in Anglo-Saxon England: Aelfric and Wulfstan* (Toronto: University of Toronto, 1977), 33.

13 Gatch, "Carolingian Preaching," 37.

14 In its fully developed form, the Office of Prone was separable from the Mass, but it occurred after the Gospel and consisted of a translation and brief explanation of the pericope, announcements of forthcoming liturgical events, catechetical instruction on the Creed and Lord's Prayer, prayers, and other devotions.

15 More specifically, it lists the fourteen articles contained in the Creed, the Ten Commandments, the two laws of the Gospel (love of God and love of neighbor), the seven works of mercy, the seven deadly sins, the seven cardinal virtues, and the seven sacraments." Strayer, *Dictionary of the Middle Ages*, 10:300. Thus the topics of the catechism were preached on four times a year, while people were required to go to confession only once a year.

16 The text can be found in the following: E. v. Steinmeyer, *Die kleinerer althochdeutsch Sprachdenkmaler* (Berlin, 1916), 29–38, and Paul Pieper, *Deutsche National-Literatur. Historisch-kritische Ausgabe*, Joseph Kürschner, gen. ed., 1, Berlin and Stuttgart (1884): 84–90. More recently, see Wilhelm Braune, Karl Helm, *Althochdeutsches Lesebuch*, 15th ed. (ed. Ernst A. Ebbinghaus; Tübingen: Niemeyer Verlag, 1969), 34–37.

17 Robinson, "For the Salvation of Simple Christian People," 10.

18 Robinson, "For the Salvation of Simple Christian People," 4.

19 Robinson, "For the Salvation of Simple Christian People," 4.

20 Berard L. Marthaler, *The Catechism Yesterday and Today: The Evolution of a Genre* (Collegeville, Minn.: The Liturgical Press, 1995), 11. See Nicholas Ayo, ed. and trans., *The Sermon-Conferences of St. Thomas Aquinas on the Apostles' Creed* (Notre Dame: University of Notre Dame, 1988). He devoted fifteen sermons to the Creed, ten to the Lord's Prayer, and thirty-two to the Ten Commandments. See *NCE* 3.227.

21 Given the five to thirty percent literacy rate among the people, preaching remained the best means of reaching the masses of people with the message of the Reformation. See Mary Jane Haemig's dissertation, "The Living Voice of the Catechism: German Lutheran Catechetical Preaching, 1530–1580" (Harvard: 1996), which is devoted entirely to the study of catechetical sermons in the sixteenth century. See Robert Kolb, "The Layman's Bible: The Use of Luther's Catechisms in the German Late Reformation," in *Luther's Catechisms—450 Years: Essays Commemorating the Small and Large Catechisms of Dr. Martin Luther* (ed.

David Scaer and Robert D. Preus; Fort Wayne, Ind.: Concordia Theological Seminary Press, 1979), 16–26.

22 Arthur Geoffrey Dickens, *The German Nation and Martin Luther* (New York: Harper & Row, 1974), 103.

23 This custom reaches back to the Lambeth Council of 1281, which obliged priests to explain homiletically to their parishioners four times a year the Creed, Lord's Prayer and Ten Commandments. See *Dictionary of the Middle Ages*, vol. 10 (ed. Joseph R. Strayer; New York: Charles Scribner's Sons), 300.

24 The tradition appears to have continued throughout the sixteenth century. For example, the constitution for electoral Saxony of 1580 prescribed: "Because there is no more necessary preaching than that on the holy catechism … pastors and ministers shall employ special diligence in commending and presenting this preaching on the catechism to the common people." Not only were they encouraged to preach the catechism, but they were warned of the consequences should they not. See Robert Kolb, "The Layman's Bible: The Use of Luther's Catechisms in the German late Reformation," in *Luther's Catechisms— 450 Years: Essays Commemorating the Small and Large Catechisms of Dr. Martin Luther*, ed. David P. Scaer and Robert D. Preus, 55–64 (Fort Wayne, Ind. Concordia Theological Seminary Press, 1979), 18. There is also a considerable bibliography of sermons on the catechisms written during the sixteenth and seventeenth centuries. Among the more famous series, one might refer to the ten sermons by Jakob Andreae that covered the six chief parts in 1561. In 1620 Johann Arndt published "The Entire Catechism in 60 Sermons." See also Günther Stiller, *Johann Sebastian Bach and Liturgical Life in Leipzig* (St. Louis: Concordia Publishing House, 1984), 48–55.

25 Haemig, "The Living Voice of the Catechism," 103.

26 For example, they recommend that on Sunday afternoons there should be a constant repetition, through preaching and exposition, of the Ten Commandments, the articles of the Creed, and the Lord's Prayer. The former teaches fear of God, the latter prayer to God. After these are spelled out "word for word," one should preach something about marriage and the sacraments.

27 These sermons were subsequently published in 1518 as *Decem praecepta Wittenbergensi praedicato populo* (WA 1:60–141=*LW* 51:14–31; WA 1:398–521). That same year Luther also published *Kurze Erklaerung der 10 Gebote* on charts or placards. See the chronology of Luther's writings in the appendix.

28 See Brecht, *Luther* I:154f; WA 1:89–94.

29 His sermons on the Lord's Prayer were published in 1519 as *Exposition of the Lord's Prayer for Simple Laymen* (*LW* 42:15–81).

30 Martin Luther, *The 1529 Holy Week and Easter Sermons of Dr. Martin Luther*, annotated with an introduction by Timothy J. Wengert (tr. Irving L. Sandberg; St. Louis: Concordia Academic Press, 1999).

31 Brecht *Luther*, II, 275.

32 Osiander's "Nürnberg Sermons for Children" are one of the first examples of catechetical preaching to utilize Luther's explanations. See Reu, *Dr. Martin Luther's Small Catechism*, 61.

33 Friedemann Hebart, "Introduction," *Luther's Large Catechism: Anniversary Translation* (Adelaide: Lutheran Publishing House, 1983), xviii–xix.

34   Bruno Jordahn, "Katechismus-Gottesdienst im Reformationsjahrhundert," *Luther: Mitteilungen der Luthergesellschaft* 30 (1959), 64.

35   Wengert, "Introduction," *The 1529 Holy Week Sermons*, 15.

36   Walter von Loewenich, *Martin Luther: The Man and his Work* (tr. Lawrence W. Denef; Minneapolis: Augsburg, 1982), 356.

37   Steven Ozment, *The Reformation in the Cities: The Appeal of Protestantism to Sixteenth-Century Germany and Switzerland* (New Haven: Yale University Press, 1975), 16. For the standard work on the topic, see Thomas N. Tentler, *Sin and Confession on the Eve of the Reformation* (Princeton: Princeton University Press, 1977).

38   Josef Andreas Jungmann suggests that these confessional booklets should be considered as "forerunners of the catechism," *Handing on the Faith. A Manual of Catechetics* (New York: Herder and Herder, 1959), 17.

39   See Johannes Geffcken, *Der Bilderkatechismus des 15. Jahrhunderts* (Leipzig, 1855). Krodel, 366.

40   *Beichtbüchlein des Magisters Johannes Wolff* (ed. F. W. Battenberg; Gießen 1907), esp. 112–17. Wolff wanted to instruct priests how to teach the laity the salutary use of the sacrament of Penance, especially the right way of confessing. Yet his comments and listing of materials for preaching suggests that it is in some ways a manual for preaching on certain subjects. He suggests that one should first teach parishioners and then in the confessional draw out of the penitent what they should produce.

41   It was modeled after Anthony of Florence's (d. 1459) *Tractatus de instructione seu directione simplicium confessorum*, an extremely popular manual geared to concrete practice. For a good discussion of its three primary versions as well as a good overview of its contents, see Steven Ozment, *The Reformation in the Cities: The Appeal of Protestantism to Sixteenth-Century Germany and Switzerland* (New Haven: Yale University Press, 1975), 28–32. For an English translation of its text, see Denis Janz, *Three Reformation Catechisms: Catholic, Anabaptist, Lutheran* (New York: Edwin Mellen Press, 1982), 31–130.

42   "Instructions on Confession," in *Luther's Catechetical Writings* (ed. John Lenker; Minneapolis, Minn.: Luther Press, 1907), 328–35.

43   *Ein kurtz Underweysung, wie man beichten sol*, 1519; WA 2, 59–65). On the original version see Brecht, *Luther*, I:152–54. These were the by-product of his sermons on the Decalogue from 1516-1517 and were published in February of 1518.

44   See Steven Ozment, *The Reformation in the Cities*, 49–51.

45   For an English translation, see *Works of Martin Luther: Philadelphia Edition*, vol. 2 (Philadelphia: Muhlenberg Press, 1915), 351–84. Luther used a slightly reworked version of his German Brief Explanation of the Ten Commandments, Their Fulfillment and Transgression of 1518, and drew on his Brief Explanation for Understanding and Praying the Lord's Prayer of 1519. He composed the explanation of the Creed "from scratch." Krodel, 373; cf. 398, fn. 110.

46   A number of features point in this direction. First, Luther uses an analogy to introduce the three chief parts that fits with the topic of confession and absolution. He describes a sick person who is diagnosed by the law and needs the medicine of the Gospel and needs to know how to take the medicine through prayer. Second, he continues the practice of cataloging sins in this document as was common. Third, he expounds the Creed and Lord's Prayer from the standpoint of persons who are renouncing their sins (and Satan) and allying themselves once

again with God. In his *Little Prayer Book* (1522) Luther referred to this work as "a simple Christian form of prayer and mirror for recognizing sin, based on the Lord's Prayer and Ten Commandments" (*LW* 43:12; WA 10 II:375).

47 Luther saw these as simply humanly devised spin-offs of the Ten Commandments (WA 7:211–28:212.3). See Krodel, 375. Luther proceeds to show how they can be incorporated into the Ten Commandments. "The five senses are comprehended in the Fifth and Sixth Commandments; the six works of mercy in the Fifth and Seventh; the seven mortal sins—pride in the First and Second, lust in the Sixth, wrath and hatred in the Fifth, gluttony in the Sixth, sloth in the Third, and, for that matter in all of them. The strange [alien] sins are covered by all the commandments, for it is possible to break all the commandments just by talking, advising, or helping someone. The crying and silent sins are committed against the Fifth, Sixth, and Seventh Commandments. In all of these deeds we can see the same thing: love of self which seeks its own advantage.… 'Self-love is the beginning of every sin'"; *LW* 43:21.

48 In it, Luther slightly reworked his Short Explanation of the Ten Commandments, Their Fulfillment and Transgression of 1518 and his Short Form of Understanding and Praying the Lord's Prayer of 1519. His explanation of the Creed is entirely new. Luther had dealt with the Decalogue, Lord's Prayer, and the subject of confession, but had not yet dealt with the Creed—although he envisioned such a work in his Sermon on Good Works (WA 6:203, 34f). At this time, he did yet not include sections on Baptism and the Lord's Supper.

49 "It did not happen without God's special ordering that for the ordinary Christian, who cannot read the Scriptures, it is ordered that he learn and know the Ten Commandments, the Creed, and the Lord's Prayer. Certainly, in these three pieces is thoroughly and completely summarized all that is written in Scripture…, also all that is necessary for a Christian to know; [it is written] in such a short and easily to be grasped form that no one may complain or pretend it is too much or too difficult to remember what he needs for salvation." Tr. Krodel, "The Making of Luther's Catechism," 374–75.

50 Ferdinand Cohrs, *Die Evangelische Katechismusversuche vor Luthers Enchiridion I: Die evangelischen Katechismusversuche aus den Jahren 1522–1526* (Berlin: A. Hofmann, 1900; Hildesheim: Georg Olms Verlag, 1978); 4. Reu similarly refers to it as an important catechetical landmark and precursor to the Small Catechism, *Dr. Martin Luther's Small Catechism*, 8–9.

51 See Krodel, "The Making of Luther's Catechism," for the most complete analysis of this "embryonic" catechism by Luther, 364–404.

52 The Augsburg Confession also affirms this connection in Article 24.6 (Latin) where Melanchthon states that no one is admitted to the Supper unless they are first heard and examined; cf. AC 25.1 (German).

53 Maurer identifies this practice as one of the roots of confirmation within Lutheranism, except that the process here is "clearly understood as being the first of many occasions rather than a once-and-for-all event"; Wilhelm Maurer, *Historical Commentary on the Augsburg Confession* (tr. H. George Anderson; Philadelphia: Fortress Press, 1986), 210.

54 "An Open Letter to Those in Frankfurt on the Main, 1533," tr. Jon D. Vieker, *Concordia Journal* 16 (October 1990): 343.

55 "An Open Letter to Those in Frankfurt on the Main, 1533," 343.

56   "An Open Letter to Those in Frankfurt on the Main, 1533," 343.

57   See Martin H. Bertram, *"Introduction" to Luther's Little Prayer Book* (*LW* 43:6).

58   From Georg Domel, *Die Entstehung des Gebetbuches und seine Ausstattung in Schrift, Bild und Schmack bis zum Anfang des 16. Jahr-hunderts* (Köln a. Rh.: Privatdruck, 1921). See Martin H. Bertram, *"Introduction" to Luther's Little Prayer Book, LW* 43:5. He mentions that "One small volume provided a variety of catalogues of sins to be used in preparation for confession, lists of ways to gain forgiveness, prayers for the festivals, acrostic prayers to the Virgin, prayers for the hour of death, prayers on the passion of our Lord, prayers guaranteeing a generous number of indulgences from the pains of purgatory if used in certain ways, prayers that guaranteed protection in childbirth or in the hour of death, catalogues of virtues, list of works of mercy, lists of the gifts of the Holy Spirit, morning and evening prayers, prayers to various saints and martyrs, the penitential psalms, and the highly regarded prayers of St. Bridget."

59   This book would go through nine editions in 1522 alone and remained an extremely popular book throughout the 1520s. Although it would be published after 1529, the Small Catechism would eventually replace it and serve the same purpose.

60   New things were constantly added. Before its appearance, Luther added eight Psalms with suggestions for prayers, the Epistle to Titus, Romans, Timothy, Peter, Jude, A Sermon on Contemplating the Holy Suffering of Christ, etc. (1523). See Brecht, *Luther*, II: 120.

61   For the most thorough analysis of this work, see Martin Nicol's chapter, "Katechismusmeditation," in his *Meditation bei Luther* (Göttingen: Vandenhoeck & Ruprecht, 1984), 150–67. For a briefer discussion in English, see Gordon Rupp, "Protestant Spirituality in the First Age of the Reformation," in *Popular Belief and Practice* (ed. G. J. Cuming and Derek Baker; Cambridge: Cambridge University Press, 1972), 155–70.

62   *Dictionary of the Middle Ages*, 301.

63   See Ian Green, *The Christian's ABC: Catechisms and Catechizing in England c. 1530–1740* (Oxford: Clarendon Press, 1996). Written in verse, it carried a forty-day indulgence for those who memorized it.

64   It covered the fourteen points of the Creed, the Ten Commandments, seven sacraments; seven works of mercy; seven virtues; and seven deadly sins.

65   It included the five bodily senses, the seven deadly sins, the contrary virtues, the seven petitions of the Our Father; the Hail Mary; the Creed; the Ten Commandments; the seven virtues, the seven gifts of Spirit, the seven Beatitudes, the seven spiritual works of mercy, the seven corporal works of mercy, the seven orders, the seven sacraments; the seven offshoots of penance, the seven privileges of the glory of paradise; the four counsels of Christ, the principal joys of paradise, and the pains of hell.

66   For a more thorough discussion of these events, see Timothy J. Wengert, *Law and Gospel: Philip Melanchthon's Debate with John Agricola of Eisleben over* Poenitentia (Grand Rapids: Baker Books, 1998), 49–50.

67   Cited in Ferdinand Cohrs, *Die Evangelischen Katechismusversuche vor Luthers Enchiridion*, 4 vols. (Berlin: A. Hofmann, 1900–1902), 4:247.

68   Cohrs 4:248. About that time, he apparently also suggested that the worship service be translated into German, a request that Luther fulfilled that Christmas with the *Deutsche Messe*.

69 The only surviving copy of the first edition was discovered in 1991 in Herzog August Bibliothek of Wolfenbüttel, Germany. See Timothy J. Wengert, "Wittenberg's Earliest Catechism," *Lutheran Quarterly*, n.s., 7 (1993): 247–60). See also Wengert's *Law and Gospel*, 54–58 for an extensive description of this work. For a translation of this text, see the collection of sources for the *Book of Concord*.

70 Cohrs, 1:169. It also brings out the importance of Luther's *Little Prayer Book* for early catechesis and "sets off the changes and improvements of Luther's *Small Catechism* in sharp relief." Timothy Wengert notes that in one form or another, this booklet was published at least twenty-six times between 1525 and 1530. See Cohrs 1:187–92 for a partial list of the printings.

71 Albrecht Peters, "*Die Theologie der Katechismen Luthers anhand der Zuordnung ihrer Hauptstücke,*" in *Lutherjahrbuch* (Göttingen: Vandenhoeck & Ruprecht, 1976), 13, observes that this matches the transformation of auricular confession into preparation for the Lord's Supper.

72 Brecht, *Luther* II:270.

73 For details on the Peasant's Revolt, see Brecht, *Luther* II:172–94.

74 For a good description of the visitations and their results, see Brecht, *Luther* II:259–73.

75 James M. Kittelson, *Luther the Reformer: The Story of the Man and his Career* (Minneapolis: Augsburg, 1986), 216.

76 James M. Kittelson, "Luther the Educational Reformer," in *Luther and Learning: The Wittenberg University Luther Symposium* (ed. Marilyn J. Harran; London and Toronto: Associated University Presses, 1983), 101.

77 C. A. H. Burkhardt, *Geschichte der deutschen Kirchen- und Schulvisitationen im Zeitalter der Reformation* (Leipzig: Verlag von Fr. Wilh. Grunow, 1879), 38f.

78 See also Kittelson, *Luther the Reformer*, 216.

79 It should be pointed out that the visitations were not without opposition. Any thorough-going reform posed the very real risk of upsetting the ways of the nobility, clergy, and laity alike. The clergy did not want to be disturbed lest they lose their position. The people did not want to be rebuked for their un-Christian ways of living. The nobility had their own designs on making church endowments their own. Finally, the visitation itself caused a political crisis leading to the Diet of Augsburg in 1530 inasmuch as it took place without permission from the regular bishops in league with Rome. Wengert, "Introduction," *1529 Holy Week Sermons*, 13.

80 Melanchthon's contributions include the following: *Annotationes in Johannem* (1523). That same year he published another catechetical work for young Latin students, namely, *Enchiridion elementorum puerilium. Vuittemberge.* It was translated into *Philipp Melanchthons Handtbüchlein, wie man die kinder zu der geschrifft vnd lere halten sol. Wittenberg.* A third work was printed in 1527 under the title, *Some Passages in Which the Entire Christian Life is Contained, in All Ways Beneficial to Keep in View and to Consider.* The latter was probably a response to Agricola's attacks in that same year. Melanchthon's works never achieved the popularity, however, of the works published by his former colleague in Eisleben (Wengert, *Law and Gospel*, 58). Agricola was busy as well. In response to the commission received from Luther he set himself to completing the project as the newly installed rector of the Latin school in Eisleben. The first result was *Elementa pietatis congesta* in 1527, which was subsequently translated under the title, *Eine Christliche kinderzucht, ynn Gottes wort vnd lere, Aus der Schule zu Eisleben.*

81 Brecht, *Luther* II:268.

82 Wengert, *Law and Gospel*, 71.

83 It was then translated into German as *Eine Christliche kinderzucht, ynn Gottes wort vnd lere, Aus der Schule zu Eisleben*. These were printed ten times in 1527–1528 (Cohrs 2:3–83).

84 Wengert, *Law and Gospel*, 72.

85 It was an immediate success, but was seen as too complicated and difficult for beginning students. So Agricola reworked it into a question-and-answer format entitled, *One Hundred and Thirty Common Questions for the Young Children in the German Girls' School in Eisleben*, dated November 18, 1527. This work proved to be very popular and went through ten printings in two years. See Wengert, *Law and Gospel*, 59–61. A translation can be found in *A Collection of Sources* forthcoming from Fortress Press. This work would experience great success and be printed ten times in 1528–1529

86 Wengert, *Law and Gospel*, 127; citing Cohrs 2:278.

87 Wengert, *Law and Gospel*, 129.

88 Wengert, *Law and Gospel*, 153.

89 These sheets themselves, as a form of presentation, carried over from the fifteenth century. See John W. Constable, "Sixteenth Century Catechisms: Their Genesis and Genius," in *Teaching the Faith* (ed. Carl Volz; River Forest, Ill.: Lutheran Educational Association, 1967), 21.

90 Edwards, *Printing, Propaganda, and Martin Luther*, 15.

91 The statistics reflect the catalog of the *Verzeichnis der im deutschen Sprachbereich erscheinen Drucke des XVI Jahrhunderts*, 19 vols. (Stuttgart: A. Hiersemann, 1983ff.). Others not incorporated in this catalog may also exist. The number of editions must take into account that shipping costs were expensive, so printers in various cities simply ran off their own copies rather than importing them from Wittenberg.

92 See Reu's chapter, "The Triumph of Luther's Small Catechism throughout Europe during the Sixteenth Century," *Dr. Martin Luther's Small Catechism*, 87–137.

93 Bruno Jordahn, "Katechismus-Gottesdienst im Reformationsjahrhundert," *Luther: Mitteilungen der Luthergesellschaft* 30 (1959): 76–77.

94 Eric Gritsch, "Whetstones of the Church," *Lutheran Theological Seminary Bulletin* 60 (1980): 4.

95 See Charles P. Arand, "Catechismal Services: A Bridge Between Evangelism and Assimilation," *Concordia Journal* 3 (July 1997): 177–91.

96 Emil Sehling, ed., *Die Evangelischen Kirchenordnungen des XVI Jahrhunderts* (Leipzig: O. R. Reisland, 1902), I:1, 700.

97 Jordahn, "Katechismus-Gottesdienst im Reformationsjahrhundert," 71.

98 See Sehling I:2, 268–69. In the Herzog Heinrich Order, the penitent is asked, "Do you know the Ten Commandments?" The answer is "Sadly, no. The papists didn't teach us that." Then the confessor continues: "Well, if you don't know them you surely aren't doing them." Then followed a basic instruction in them and then confession; trans. William Weedon, in "Catechesis and Liturgy," an unpublished paper.

99 See Bryan Spinks, *Luther's Liturgical Criteria and his Reform of the Canon of the Mass* (Notts [England]: Grove Books, 1982), 32.

100 Bornkamm, Heinrich, *Luther in Mid-Career, 1521–1530* (tr. E. Theodore Bachmann; Philadelphia: Fortress Press, 1983), 134.

101 Irwin J. Habeck, "Profit and Peril in Preaching on the Catechism," *Wisconsin Lutheran Quarterly* 76 (1979), 133. See also Carl Meusel, *Kirchliches Handlexicon*, Vol. III (Leipzig: Justus Naumann, 1891), 723.

102 Meusel III:723. Other church orders like that of Wolfenbüttel Church Order of 1569 also prescribed that the pastor should preach on the catechism quarterly, Sehling I:711.

103 Habeck, "Profit and Peril in Preaching on the Catechism," 132.

104 Sehling, *Die Evangelischen Kirchenordnungen*, I:701.

105 Robin A. Leaver, "The Chorale: Transcending Time and Culture," *Concordia Theological Quarterly* 56 (1992): 123–44.

106 Robin A. Leaver, "Luther's Catechism Hymns: 8. Confessional Substance," *Lutheran Quarterly*, XII (1998): 322.

107 Christopher B. Brown, "Singing the Gospel: Lutheran Hymns as a Source for the Popular Reception of the Reformation," Unpublished paper, 7.

108 Marilyn Harran, *Martin Luther—Learning for Life* (St. Louis: Concordia, 1997), 226.

109 Harran, *Martin Luther—Learning for Life*, 232.

110 Robin A. Leaver, "The Chorale: Transcending Time and Culture," *Concordia Theological Quarterly* 56 (1992): 133. See C. Mahreholz, "Auswahl und Einordnung der Katechismuslieder in den Wittenberger Gesangbüchern seit 1529," *Gestalt und Glaube: Festschrift für Vizepräsident Professor D. Dr. Oskar Söhngen zum 60. Geburtstag* am 5. Dezember 1960 (Witten and Berlin, 1960), 123–32; P. Veit, *Das Kirchenlied in der Reformation Martin Luthers: Eine Thematische und Semantische Untersuchung* (Wiesbaden: Steiner Verlag, 1986), 68–72.

111 Trans. in Robin A. Leaver, "Luther's Catechism Hymns: 1. Lord Keep Us Steadfast in Your Word," *Lutheran Quarterly*, XI (Winter 1997): 400.

112 Robin A. Leaver, "Luther's Catechism Hymns: 8. Confessional Substance," *Lutheran Quarterly*, XII (1998): 322.

113 Robin A. Leaver, "Luther's Catechism Hymns: 2. Ten Commandments," *Lutheran Quarterly* XI (Winter 1997): 410–21.

114 Robin A. Leaver, "Luther's Catechism Hymns: 3. Creed," *Lutheran Quarterly* (Spring 1998): 79–88.

115 Leaver, "Luther's Catechism Hymns: 3. Creed," 79–88.

116 Luther's six principle catechism-chorales became a basic feature of Lutheran worship, especially at Sunday vespers, at which time it became customary to expound the catechism in the sermon. See Leaver's analysis, "Luther's Catechism Hymns: 5. Baptism, *Lutheran Quarterly*, XII (Summer 1998): 161–69.

117 Robin A. Leaver, "Luther's Catechism Hymns: 6. Confession," *Lutheran Quarterly* XII (Summer 1998): 171–80.

118 Leaver, "Luther's Catechism Hymns: 1. 'Lord Keep Us Steadfast in Your Word'," 397–410.

119 See Wichmann von Meding, "Luthers Katechismuslieder," *Kerygma und Dogma* 40 (October 1994): 250–71.

120 Brecht, *Luther*, II, 135.

3

A Guide
from Font to Grave

The Design and Plan
of Luther's Catechisms

By the end of the 1520s, the catechism had become one of the most important vehicles by which the message of the Reformation moved out from the university and into the parishes and homes of average people. Where other writings reached the intelligentsia of the day, the academics, and the churchmen, catechisms took the message of the Reformation directly to the people. In the process, they quickly became the best-sellers of their day.[1] The publishing success of catechisms in general and the Small Catechism in particular helps to explain why "in a relatively short span of time, masses of people cast aside religious values and practices sanctioned by centuries of tradition in favor of new ones."[2] Its many printings and numerous editions enabled the catechism to have a longer-lasting effect in spreading the message of the Reformation than any other innovation of the sixteenth century.[3]

The large numbers of catechisms that were sold and bought does not, however, explain how the catechism reached most people with the message of the Reformation. Even though the Small Catechism was a tremendous publishing success, most people could not read it. Illiteracy remained a massive impediment to any effort aimed at lifting the level of religious knowledge among the laity throughout the sixteenth century. To be sure, the Small Catechism targeted an increasingly literate population that could read in the vernacular.[4]

Even with that audience in view, however, the literacy rate throughout the empire was perhaps five percent at most. Even though the Reformation spread fastest in the cities where the literacy rate was higher, it still probably never achieved a rate higher than thirty percent.[5] So only a small fraction of the total population was literate. This would have included members of the nobility and those at their courts, bureaucrats and civil servants, merchants, masters and mistresses of crafts, midwives and physicians, notaries, and laity affiliated with religious orders.[6] Thus, in sixteenth-century Germany, oral transmission remained "the primary mode of communication, in which information was received by face-to-face contact within small communities."[7]

So, how would most illiterate or semi-literate people have learned the catechism? It appears that the reformers utilized a "two-stage communication process"[8] that integrated traditional means of teaching with the new technology of the printing press. First, they took advantage of the increased lay literacy rate and targeted those who could read, people who also happened to be the so-called "opinion makers" of the day, namely, preachers, teachers, and government officials. Most villages would have had at least one or two persons—perhaps the village priest or village officials—able to read and write.[9]

Second, these in turn passed on the message to much larger numbers of non-reading people in much the traditional manner, that is, orally. As a result, the majority of people would have learned the evangelical message from sermons and conversations rather than from books, pamphlets, or even pictorial media.[10] Even the printed word was mediated by the spoken word, reading aloud to oneself or others, or by the discussion of things in print.

The Small Catechism itself reflects this two-fold strategy.[11] It targets pastors and parents who would in turn share it orally with children and the household. Toward that end, Luther recommends a method appropriate for such oral instruction. With this oral communication in view, Luther not only wrote the Small Catechism in the vernacular, but composed it more for the ear than the eye. To that task, Luther brought a pastor's heart, a poet's touch, and considerable language skills that he had honed in the pulpit. In the process, he used the catechism as an instrument for learning the basics and as a companion for a lifetime of learning.

A HANDBOOK OF INSTRUCTION
FOR PASTORS AND PARENTS

In the preface to the Small Catechism, Luther calls upon a coalition consisting of three groups—government officials, pastors, and parents—to take responsibility for the teaching and training of the young in the faith. While his call for pastors and parents to undertake the task placed him squarely within the church's tradition, the call for government officials reflects the growing role and importance of secular authorities over the preceding two centuries.

Of these three groups, Luther placed the greatest emphasis upon the family. From the very beginning of the evangelical movement, parents were enlisted as valued allies in the formation of holy households. Luther regarded the family as the fundamental, legitimate, and divinely ordained locus for good and useful works in a clear rejection of monastic values and piety. By mid-decade, however, the visitations revealed the difficulties of relying on parents alone. They did not have the time, were unskilled, or were unwilling to carry out their task.

Recognizing the failure of parents to carry out their responsibilities, the Reformers turned increasingly to other authorities for assistance: pastors, schoolteachers,[12] and secular authorities.[13] The Latin translation of the Small Catechism reflects this reality in its headings: "how the teacher should present...."[14] These other authorities were to supplement, not replace, the role of parents. In the coalition, each must tend to their respective duties: pastors must see to their congregations, housefathers, acting as pastors and bishops in their own homes, must attend to their households.[15]

Despite this reality, Luther continued to affirm the centrality of the home. "Education begins in the home, and is reinforced in church through catechism classes, sermons on the catechism, and the learning of hymns that reinforce catechetical teachings."[16]

"PARISH PASTORS"

The title pages and prefaces of Luther's catechisms identify pastors as their immediate target audience. More precisely, the title page of the Small Catechism reads: "Enchiridion. The Small Catechism for secular (*gemeine*) Pastors and Preachers." With the reference to "secular pastors," Luther targets parish clergy rather than the monastic clergy.[17] Traditionally, the burden of catechizing the laity had generally fallen to these parish clergy from at least the eighth century and the Carolingian reforms.[18] By calling upon them, Luther placed a renewed emphasis on the importance of pastors for teaching the young. Brecht puts it well, "Luther was aware of how difficult any sort of elementary instruction was. Nevertheless, he considered it one of theology's most noble tasks."[19] In the preface to his commentary on Zechariah, Luther ranked above the most subtle theologians those who could give good catechetical instruction. "One ought ... to regard those teachers as the best and the paragons of their profession who present the catechism well.... But such teachers are rare birds. For there is neither great glory nor outward show in their kind of teaching; but there is in it great good and also the best of sermons, because in this teaching there is comprehended, in brief, all Scripture" (*LW* 20:155–57; WA 23:485–86). Catechetical instruction emerged as one of the primary tasks of a Lutheran pastor.

Indeed, in the sixteenth century, many "pastors conducted their ministries in many respects as educational programs."[20] By the end of the century, when the superintendent and local pastors came on their annual visitation, they would conclude their visit by ringing the church bell, calling the children together, and examining them on their knowledge of the catechism.

Although Luther pleaded with parish pastors to catechize the young, they were for the most part entirely ill-equipped to carry out the task. Early in the 1520s, the Wittenberg Reformers knew that clergymen throughout the Electoral domains left much to be desired. While the regular clergy were educated, the secular clergy often came from the peasant class and thus their level of learning was low and the minimum knowledge expected of them was very basic.[21] But the reformers did not know the extent of the deterioration of religion in village parishes until they had taken part in the parish visitations. The first exploratory visitations of 1525–26 jolted the Wittenberg theologians out of their "merely conventional and usually calm recognition that clergymen were inadequate to the task of administering reformed parishes."[22]

By 1529 nearly every prominent reformer participated in the visitations and had personally witnessed the parish disarray. The experience of the visitations revealed that a basic knowledge of Christianity was lacking, especially in the villages, and pastors were in no position to supply it. In the preface of the Small Catechism Luther lamented that "many pastors are quite incompetent and unfit for teaching" (SC Preface 2).

When Luther prepared the catechisms, he did so with two goals in mind. First, he wanted to acquaint the pastors themselves with the most elementary tenets of the evangelical faith. In other words, he wrote catechisms with a view toward educating the priests and improving their own theological ability. The Large Catechism, especially, might be regarded as something of a manual in the training of theology.[23] This also explains Luther's exhortations to pastors in the preface that they use the catechism as a prayer book and never stop studying the catechism, but to practice it daily.

Second, the Small Catechism served as something of a manual of pastoral care. It was to assist the pastor in his own catechizing of the people. If pastors were unable to catechize in their own words, they could simply use Luther's text and read it aloud. This would take place primarily in the catechetical services in which the pastor would either read the catechism or preach on the catechism. As a manual of pastoral care, the Small Catechism provided a collection of handy materials useful in various contexts such as confession and absolution, the preparation for the Lord's Supper, and the conducting of occasional worship services.[24] A year later, Luther called for the creation of a new clergy, a supply of "ordinary pastors who will teach the Gospel and the catechism to the young and ignorant" (*LW* 46:231).[25]

"Head of the Household"

While Luther addressed the catechisms to pastors, he still envisioned the head of the household as the primary teacher. When the catechism first appeared in January 1529 on large sheets of paper, each sheet bore the title, "How the House Father Should Present the Ten Commandments [or Creed, etc.] to the members of the household." These headings for the five chief parts carried through into the Small Catechism.

For Luther, the housefather was not coextensive with the biological father, and the household was not coextensive with the nuclear family. To be sure, a household included the core family based on marriage: the husband, wife, and children, as well as parents and multi-generational blood relatives living under the same roof. But the household also included all persons living in the house, such as domestics and other dependents who were part of the family, as well as guests living in the house on a temporary basis.[26] The household was thus the basic social structure and economic unit in society. In this connection, Luther might have had in immediate view those more well-to-do families in which the head the household would be somewhat literate.

In one sense, Luther's focus on the family was not new. He simply took over the concept of domestic catechization from the Middle Ages and before that from the ancient church.[27] Within the history of the church, families had always been considered an important setting for catechizing the young in the faith. Ecclesiastical mandates from the Carolingian era placed a modest responsibility upon both parents and godparents to teach their children the Creed and the Lord's Prayer by rote and in their mother tongue.[28] Throughout the late Middle Ages, the church frequently singled out parents for admonition and exhortation to instruct their children. Gerson, in his ambitious catechetical program, entrusted a number of elements of instruction to parents.

In another sense, though, Luther gave the head of the household an emphasis and value not seen before. He ascribed to the housefather all of the titles that were at one time reserved exclusively for the clergy.[29] For example, in his Third Catechism Series of 1528 Luther refers to the father and mother as the bishop and bishopess of the household (*LW* 51:136–37; WA 30:I, 58).

By assigning the role of the housepastor to the head of the house, Luther shows that he envisioned the home as something of a house-church with the head of the house as the pastor. Again, there were precedents such as Stephan of Landskron who exhorted the father to lead the household in religious exercises on the Sabbath.[30] In a similar way, Luther had composed the Small Catechism "in an effort to create just such a scene: the pious family gathered around this digest of biblical teaching, praying and studying it together in preparation for daily service to God."[31]

To that end, the Small Catechism provides the household with something of a liturgy, that is to say, the parts of the catechism framed and shaped a Christian ethos for daily living: Upon waking, make the sign of the cross and say the invocation followed by thanks for protection the previous night with prayer to be kept from sin during the coming day. Go to work joyfully. At meals, fold hands and pray. In the evening, call upon the triune Name. Give thanks for the day. Pray for protection during the night. Go to sleep in peace.

Still, Luther knew that some parents were simply unwilling to follow these "instructions" themselves. Consequently, he pleaded with parents in the Third Catechism Series to grant their children some time off that they might attend the catechism sermons. "Give them an hour off that they may come to know themselves and Christ more fully" (*LW* 51:136; WA 30:I, 58). But Luther did not simply scold or exhort parents to carry out their duties, as had often been done by church leaders during the Middle Ages (and would be later by too many of his adherents). He also recognized that many parents were simply ill-equipped to carry out their divinely ordained task and so Luther provided them with assistance for doing so. The explanations in the Small Catechism were thus "aimed more at adults than children and were to be used by them so that they could explain the various texts of the lay Bible to their children."[32] This comes through particularly in the first person perspective of the housefather from which much of the catechism is written. For example, in the First Article the housefather speaks of "wife and children" as gifts from God.

Theological-Pedagogical Conception of the Catechism

In the preface to the Small Catechism, Luther sets forth his theological and pedagogical conception of the catechism by which he hoped to lead a person step by step into the maturity of faith. Within this process the catechism provided the basics of the Christian faith that in turn laid the foundation for a lifetime of growth.

While the Small Catechism provides the milk of the Word, it at the same time prepares the digestive system for the meat of the Word (much of which can be found in the Large Catechism).[33] To that end, Luther proposes in the preface of the Small Catechism a three-stage process that again has in view those who are illiterate or semi-literate. In the first stage, he wants catechumens simply to learn the bare texts of the catechism itself. (SC Preface 7–10).[34] In the second stage they are to learn the meaning of these texts through such explanations as those found in the Small Catechism itself (SC Preface 14–16). Finally, the pastor should take up a larger catechism which allows the various components to be explored in greater depth (SC Preface 17–18). In these three steps, Luther followed the time-honored procedure of moving from the simple to the complex. While there is nothing new about Luther's first step, the next two steps illustrate a new emphasis in catechetical instruction.

Stage I: Learn and Remember the Basics

Luther's first stage clearly presupposes an oral communication of the catechism's texts; that is, it assumes that those who learn it will do so by hearing it and not by reading it. Accordingly, it will only do them any good if they remember what they hear. The whole point of Luther's first stage is to provide a way in which the texts of the catechism can be learned by heart and be reproduced by heart. His approach and method reach back at least a millennium in the tradition of the church. Over that period of time and prior to the invention of the printing press, the church lived in a predominantly oral-aural culture. That situation, as well as the nature of the learners encountered by teachers, had not changed significantly by Luther's day. At the same time, Luther appropriated the theological concerns for learning the catechism that the ancient church fathers themselves had voiced, namely, that it must be internalized before it can be confessed (along the lines of Romans 10).

Learn the Text by Heart

In his first stage, Luther insists that before pastors teach the catechism they must settle on a single text of the Ten Commandments, Creed, and

Lord's Prayer. Once a pastor has adopted a single text, he must "stick with it, and always use the same one year after year."[35] To drive the point home, Luther emphasizes repeatedly that the pastor should at all costs avoid making any changes or introducing any variations in the text—not even a "single syllable." Even if a new and improved version comes out, it would be better to stay with the old text. Not only should a pastor avoid introducing changes to the text, he should also avoid presenting it or reciting it differently to the catechumens. Although his method seems very rigid to the modern pedagogue, Luther's concern is to avoid confusing people. If hearing the catechism is the only way that they can learn it by heart, it is important that it be used repeatedly in the same way.[36]

Luther's method of having the catechist present the catechism, followed by recitation on the part of the catechumen, also reflects the reality of an oral age in which a person will learn the catechism only in conversation with another person. In this case, the conversation takes the form of a *traditio* (presentation) and *redditio* (recitation) of the catechism's texts. Thus after selecting texts for the chief parts, the pastor is then to read it to children and the unlettered "word for word so that they can repeat it back to you and learn it by heart."[37] In a similar way, the heading of each of the chief parts exhorts the head of the household to "present" (*furhalten*) that particular portion orally to the members of their household who then repeat it back through recitation (LC Short Preface, 16–17). Luther also insisted that "children should be taught the habit of reciting them daily when they rise in the morning, when they go to their meals, and when they go to bed at night" (LC Short Preface, 16). Not only should children recite them daily, but the parents were also encouraged to examine children and servants (i.e., the household) once a week and keep them at it until they know it (LC Short Preface, 4). Through such recitation and repetition, the catechism would become engraved upon the mind and the heart.

Illiteracy was not the only obstacle preventing people from learning the catechism. In some cases, it was a matter of people stubbornly refusing to learn. By 1529 Luther would have none of that. His adamancy on this point emerges in his recommendations for punishing those who resist learning the catechism. He suggests that parents should not give the children food or drink if they refuse to learn it (LC Short Preface, 17) and that they should dismiss the servants if they refuse (LC Short Preface, 17). In the Small Catechism he stresses that such people should be told that they are not Christians, and should not be allowed to be sponsors for children in Baptism nor admitted to the sacrament. Parents ought to deny them food, employers should dismiss them, and princes should drive out such coarse people from the country.

These strictures seem harsh and decidedly unevangelical by twenty-first-century standards. Luther acknowledges that one cannot force anyone to believe in the vertical realm, but he also recognizes that in the horizontal realm children must grow up to become functioning and useful citizens. In the horizontal realm, obstinacy must be met by the Law.

The Importance of Memory

At first glance, Luther's first stage may appear to be nothing more than a form of mindless rote learning. But his concern and approach reaches well back into the early church. In presenting the Creed to the catechumens, the church fathers universally exhorted the catechumen to learn it by heart. For example, Cyril urged his students, "This is what I want you to retain verbatim, and which each of you must carefully recite, without writing it on paper, but by engraving it by memory in your hearts" (Cyril, Catechesis V, 12). Augustine emphasized the same theme:

> Receive, my sons, the rule of faith, called the Creed. On receiving it, write it in your heart, and every day recite it among yourselves. Before you fall asleep, before you proceed to anything, gird yourselves with your Creed. No one writes down the Creed just to be read; he stamps it on his soul, lest forgetfulness should lose what diligence had given him. Your book is your memory.[38]

Augustine continues: "Say it on your beds; ponder it in the streets, do not forget it during meals; and even when your body sleeps, keep watch over it in your heart."[39]

The emphasis on memory in the church fathers as well as in Luther reflected an intersection of pedagogical realities (oral learning and high illiteracy among the people) and theological concerns (that the word take deep root in the heart).

In an oral culture in which most people cannot read, and thus the spoken word is the primary means of communication, a person "knows" only that which he or she can remember. With this in view, Luther emphasizes that it is vitally important to learn the parts of the catechism so that their contents "may penetrate deeply into their minds and remain fixed in their memories" (LC Short Preface, 27). In other words, he wants it learned "by heart" which suggests a "repetition which has been internalized, which has become part of us, that is second nature, and thus something which is literally spoken or sung "from the heart."[40] Margaret Krych has suggested that we truly do not learn something until it is overlearned.[41] "Until something is 'overlearned' (for example, the alphabet is learned so well by most people that it almost cannot be forgotten), it will assuredly be forgotten eventually. So the catechism should be overlearned or reviewed often enough that they 'know it'—that is, have it at their fingertips."[42]

Luther wants God's Word to become a Christian's constant companion in order that it may shape new attitudes, thoughts, and actions. When the Word is our constant companion, it has the opportunity to change the way we think and act. For it is through the Word that the Spirit bestows his blessings, and it is through the Word that the Spirit routs the devil and his cohorts. Luther took his cue from Deuteronomy. With regard to the Shema ("Hear O Israel, the Lord your God is One") in Deuteronomy 6, Luther states, "he [God] simply wants these words to meet us everywhere and to be in our memories" (*LW* 9:69). He continues:

> Therefore it is not without reason that the Old Testament commands men to write the Ten Commandments on every wall and corner, and even on their garments. Not that we are to have them there merely for a display, as the Jews did, but we are to keep them incessantly before our eyes and constantly in our memory, and practice them in all our works and ways. Everyone is to make them his daily habit in all circumstance, in all his affairs and dealings, as if they were written everywhere he looks, and even wherever he goes or wherever he stands. (LC 331, 332)

In other words, the Shema of Deuteronomy was for the Israelite his constant companion through life—sleeping and waking, it was ever before his mind (Deuteronomy 6:4). For it was his very life: this faith of Israel in the One True God. It needed to be repeated as Israel often forgot.[43]

Stage II: Understanding the Basics

Learning the texts by heart does not exhaust the task of learning the catechism. Thus in his second stage, Luther wants the pastor to lead the catechumen into an understanding of the catechetical texts. This stage bears some similarities to the first stage in as much as Luther also advocates that when these explanations are chosen they should be adhered to closely without "changing a single syllable" (SC Preface 8). But in order to promote an understanding of the texts, Luther suggests that ample time be allowed for this stage, since it deals with lengthier explanations. In other words, pastors should not overwhelm the catechumen otherwise "they will hardly remember a single thing."[44]

Although Luther is not the first to provide explanations of the catechism's texts, his catechisms exhibit several characteristics and features which set them apart from many other catechetical writings in their efforts to promote an understanding of its contents. Three features in particular stand out: Luther's form of questions and answers; the literary characteristics and rhetorical qualities of his explanations; and his use of woodcuts alongside the text.

The Question: "What Is That? Answer"

In spite of the extraordinary influence of the Small Catechism upon the entire genre of catechisms, Luther was not the first to use a question and answer format, as he himself traces the method back to the etymology of "catechism" among the ancient Greeks. For a "catechism" (according to the Greeks) is a way of teaching with questions and answers, just as a schoolmaster has his pupils recite their lesson to see if they know it or not.[45] Within the church, the use of questions and answers in catechetical instruction can perhaps be traced back ultimately to the creedal questions asked in Baptism.[46] There the candidate was asked, "do you renounce the devil…?" and "do you believe in God the Father…?"

In the Middle Ages, the first catechetical work known to use a question-and-answer format, and thus constitute a milestone in the history of catechisms, is the well-known work, *Disputatio puerorum per interrogationes et responsiones*, attributed to Alcuin (735–804). In chapters 11 and 12 the author of this writing presents a Latin explanation of the Creed and Lord's Prayer in a series of questions.[47] These questions were later incorporated into a commentary on the Psalms by Bishop Bruno of Würzburg (d. 1045).

Luther had not used the question-and-answer format in his earlier catechetical writings, such as the *Brief Explanation* (1520) and the *Little Prayer Book* (1522). The following year, in 1523, he does append "Five Questions and Answers for Those Desiring to Go to the Lord's Supper" to a sermon. He asked: 1) Why do you take the sacrament? 2) What do you believe or confess that the sacrament is? 3) What are the words that Jesus used regarding the sacrament, and is your faith adequate? 4) Why do you receive the sign? 5) How will you use the sacrament? (WA 11:79–80).

Several years later, in his *German Mass*, Luther expressed his thoughts on the content and form that a catechism might take. Using the Lord's Prayer as an example, he suggests questions along the line of: What should you do when you pray? What is meant when you say Our Father in Heaven? How do we profane or dishonor God's name? What does it mean to believe in God the Father Almighty? What does it mean to believe in

Jesus Christ, his only Son? (*LW* 53:65). He goes on to suggest that questions could also be developed from or based on his *Little Prayer Book*.

Although Luther was not the first to employ a question-and-answer format, his questions in the Small Catechism are unique for their simplicity and consistency. This is especially evident when contrasted with other catechisms of his day. For example, compared with the "verbose and often aimless 130 questions" of Johann Agricola, Luther asks essentially one, and he asks it 23 times throughout the course of the catechism: "*Was ist das?*"[48] This has been translated into English most famously as "what does this mean?" It would, however, be more correct to translate it as "What is that?" or "What is this?" It introduces nearly every single "explanation" in the Small Catechism. Rather than ask a variety of questions that may require inductive or deductive reasoning, Luther asks only one—and that one is a fairly simple one. By asking basically one question, he follows the advice that he himself gave in the Large Catechism where he states, "Because we preach to children, we must talk babytalk to them."[49]

Wengert points out that Luther was 45 years old at the time and one of the first theologians in the West to witness his own child (Hans was about three years old at the time) learn to speak and ask simple questions ("What is that?" "That is a bird."). It was an experience that no doubt contributed to the clarity and simplicity of Luther's questions as well as the answers. Here it should also be noted that Luther identifies children as the target audience of the Small Catechism, whereas in his earlier writings he identified adults as their audience.

Luther's question, though a simple child's question, also provides a clue as to how he regarded the purpose or character of his explanation. Luther's intention in using "*Was ist das?*" is not to ask a question that implies some hidden meaning that needs to be brought to light by someone who has an expertise on the subject. As Wengert explains, "Luther is not so much interested in the deeper hidden meanings of these chief parts as in basic definitions, such as "What is the First Commandment? or Amen? or Baptism?"[50] "What is a god"? This idea is supported by the next word that appears in Luther's text, namely, "*Antwort.*" "*Was ist das? Antwort,*" appear alongside one another centered on the page in Luther's catechism.

Together, the question and answer look backwards and forwards. The *das* in the "What is this?" refers back to the text under consideration. The word "*Antwort*" indicates that the text which follows (namely, Luther's explanation) is a statement that is not open for discussion. Note that Luther does not say, "explanation" or "interpretation." In other words, Luther's "answer" is less an explanation in the modern sense than a restatement of what was just said. What follows is intended as the response of the catechumen. As such, it takes on the character of a confession. For example, the closing statement of the Creed, "This is most certainly true" clearly indicates that what was just covered is nothing other than the truth.

The relation between Luther's question ("what is that?") and his explanation ("answer") might be illuminated through the use of rhetorical tools.[51] The text with which Luther works is the *propositio*, that is, a brief listing of points that will be treated in greater detail.[52] Luther's question (*Was ist das?*) and answer (*Antwort*) function as the copula that connects the *propositio* with the following *explanatio dicti superioris* (explanation of what was said above). The answer or "explanation" of Luther's Small Catechism takes the form of what rhetoric calls an *amplificatio* or elaboration. The answer that follows is an epexegetical statement of the text just read. That is to say, the answer restates, expands, and elaborates upon the original text itself. Accordingly, Krodel suggests that a correct translation would be: "What is this [that I have just said]?" [To] answer, [I shall now elaborate on what I said]. In brief, "*Was ist das? Antwort,*" takes on the character of a "that is." So the First Commandment would read, "We should have no other gods," that is, "we should fear, love, and trust in God above all things." Here it should be noted that after Luther quotes the First Commandment in the Large Catechism, he then opens his explanation with the very words, "*Das ist.*"[53] The answer then provides a text or statement for the hearer to ponder and reflect on. Through this "explanation" the author tries to persuade the reader to undertake a specific action.

Luther occasionally asks several other questions in the course of the Small Catechism. In the Lord's Prayer he asks an additional question in the first three petitions, namely, "How is this done?" In the fourth petition he asks a unique one, "What is meant by daily bread?" This was most likely due to the fact that he had radically shifted the definition of bread to speak primarily of First Article gifts and the sustenance of bodily life.[54] In the sacraments Baptism and the Lord's Supper, he asks four questions, of which the first three are identical. Again, it may be that he has taken questions from the discipline of rhetoric, particularly, the teaching genus.[55] His first question, like all the others in the catechism, asks "*Was ist das*" which corresponds to the *quid est* (what is it?) of rhetoric. "What is Baptism?" "What is the Sacrament of the Altar?" It seeks to inquire into the essence of the matter under discussion. The second question, "What is the benefit of such eating and drinking?" corresponds to the *qui effectus* (what is the effect?) of rhetoric. Each of these questions was concerned with definition and under-standing the topic from all vantage points.

Characteristics of the "Explanations" in the Small Catechism

In a culture that was predominantly oral (for both children and adults), the printed word was most often mediated by the spoken word, either by reading aloud to oneself or by being read aloud to others.[56] Thus catechisms within the sixteenth century did not presuppose universal lit-eracy and as a result were published with a view toward being read aloud within a group, rather than scanned silently in the privacy of one's own room. R. W. Scribner notes that many writers were "aware that their works would be mediated through hearing."[57] In many instances, Luther's expla-nations in the Small Catechism were arguably composed more for the ear than for the eye.[58] As a result, his text has the character of living speech. In version after version of his sermons (especially the 1528 series), Luther not only simplified the complexities of the faith, but worked on the language of the explanations so that anyone could easily retain them in mind and heart. As a result:

> There is a strange rise and fall, cadence and rhythm in these sentences, to which nothing else in our literature can be compared. And these pleasing rhythms clothe a body of thoughts which by no means can be said to invite musical, rhythmical language. It is a masterful use of the language of the common people, combined with a genius for the tonal qualities of language.[59]

Although this is true for the entire catechism, "Luther's art of formulating his thoughts reached an apex in the explanations of the three articles of the Creed." Here "he used the many possibilities of the German language in a masterly way. The explanation of each article is one single, rhythmic and melodious sentence, which can be easily committed to memory and recited."[60]

In addition to learning by repetition, an oral population must clothe truths in words that are memorable or that relate to each other through the use of mnemonic devices.[61] Luther utilizes a wide range of rhetorical and mnemonic devices throughout the Small Catechism in order to ren-der it memorable. As will be seen, many of these are simply lost in most English translations.

Luther frequently uses two of the most common techniques to help the memory, namely, alliteration and assonance. In alliteration, the opening consonants share the same sound. Any number of examples can be found in the Small Catechism, for example, *Notdurft und Nahrung* (needs and nourishment); *Leibes und Lebes* (body and life); *behütet und bewahret* (protects and defends); *Tod und Teufel* (death and the devil); in *Worten und Werken* (in words and deeds); *Lehret und Lebes* (doctrine and life); *Haus und Hof* (house and home); *verlorenen und verdammten* (lost and condemned); *abspannen, abdringen, abwendig* (entice, force away, turn against). In the case of asso-nance, the opening vowels of two or more words sound the same. Some examples include: *lehret und lebet* (teaches and lives); *reichlich und täglich* (richly and daily), *lügen und trügen* (lies and deceives).

Another characteristic of oral speech is that the spoken word disappears the moment it is uttered. Unlike reading, a person does not have the lux-ury of dwelling on the word, much less the opportunity to "backscan" across the text just read. Moreover, the mind moves ahead more slowly in oral listening. One way of overcoming this in oral communication is to uti-lize repetition, that is, a person repeats what he or she just said but with slightly different words. It uses "clusters of integers such as parallel terms or phrases or clauses, antithetical terms or phrases or clauses."[62] The Small Catechism provides a number of good examples for such a technique: lie and deceive, house and home, wife and child, clothing and shoes, gold or silver, body and soul, eyes and ears, and all my senses. In each one of these, the hearer has the opportunity to pause for a moment and ponder the thought being expressed. Oral speech also tends to minimize the use of subordinate clauses and instead is additive through the use of coordinating conjunctions. Luther makes occasional use of these. For example, in the Second Article he concludes, "that I may be his and live under him in his kingdom and serve him in everlasting righteousness...."

Because images linger in the memory, oral speech often employs con-crete terms rather than abstract concepts, that is, words that can be pic-tured in the mind. Oral cultures must conceptualize and verbalize their knowledge with more or less close reference to the human-life world.[63] As a rule, very few generalizations can be found throughout Luther's expla-nations. Instead, Luther refers to the everyday activities of his readers and employs many down-to-earth expressions that would be familiar to the people of his day. So where Luther could have used a more abstract term like "family," he writes "wife and child." Instead of writing "economic livelihood," he speaks of field and cattle. Instead of referring to shelter, he has house and home, clothing and shoes. In other words, Luther uses readily understood examples from daily life in order to convey the cate-chism's teaching. Luther's explanations might be called *Kleinmalerei*, that is, vivid miniature word paintings. As Reu puts it, "Each stroke of the brush in the hand of this master painter makes God greater before the eye of the child."[64]

As any orator well knows, stories provide a more effective way to communicate the truth than does an abstract discourse. Out of the various items listed in the Creed (the *propositio*), Luther creates a story, not a *fabula*, but a *historia*. His *narratio* thus serves as an *expositio* of the *propositio* (the texts of the Creed's articles). His explanation of the First Article gives a description of the God of Creation not as a concept removed far from daily life, but as a description of the God who creates and sustains all that exists, especially me, and does all this for no other reason than his fatherly goodness and mercy. Luther's mastery reaches its pinnacle in the Second Article where he portrays Christ as the conquering hero, the one who wages battle upon the forces of death and the devil. In the Third Article, the narrative stretches from the creation of faith and conversion of the individual to the resurrection and granting of eternal life. Luther's narratives explains the text by expanding and amplifying it. For example, "heaven and earth" are expanded to include "me and all creatures" which is then expanded to include body and soul, house and home, etc.

Three characteristics of Luther's narrative stand out. First, wherever he can, he uses a verb instead of a noun because it is more understandable and dynamic. Creator is explained by the verbs create, give, sustain, provide, protect, and preserve. "Lord" is explained by the verbs redeem, purchase, and obtain. "Holy" in the Third Article is explained by call, enlighten, gather, and preserve. Second, he uses concrete and familiar everyday nouns, with which the hearer can identify as the objects of the verbs. Everyone would have been familiar with body, soul, limbs, senses, reason, faculties, food, and clothing, house and home, family and property, necessities of life, danger, and evil. Finally, the story is somewhat autobiographical. The story makes the hearer a participant. It is empathetic in that it draws the hearer into the story in such a way that he or she becomes a part of the communal story itself. "Each statement defines and expresses my existence, it puts a stamp on me, so to speak, the way in which in Baptism the sign of the Cross is placed upon me."[65] This makes the story not so much a past event as much as it makes the story contemporaneous with the life of the hearer. In a sense, the past, present, and future merge so that the sense of time disappears. Luther's extensive use of the first person pronoun, in which the *pro me* character of faith is also expressed brings this out. Thus God has created me, redeemed me, sanctified me. In the Second Article, Luther brings out the contemporaneity of Christ's saving work by using such words as "My Lord" and "done for me."

Luther's explanations of the Decalogue and Lord's Prayer may not use narrative as much, but do utilize what might best be described as a formulaic pattern into which he can insert the particulars of each commandment or petition. In each of the commandments, Luther uses the formula "we should fear and love God so that we do not … but that we…." Into each he inserts the particulars of the commandment under discussion. In the Lord's Prayer Luther creates a similar pattern as he opens each of his explanations by saying that "God's name is indeed hallowed without my prayer but we pray that it may be hallowed among us also. God kingdom comes indeed without our prayer, but we…." Finally, Luther uses antitheses to good effect as well. For example, in the Second Article he paints the contrast, "Not with gold or silver, but with his innocent suffering and death."

Luther manages to combine all of these various features into a sense of harmony and rhythm. It can be observed in the familiar combinations like *lügen und trügen, reichlich und täglich, lehret und lebet, mit aller Notdurft und Nahrung des Leibes und Lebes, behütet und bewahret, erworben und gewonnen, Tod und Teufel, gnädiger und guter Wille, in Worten und Werken*, etc. In English we have similar striking combinations like, "love and trust," "love and esteem," "help and befriend," "improve and protect," "property and living," "heaven and earth," "thank and praise," "lives and reigns," etc. Reu encouraged the German-speaking people of his day, "Read your Catechism aloud and with correct accentuation and I believe even the unmusical ear should perceive something of the musical force of these rhythmical periods and clauses."[66]

Woodcuts and Bible Stories

In order to help the catechumen remember the texts, Luther (along with his printer)[67] supplemented the written texts of the Small and Large Catechism with a number of woodcuts. In the introduction to a passional which was added to his *Little Prayer Book* in 1529, Luther explained the importance of providing woodcuts. "Children and simple people are more apt to retain the divine stories when taught by picture and parable than merely by words or instruction" (*LW* 43:43). These thus provided important aids in the learning process, especially for the illiterate.

For those "with little or no reading ability in the narrow sense, listening or looking would have been the major means of acquiring their knowledge of the Reformation."[68] From early on, then, looking (at pictures) and listening (to the text being read) were at least as important as reading for those members of the household who could not read. At the same time, however, they also provided a meeting ground of the illiterate, semi-literate, and literate. All could participate in the communal activity of learning the catechism together. The printing press not only made possible the wide distribution of the printed word, but of the picture as well.

Woodcuts were probably the first item of mass circulation. "At the beginning of the sixteenth century the German woodcut reached the peak of its artistic development, combining simplicity of line [and hence the ease with which they could be 'read'] with sophistication of expression."[69] Their popularity was probably due in part to their durability and cost of production. Like homemade gin, they were "cheap, crude, and effective."

Luther recognized the value of images in woodcuts on several fronts. Medieval culture had been filled with stained glass windows and stories of the saints. He knew that in an oral culture images provided an important tool for stimulating the imagination. "Without images we can neither think nor understand anything (WA 37:63)."[70] Images also possessed an important rhetorical and emotional impact. For these reasons, images or woodcuts could and should be used in the educational enterprise. While picture catechisms were not entirely uncommon,[71] Luther's use of them was distinctive in at least two ways. First, whereas other manuals of the day might include one or two woodcuts, Luther's Small Catechism included more than twenty.[72] Second, whereas other manuals included woodcuts that told sensational although allegedly true stories,[73] Luther's focused on the narratives taken from the biblical text.[74] In this connection, however, one should note that the Small Catechism's use of woodcuts was not to be considered in isolation from the written word. Conversely, the printed word should not be read in isolation from the woodcut, but should be considered in relation to the visual form of communication. In the Small Catechism, Luther created an interplay or reciprocal relationship between the text of his explanations and the biblical narratives which they depicted. There are two dimensions where the text served the picture and the picture in turn served the text.

First, there is a sense that "pictorial representation ... can never escape the danger of ambiguity."[75] For that reason it requires an explanation to be provided by the spoken or printed word. Like other pictures or artwork, woodcuts often raise more questions than they answer. The picture summarizes a narrative by providing a "snapshot" of the story, but the meaning of the pictures is not always self-evident or self-explanatory. The narratives that they portray would raise questions not only about the story being portrayed by them (What's going on? Who are they? What are they doing?), but about the meaning and application of the stories as well. The addition of the printed word of the commandment and explanation enabled the catechism to spell out the message of the woodcut unambiguously.[76] In the case of the Small Catechism, the "*Was ist das? Antwort*" provided the meaning to the story being portrayed.

Second, unlike today's video age in which the word serves the picture and is subservient or auxiliary to the image, in Luther's catechism the picture portrayed by the woodcut would serve the printed word. The pictures made a direct visual point, while the printed explanation required only simple reading skills.[77] In other words, woodcuts allowed the printed text to be kept brief and simple since a picture, as has often been said, is worth a thousand words. Furthermore, as an illustration in a book, woodcuts reinforced the message of the printed word. They provided a concrete, and easily remembered illustration of the text under consideration. For example:

> Today people do not always remember that Luther connects hallowing God's name to the preaching of the Word of God. However, in Luther's catechism the reader, or even the child too young to read, would have seen on the page facing Luther's succinct explanation of that petition [commandment] a picture of people in contemporary dress listening to a preacher delivering a sermon.[78]

The woodcuts provided in the Small Catechism connected each explanation of the Catechism with easy-to-remember stories of the Bible in the contemporary dress of Luther's day.[79] One could imagine the head of the house reading the text and then holding up the picture for all to see.[80]

STAGE III: THE LIFELONG PRACTICE OF THE FUNDAMENTALS

Luther regarded the texts of the catechism to be of such fundamental importance that a Christian should daily make use of them throughout life (LC Preface, 19). He knows that the basics in any field are of such a nature that one never leaves them behind. In the same way a pianist practices scales, a basketball player his shots, so also the Christian practices her catechism. The basics lay a foundation for everything that follows. Once students have learned their ABCs, they can go on to learn the grammar of speaking and writing.[81] Scales and arpeggios form the basis for a pianist's repertoire so that a pianist both practices them and then uses them to learn new pieces. A map is drawn in order to be used. It is not enough to learn the map, but one must then take it upon the journey and use it to find one's way to the destination of the journey. In a similar way, these fundamentals of the catechism as contained in its texts, lay the foundation for a person's lifelong spiritual formation.

By providing the basics, the Small Catechism and Large Catechism were intended to be more of a daily companion for meditation and spiritual guidance than one time instructional textbooks for confirmation. One exercises himself in the basics of the Small Catechism through its ongoing study and meditation. Luther brings this out in the longer preface to the Large Catechism[82] in which he addresses adults who considered the catechism as a simple teaching, easily mastered in an hour or in a single day. Here Luther speaks of his own need for daily study of the catechism.

> Yet I do as a child who is being taught the Catechism. Every morning, and whenever else I have time, I read and recite word for word the Lord's Prayer, the Ten Commandments, the Creed, the Psalms, etc. I must still read and study the Catechism daily, yet I cannot master it as I wish, but remain a child and pupil of the Catechism, and I do it gladly." (LC Long Preface, 7–8)

Such statements were not simply examples of hyperbole or false modesty on Luther's part. Luther conceives of them being used less for "study" in our modern sense than for "meditation" or "contemplation." With this understanding, Luther recognized several important truths about the texts of the catechism and the contents of the Small Catechism.

Fullness of Words

Luther calls for the continual study of the catechism because its contents echo themes that are central to the revelation of God in salvation history, themes that Scripture returns to time and again. These provide the daily food for the Christian. Luther took his cue from Deut 6:7–8, "keep these always before you." Luther adds, "God himself is not ashamed to teach it [the Catechism] daily, for he knows of nothing better to teach, and he always keeps on teaching this one thing without varying it with anything new or different" (LC Long Preface, 16). Focusing on these themes can keep a Christian from being distracted by peripheral concerns, tasks, and matters that in the end are not of eternal consequence.

In addition, there is a sense where we continually need to relearn lest we forget and fall away (a prominent theme in the Old Testament): "Even if their knowledge of the Catechism were perfect (though that is impossible in this life), yet it is highly profitable and fruitful daily to read it and make it the subject of meditation and conversation. In such reading, conversation, and meditation, the Holy Spirit is present and bestows ever new and greater light and fervor, so that day by day we relish and appreciate the catechism more greatly" (LC Long Preface, 9). Taking God as our teacher, Luther urges continual reflection upon and appropriation of these materials. The Gospel exhibited by these texts is so rich and broad that we can never learn it fully (LC II 33).

There is a depth to the catechism that cannot be exhausted in a single session. Instead, the words and contents of the catechism contain the highest mysteries of the faith. Thus he writes, "anyone who knows the Ten Commandments perfectly knows the entire Scriptures" (LC Long Preface, 17). Again, "What is the whole Psalter but meditations and exercises based upon the First Commandment?" (LC Long Preface, 18). The Commandments always open new avenues of thought and open new ways of looking at Scripture and at life. For example, the first line of Luther's explanation to the First Commandment provides enough for one to think about and live out for many years. Many other lines of Luther do the same thing. "One goes ahead to them, the way Pablo Casals, the [twentieth] century's great cellist, went to his piano each morning and set his day by playing and reflecting on one of Bach's Two-part Inventions. The catechism is the basic 'two-part inventions' of the Christian church."[83]

Exploration of Scripture

The church had always considered texts such as the Creed as handy summaries of Scripture's message. Luther describes the Large Catechism as "a brief compend and summary of the Bible's central contents" (LC III, 19). Luther's understanding of the catechism as a brief summary of the Holy Scriptures (LC III, 19) in a readily accessible form would be reinforced by a "nickname" that it acquired, namely, the "layman's Bible." In a sermon on September 14, 1528, Luther referred to the catechism as a "children's sermon or lay Bible" (WA 30:I, 27, line 26). This title would stick throughout the sixteenth century and eventually find its way into the *Book of Concord* and its Catalog of Testimonies.

Although the catechism did not set forth the entire doctrinal content of the Scriptures, it captures and thus provides an introduction to the most important themes in the Scriptures for the average person. For example, the prominence of the First Commandment in Luther's Small Catechism captures well the prominence that it has in the entire Scriptures, particularly, the Old Testament. Not only is idolatry the sole reason for which Israel is taken into captivity as the judgment of God, but time and time again Deuteronomy brings up the need to fear and love God as the key to

Israel's response to God. In the First Article of the Creed, Luther captures the heart of the biblical witness with his stress on creation as the foundation for the First Commandment and his stress on the continuing creative work of God whereby he continues to provide for human needs. The Second Article focuses on the three events in Christ's life that the church regards as the key to understanding the significance of Christ, namely, his incarnation, suffering and death, resurrection and exaltation. It corresponds with the major points of not only the Gospels, but with Paul's entire treatment of Christ. The Third Article orients the entire doctrine of the Holy Spirit to Christ as the one who extends and implements the work of Christ. This, too, corresponds not only with the role of the Spirit in moving forward the work of Christ in the Gospels (incarnation, Baptism, temptations, etc.), but the place of the Holy Spirit in Acts and the Epistles as the one who brings Christ and believers together.

In fact, by providing a summary of the central themes and contours of Scripture, the catechism actually provides a springboard for the further exploration of Scripture, as Luther himself proposes. "When these parts have been well learned, you may assign them also some Psalms or some hymns, based on these subjects, to supplement and confirm their knowledge. Thus our youth will be led into the Scriptures so that they make progress daily" (LC Short Preface, 25). Not only does the catechism lead them into Scripture, it provides a framework for incorporating new insights from Scripture. Again, Luther suggested that once people know the catechism, they may proceed to learn more, "relating to these teachings of the Catechism all that they learn in the Scriptures, and thus advance and grow richer in understanding" (LC II, 70).

A reading of the Small Catechism quickly reveals that it does not deal with every article or theme in Scripture or Christian doctrine. Startling by their omission are such terms as "Trinity," not to mention such themes in Christology as the states and offices of Christ or a discussion on the attributes of God. While not dealing explicitly with these themes, the catechisms provide a springboard for thinking about them in a way that is faithful to the contours of Scripture itself.

The doctrine of the Trinity provides a good example. In his catechisms, Luther does not use the traditional language and categories of dogmatics. The Small Catechism contains no introduction to the Trinity and does not mention, let alone discuss, such classical terms as "person," essence," and "Trinity." The Large Catechism offers little more. What Luther provides is a description of the three works of the three persons of the Trinity. He places the doctrine of the Trinity within the narrative of salvation history, which corresponds well with Scripture's own approach.[84] Indeed, Trinitarian reflection in the New Testament and in the centuries leading up to Nicea generally focused its attention on what is called the economic Trinity.[85] In other words, the Trinity was considered within the framework of the threefold structure of salvation that focused attention on the way in which the three persons were manifested in our world soteriologically. This had several ramifications. First, discussion begins with the three persons and then proceeds to their unity. Second, the Father provides the focal point for understanding their unity. Third, the focus of Christian reflection was the self-expression and historical unfolding of the one God (Father) in the economy, in the incarnation of the Son and the sending of the Holy Spirit, and the return of all things to their point of origin in God. All things proceed *a Patre ad Patrem*. Here the Father is understood to be related to us "through Christ and in the Spirit." This approach is apparent in the Creeds and Rules of Faith, as well as the doxologies and prayers of the church. Thus Luther's treatment provides scriptural trajectories for reflecting on the doctrine of the Trinity.

Life as a Catechumenate

Luther also recognized that while the catechism leads a person into the Scriptures, it also functions as a catalyst for bringing the same Scriptures into the life of Christians. As such, it equips Christians to interpret their life experiences theologically in light of the Gospel, and thus prepares them to stand firm amidst the turbulence of life. Here Luther takes the long view and considers the Christian life in light of the eschaton. After returning from the Wartburg to Wittenberg, Luther made the following statement in his first sermon:

> The summons of death comes to us all, and no one can die for another. Everyone must fight his own battle with death by himself, alone. We can shout into another's ears,[86] but everyone must himself be prepared for the time of death, for I will not be with you then, nor you with me. Therefore everyone must himself know and be armed with the chief things[87] which concern a Christian. (*LW* 51:70; WA 10 III:1.7–2.2)

The Christian exercises his or her faith daily in the battle with the devil and death with the result that through this battle faith is strengthened (*LW* 51:71). Two years after publishing the catechism, Luther rejoiced in this goal. "[P]raise be to God—it has come to pass that man and woman, young and old, know the catechism; they know how to believe, to live, to pray, to suffer, and to die. Consciences are well instructed about how to be Christians and how to recognize Christ" (*LW* 47:52–53).

The catechisms exhibit little interest in conveying an abstract theoretical knowledge or a body of facts organized for transmission from one generation to the next. Doctrine is not abstract theory to be contrasted with practical skills and how-to steps for daily living. If anything, the Reformers (and the church fathers before them) viewed doctrine as pastoral care. This is what made the study of doctrine so important. This is why they were willing to engage (however reluctantly) in doctrinal debates. Doctrine provides the Christian with a diagnosis of the innermost needs of human beings. It provides a framework for interpreting life and the experiences of life in the light of the triune work of God. Doctrine provides a foundation for faith and life in order to make sense of a world that often seems confusing and meaningless. Most importantly, it brings God and his gifts into our very lives. Of course, for Luther "that knowledge was to be tested in the stress and strain of everyday spiritual and corporeal life."[88] The catechism's concern for pastoral care comes through in several ways.

First, it emerges in, and in turn, explains the thoroughly existential ordering of Luther's catechisms as a whole as well as the existential starting point for the explanations of its individual parts.[89] In each instance, Luther begins at the point where people encounter and experience life with its demands and gifts, its disappointments and joys. This is most readily seen in his treatment of the First Commandment in the Large Catechism. There Luther defines a god in terms of a person's trust. In other words, whatever one's heart clings to, that is one's god. The First Article begins at the point where I experience the creative activity of God. The Second Article begins with my experience of bondage under sin. The Third Article begins with my inability to trust. Each petition of the Lord's Prayer approaches God from our experience as people in need of God's help. It recognizes that our relation to God will always be one of speaking out of actual outer or inner need.

Second, the Large Catechism focuses less on expounding the biblical text than on actualizing and applying those texts to one's life. It shows how these texts might address the needs of practical Christian living in different situations and at different times. The First Commandment entails different things for a newlywed with a child on the way than it does for a single person or for an older person with elderly parents. It is in the face of need that one truly learns the difficulty of this commandment. The Fourth Commandment is examined from the perspective not only of children, but also of parents with all their responsibilities. The seventh commandment focused on what it entails for people in all walks of life. Luther expounds it for employers, employees, artisans, workmen, day-laborers, businessmen, merchants, maids, etc. (LC I, 225–27). In the Sixth Petition of the Lord's Prayer, Luther highlights the different temptations that afflict a person as he moves from youth into adulthood into old age. Luther makes it clear then that in a very real sense, "the catechism is not really learned until life strikes."[90] As Luther himself puts it, we shall never finish learning it, "since doctrine does not consist in words and sermons, but in life" (WA 32:210–32). This means that the entire Christian life becomes a catechumenate.[91]

CONCLUSION

Luther designed his catechisms to accompany the Christian from the Baptismal font (from which he or she received new birth) to the grave (from which he or she will rise to new life). Along this journey the catechism keeps the Christian centered on chief articles of the Christian faith. In doing so, it provides the Christian with a defense against spiritual assaults on the one hand and assists Christians in making sense of their lives on the other hand. To that end, the catechisms provide an invaluable service to the novice and veteran of the faith alike.

NOTES

1 Between 1522 and 1529 sixty editions of thirteen different instructional booklets of one form or another were printed in Wittenberg. See Timothy J. Wengert, "Wittenberg's Earliest Catechism," *Lutheran Quarterly*, n.s. 7 (Fall 1993): 250. For the many editions published throughout Europe during the sixteenth century, see J. M. Reu's *Dr. Martin Luther's Small Catechism* (Chicago: Wartburg, 1929), 25–60.

2 Wengert also notes, "The amazing success of these booklets places in question the common opinion that Luther and Lutheranism's influence among the simpler folk waned after the Peasants' War. If anything, it increased as the reformers themselves developed media for getting their particular message across." Wengert, "Wittenberg's Earliest Catechism," 258, note 20.

3 John Bossy, *Christianity in the West, 1400–1700* (Oxford: Oxford University Press, 1985), 119.

4 Latin had long served as a line of demarcation between the clergy and the laity and thus served to buttress a social hierarchy that elevated the clergy above the laity. That began to change in the fifteenth century as the use of the vernacular increased.

5 It also must be kept in mind that only about 10% of the people in the Holy Roman Empire lived in cities and that these cities ranged from 2,000 to 50,000 in population. In Luther's day, Wittenberg itself was probably closer to 2,000 in population.

6   Bast, *Honor Your Fathers*, 8. This is not to say that all members of the nobility
    were literate. Some individuals like Franz von Sickingen would have had books
    read to them.

7   R. W. Scribner, "Oral Culture and the Diffusion of Reformation Ideas," *Popular
    Culture and Popular Movements in Reformation Germany* (London: Hambleton
    Press, 1987), 50.

8   Mark U. Edwards, Jr., *Printing, Propaganda, and Martin Luther* (Berkeley: Univer-
    sity of California Press, 1994), 37.

9   R. W. Scribner, "Oral Culture and the Diffusion of Reformation Ideas," 50.

10 Edwards, *Printing, Propaganda, and Martin Luther*, 37.

11 It should also be noted that Luther's *Brief Explanation of 1520* is explicitly tar-
    geted at the illiterate as he introduces it with the words, "the ordinary Christian,
    who cannot read the Scriptures..." PE 2, 354.

12 Melanchthon provides some specific instructions for schoolmasters on teaching the
    catechism to different grade levels in his *Instructions for the Visitors* (*LW* 40:315, 318).

13 Earlier in the decade Luther had already urged government officials to undertake
    the responsibility of providing education for the young. See *To the Councilmen of All
    Cities in Germany that they Establish and Maintain Christian Schools* (*LW* 45:339–78;
    WA 15:27–53). Gerald Strauss strongly criticizes this shift "of educational
    authority from private to public jurisdiction, from voluntary to compulsory par-
    ticipation, and from associative to institutional organization." *Luther's House of
    Learning: Indoctrination of the Young in the German Reformation* (Baltimore and
    London: Johns Hopkins University Press, 1978), 7. For a counter response see
    James M. Kittelson, "Successes and Failures in the German Reformation: The
    Report from Strasbourg," *Archiv für Reformationsgeschichte* 73 (1982): 152–75.

14 In addition to Latin schools, a few schools provided instruction in the vernacular.
    See Elbert Vaughan Wills, "The Elementary-School Ordinance From the Würt-
    temberg Church Code of 1559," *Lutheran Church Quarterly*, II (July 1929),
    355–57 for a discussion of the use of the catechism in these schools.

15 Bast, *Honor Your Fathers*, 101.

16 Marilyn Harran, *Martin Luther—Learning for Life* (St. Louis: Concordia, 1997), 214.

17 By addressing "ordinary pastors," Luther refers to the traditional distinction
    between regular clergy (the monks, canons and nuns, who had withdrawn from the
    world to live under a rule, called in Latin a *regula*) and the secular clergy (those
    who worked among the laity in the world, which in Latin was called the *saeculum*).

18 Having withdrawn from the world to save their souls, ancient canon Law and
    monastic rules discouraged monks from providing direct service to lay congrega-
    tions. They were not supposed to preach and administer sacraments to the laity
    because that was the right and duty of the secular clergy. To be sure, that would
    eventually change with the result that monks became the backbone of missionary
    work. Following the adoption of the Rule of St. Benedict, regular clergy focused
    on the educational and cultural revival of the church. This included teaching and
    learning Latin grammar, reading, copying of Scriptures and liturgical books, etc.
    See Joseph H. Lynch, *The Medieval Church: A Brief History* (London, New York:
    Longman, 1992), 77–83.

19 Brecht, *Luther*, II, 274.

20 Kittelson, "Luther the Educational Reformer," 105–6.

21 Bernard Hamilton, *Religion in the Medieval West* (London: Bernard Hamilton, 1986), 68ff. In 1471, Bishop Wedego of Havelberg had stated that men desiring a pastorate should be able to recite the Lord's Prayer and the Apostles Creed; they had to know what the seven sacraments were and be sufficiently familiar with Latin to read the Mass. They were in any case to know more than the laity. These criteria for admission to the priesthood were so low-level that one need not have completed a course at a grammar school in order to fulfill them. Susan C. Karant-Nunn, *Luther's Pastors: The Reformation in the Ernestine Countryside* (Philadelphia: The American Philosophical Society, 1979), 20.

22 Karant-Nunn, *Luther's Pastors: The Reformation in the Ernestine Countryside*, 23.

23 Friedrich Mildenberger, *Theology of the Lutheran Confessions* (tr. Erwin L. Lueker; Philadelphia: Fortress, 1986), 142.

24 These include the order of confession, the Baptismal booklet, and the Marriage booklet, each of which has a liturgical character and none of which contain the superscription addressed to the head of the household.

25 See Kittelson's analysis of the shift that occurred in Luther's thinking on the need for schools from his 1524 writing, *To the Councilmen of All Cities in Germany That They Establish and Maintain Christian Schools* (*LW* 45:339–78) to his 1530 *Sermon on Keeping Children in School* (*LW* 46:207–58) where he argues for boys of lesser ability to remain in school in order to provide a ready reserve of pastors in case of emergency, "Luther the Educational Reformer," 100–1.

26 See Hans-Werner Goetz, *Life in the Middle Ages from the Seventh to the Thirteenth Century* (Notre Dame: University of Notre Dame Press, 1993), and David Herlihy, *Medieval Households* (Cambridge, Mass.: Harvard University Press, 1985).

27 See Reu *Dr. Martin Luther's Small Catechism*, 1–6, on the catechization of the young in the early church and Middle Ages.

28 Bast, *Honor Your Fathers*, 57.

29 In fact, Luther could apply every high and respectable title, such as ruler, bishop, doctor, pastor, preacher, judge, schoolmaster, to the parent (WA 16:490, 30ff).

30 "Stephan Landskron proposed that following the first meal, the father should go with his household to a sermon. Thereafter he should sit at home with his wife and his children and the rest, and ask them what they had learned from the sermon, sharing with them what he had learned. Then he should listen to see if they know and understand the Ten Commandments, the Seven Deadly Sins, the Lord's Prayer and the Creed, and he should teach them. He should have them bring him a little drink, and sing him a nice song about God, our dear Lady, or the dear saints. For he who was joyful with his flock like this would be passing the time is a good way, and Christ our Lord would be there also. For as he promises in the Gospel, 'Where two or three are gathered in my name, I am there in their midst'"; quoted in Bast, *Honor Your Fathers*, 59.

31 Robert Kolb, "The Layman's Bible: The Use of Luther's Catechisms in the German Late Reformation," in *Luther's Catechisms—450 Years: Essays Commemorating the Small and Large Catechisms of Dr. Martin Luther* (ed. David Scaer and Robert D. Preus; Fort Wayne, Ind.: Concordia Theological Seminary Press, 1979), 22.

32 Wengert, "Forming the Faith through Catechisms: Moving to Luther and Today," *Formation in the Faith: Catechesis for Tomorrow*, Symposium Papers, no. 7 (St. Louis: Concordia Seminary Publications, 1997), 43.

33 In *A Simple Way to Pray*, Luther uses similar imagery when he says, "To this day I suckle at the Lord's Prayer like a child, and as an old man eat and drink from it and never get my fill" (*LW* 43:200). Behind its seemingly simple language, then, one can discern profound theological depth. Although the Small Catechism does not address every topic of Christian doctrine, it opens the way for further thinking and conversation on other issues.

34 Here Luther, following his own advice, retained the wording of the Decalogue (which was often abbreviated for the sake of helping people memorize it) that was used during the Middle Ages. This explains why certain elements are not always present as we might expect, such as the promise attached to the Fourth Commandment.

35 Wengert, *A Contemporary Translation*, 74.

36 As many pastors today recognize, to introduce even minor translation changes into the wording of Lord's Prayer creates havoc when a congregation attempts to pray it aloud together.

37 Wengert, *A Contemporary Translation*, 75. A good example from the fifteenth century is Johannes Wolff who provides a detailed example of public instruction by the priest developed through practice with his own congregation. "The method was so simple and foolproof, he boasted, that everyone would learn it 'whether they liked it or not,' even those 'as dull as a beast, a horse, an ass, or a stone.'" Each Sunday, after reading the Creed, the pastor was to recite the Ten Commandments "slowly in German, counting them off on their fingers, with frequent pauses so that the congregation could repeat the words: The preacher will say, 'you shall only pray…' and the people will respond, 'You shall only pray…' Preacher: '…to the one God'; people: '…to the one God.'" This was in turn supplemented by frequent preaching on the Decalogue, which Wolff strongly encouraged for people who heard them forget them and others know nothing about them at all. Bast, *Honor Your Fathers*, 24.

38 See his sermon *De Symbolo ad Catechumenos*, dating from the last years of Augustine's life. Cited in Robert I. Bradley, *The Roman Catechism in the Catechetical Tradition of the Church: The Structure of the Roman Catechism as Illustrative of the "Classic Catechesis"* (Lanham, Md.: University Press of America, 1990), 31, and translated from PL 40:627.

39 Harmless, *Augustine and the Catechumenate*, 276. Augustine cites Jeremiah 31:33 about writing it on the heart. He also recalls Paul's comments in Romans 10:8. What you will hear is what you will believe; and what you will believe is what you will recite.

40 Carl Schalk, "Worshipping from Memory or 'By Heart'," *Lutheran Education*, September/October 1990, 56.

41 In our day and age we call it "muscle memory." Learning to dribble a basketball or playing scales on a piano requires repetition over time. Only after a person has learned the scales or learned to dribble can that person then go on to play music or play the game of basketball.

42 Margaret A. Krych, "The Catechism in Christian Education," *Word and World*, 10 (1990): 43–47.

43 See Virgil Thompson, "The Promise of Catechesis," *Lutheran Quarterly* 4 (Autumn 1990): 259.

44 Wengert, *A Contemporary Translation*, 75.

45 *LW* 53.

46 See John Constable, "Sixteenth-Century Catechisms: Their Genesis and Genius," *Teaching the Faith: Luther's Catechisms in Perspective* (ed. Carl Volz; River Forest, Ill.: Lutheran Educational Association, 1967), 20–21.

47 See Joseph Anthony Slattery, "The Catechetical Use of the Decalogue from the End of the Catechumenate through the Late Medieval Period," Ph.D. thesis (Catholic University of America, 1979), 115–16.

48 The question, "What is this?" appears 23 times in the Small Catechism. In the first three chief parts, Luther asks a different question only four times, "How does this happen?" occurs in the first three petitions of the Lord's Prayer and, "What then does daily bread mean?" ("*was heißt denn täglich Brot?*") in the fourth. Only the sacraments contain a variety of questions.

49 Large Catechism I, 77: "*Weil wir den Kindern predigen, müssen wir ihn lallen.*" See Wengert, "Forming the Faith through Catechisms," 39.

50 Wengert, *A Contemporary Translation*, 8.

51 Gottfried Krodel has proposed the use of rhetorical analysis for Luther's catechism and gives an example of it with regard to the three articles of the Creed. See his forthcoming article, "Luther's Work on the Catechism in the Context of Late Medieval Catechetical Literature," in the *Concordia Journal* 25 (October 1999): 380–83. There he points out that Luther would not have been unaware of rhetoric. See Neil R. Leroux, "Luther's *Am Neujahrstage*: Style as Argument," *Rhetorica* 12 (1994):1–42.

52 Krodel points out that Luther does not have to "search for, or discover, or invent the materials" to be treated by him, "Luther's Work on the Catechism," 381.

53 He also introduces the explanations of the three articles in *Brief Explanation* with *Das ist*. See WA 7:215.26, 217.5, 218.24; PE 2:369, 370, 372. In the *Brief Explanation*, the explanations of the individual sections of the LP are introduced with: "*Die Meinung ist.*" As Krodel notes, *Meinung* for Luther designates content, substance, intention, goal, plan, and confession or even *rechte Auslegung*.

54 See Paul Robinson's article in *Lutheran Quarterly*, "'What is Meant by Daily Bread?': Luther's Catechisms and the Medieval Sermonic Tradition" (Winter, 1999–2000): 435–47.

55 Rhetoric generally dealt with three or four types of speech. The traditional three included: the *genus demonstrativum*, which contains praise and blame; the *genus deliberativum*, which engages in persuasion and disuasion; *genus iudicale*, which deals with texts involving controversies and litigation and whose purpose was to refute the opponents. In bringing dialectics into rhetoric, Melanchthon added a fourth for the teacher and theologian, the *genus didascalium*. For a brief overview of Melanchthon's rhetoric, see Timothy Wengert, "Philip Melanchthon's 1522 Annotations on Romans and the Lutheran Origin of Rhetorical Criticism," in *Biblical Interpretation in the Era of the Reformation* (ed. Richard A. Muller and John L. Thompson; Grand Rapids: Eerdmans, 1996), 128.

56 Scribner, *Popular Culture and Popular Movements in Reformation Germany* (London: Hambledon Press, 1987), 50–51.

57 Scribner, *Popular Culture and Popular Movements in Reformation Germany*, 54.

58 While focusing on the theological content of the Small Catechism, it is easy to overlook its rhetorical and literary qualities. This is a particularly challenging

task for translators of the catechism. See Charles P. Arand and James W. Voelz, "Classic Catechism—1995," *Concordia Journal*, 22 (January 1996): 66–75.

59   *Zur Sprache und Geschichte des kleinen Katechismus* (Leipzig: Verlag der Dürr'schen Buchhandlung, 1909), 15–16. Tr. Fred Kramer in J. M. Reu, "Why Luther's Catechism Is So Dear to My Heart," Appendix 19 of Paul I. Johnston's Ph.D. dissertation, "An Assessment of the Educational Philosophy of Johann Michael Reu" (Urbana, IL: University of Illinois, 1989), 924.

60   Martin U. Brecht, *Doctor Luther's Bulla and Reformation: A Look at Luther the Writer* (Valparaiso, Ind.: Valparaiso University Press, 1991), 5.

61   Such as organizing items into lists of seven during the Middle Ages (seven deadly sins, seven virtues, etc.). See Walter Ong, *Orality and Literacy: the Technologizing of the Word* (London: Routledge, 1982). See also chapter two of Thomas Winger's, "Orality and the Interpretation of Written Documents" in "Orality as the Key to Understanding Apostolic Proclamation in the Epistles," Th.D. Thesis (St. Louis: Concordia Seminary, 1997), for a good overview of the subject.

62   Ong, *Orality and Literacy*, 38.

63   Ong, *Orality and Literacy*, 38.

64   Reu, cited in Paul I. Johnston, "An Assessment of the Educational Philosophy of Johann Michael Reu Using the Hermeneutic Paradigms of J. F. Herbart and of J. C. K. von Hofmann and the Erlangen School: A Thesis Submitted in partial fulfillment of the requirements for the degree of Doctor of Philosophy in Education" (Urbana-Champaign: University of Illinois, 1989) 4:922.

65   Krodel, "Luther's Work on the Catechism," 383.

66   Reu, "Why Luther's Catechism Is So Dear to My Heart," 923. Take the Second Article: *Ich glaube, dass Jesus Christus, wahrhaftiger Gott, vom Vater in Ewigkeit geboren, und auch wahrhaftiger Mensch, von der Jungfrauen Maria geboren, sei mein Herr, der mich verlorenen und verdammten Menschen erlöset hat, erworben und gewonnen von allen Sünden, vom Tod und von der Gewalt des Teufels, nicht mit Gold oder Silber, sondern mit seinem heiligen theuren Blut und mit seinen unschuldigen Leiden und Sterben, auf dass ich sein eigen sei und in seinem Reich unter ihm lebe und ihm diene in ewiger Gerechtigkeit, Unschuld und Seligkeit, gleichwie er ist auferstanden von Tod, lebet und regieret in Ewigkeit. Das ist gewislich wahr."*

67   The consistency in using the same woodcuts throughout the various editions suggests that Luther played an active role in at least identifying the biblical narratives to be used. Reu notes, "Luther, who had good insight into the importance of illustrations ... designated the biblical events that were to be represented by pictures and Schirlentz used the corresponding cuts which he had on hand or could easily get," Reu, *Dr. Martin Luther's Small Catechism*, 31. While the same events are depicted in the woodcuts, often the quality and detail of the woodcuts will improve from one edition to the next. For example, compare the woodcuts from the Small Catechism and the Large Catechism.

68   R. W. Scribner, *For the Sake of Simple Folk: Popular Propaganda for the German Reformation* (Oxford: Clarendon, 1994), 3. This book provides a very helpful treatment of the role and interpretation of woodcuts as a medium of communication during the sixteenth century.

69   Scribner, *Popular Culture*, 277–78.

70   Scribner, *Popular Culture*, 299. Quoted from WA 37:63, line 26.

71   See the classic in this area, Geffcken, *Der Bildercatechismus des funfzehnten Jahrhunderts und die catechetischen Hauptstücke in dieser Zeit bis auf Luther* (Leipzig: T. O. Weigel, 1855).

72   Wengert suggests that these were at the time being prepared for a new edition of Luther's *Prayerbook*. If so, their inclusion in the Small Catechism may also say something about its purpose. Wengert, "Forming the Faith through Catechisms," 44.

73   For example, In the *Soul's Consolation* (1474), the First Commandment was illustrated by the story of a man who loved temporal things more than God. "After his death an autopsy revealed that his heart was missing from his body. His friends, knowing his character, ran to his storehouse of treasures, and there lying among them they found his bleeding heart." The moral of the story was, "where your treasure is, there also is your heart." See Steven E. Ozment, *Reformation in the Cities* (New Haven: Yale University Press, 1975), 27, for other examples.

74   The 1531 edition includes the following. Ten Commandments: 1. Moses receiving the tables of the Law while the people are dancing around the golden calf (Ex 32); 2. Stoning of Shemeth's son, who blasphemed the name and cursed (Lev 24); 3. Man outside gathering wood while a congregation is gathered at church to hear God's Word (Num 15); 4. The sin of Ham (Gen 9); 5. Cain killing his brother (Gen 4); 6. David looking at Bathsheba washing (2 Sam 11); 7. Achan the thief (Joshua 7); 8. Two false witnesses against Susanna, Apocrypha, ii); 9. Jacob craftily seeking to gain the stronger sheep or cattle (Gen 30); 10. Joseph fleeing temptation by Potiphar's wife (Gen 39). Creed: First Article, the Creation of the World (Gen 1); Second Article, Christ upon the cross; the Third Article had the Holy Spirit appearing as tongues of flame in the disciples' mouths (Mt 27, Jn 19, Lk 23, Mk 15). Lord's Prayer: Introduction: Pastor preaching to congregation; First petition: pastor preaching to congregation; Second petition: man outside gathering wood while congregation is gathered in church to hear God's word; Third petition: Christ carrying his cross and being mistreated; Fourth petition: Jesus feeding the five thousand (Jn 6); Fifth petition: the unmerciful servant (Mt 18); Sixth petition: temptation of Christ. Christ has a sheep with him while the devil is portrayed as a lion seeking to devour (Mt 4); Seventh petition: Canaanite woman pleading with Christ (Mt 15). Baptismal booklet: an infant is being baptized. Lord's Supper: the Eucharist is being celebrated. There seems to be a strong tradition of certain images or narratives being used for certain parts of the catechism. For the most part, the woodcuts for the Ten Commandments, the Creed, and the Lord's Prayer remain consistent through a number of editions. A couple exceptions can be found in the Second Petition. The 1529 edition had the outpouring of the Spirit where the 1531 edition used the same woodcut as that used for the Third Commandment, while a 1553 edition had a man praying beside his window in his room. Third Petition: the 1531 edition had Christ carrying his cross and the 1553 edition had Christ in Gethsemane.

75   Scribner, *Simple Folk*, 6.

76   See Scribner, *Simple Folk*, 6, where he describes the process from a 1524 pamphlet, *A Dialogue Between a Christian and a Jew … concerning Christ the Cornerstone*. "A Jew and an evangelical Christian fall into conversation in an inn, and the Jew produces a woodcut he has picked up on his travels. The Christian uses the woodcut to explain to the Jew the main points of evangelical belief as the woodcut depicts them. When they part, the inn servant, who has listened to them with interest, promises to set their conversation down in print, along with the

woodcut. This case shows the ideal balance of oral, visual, and printed means of communication as it is found during the Reformation."

77 Scribner, *Popular Culture*, 278.

78 Wengert, "Forming the Faith through Catechisms," 43–44.

79 Wengert, "Forming the Faith through Catechisms," 43.

80 To this day, when parents read a picture book to a young child they will first read the text and then hold the book up so that their child can see the picture which depicts the narrative just read aloud.

81 The catechism thus functions for the Christian in the way that the periodic table of elements does for the chemist, the Mass-Luminosity diagram does for the astronomer, or the circle of fifths for the musician. James Arne Nestingen, "Preaching the Catechism," *Word and World* 10 (Winter 1990): 33–42.

82 Luther added the longer preface to the Large Catechism in 1531 in which he addressed pastors. The shorter preface of the Large Catechism (1529) addressed the needs of children and was probably an original part of the sermon address.

83 Martin E. Marty, "The Challenge of Catechesis: The Changing Cultural Landscape," in *Formation in the Faith: Catechesis for Tomorrow* (Concordia Seminary Publications, 1997), 10.

84 Peters, II, 38.

85 Trinitarian thinking today generally recognizes two ways of approaching the doctrine of the Trinity, ways that are not necessarily contradictory. As a rule, the Scriptures and the early church are seen as approaching the issue from the standpoint of the economic Trinity which emphasizes the structure of God's work and focuses on the relationship of the three persons to the world. It thus begins reflection on the three persons and then raises the question of their unity. By contrast, the so-called immanent Trinity, as it became prominent after Nicea and with Augustine, focuses on how God relates to himself (hence the language of unbegotten, begotten, and proceeding) rather than on how God relates to the world. It generally begins reflection on the oneness of God and then asks, how are they three? It may not be the primary language of proclamation, but does provide an important backdrop for the economic Trinity by guarding against subordination of every kind. See Catherine M. LaCugna, *God for Us: The Trinity and Christian Life* (San Francisco: Harper, 1991), especially chapter one, "God's Economy Revealed in Christ and the Holy Spirit."

86 That is, "we preachers can preach as loud and as much as we want, but finally it is up to you people." Quoted in Krodel, "Luther's Work on the Catechism," 403, fn 166.

87 Luther wrote *Hauptstück*. Here Luther not only refers to the three articles of the Creed, but to the first three chief parts of the catechism. Krodel notes this one modification, that the third chief part deals not with the Lord's Prayer, but with the evangelical life of the Spirit manifested in love, patience, and forbearance.

88 Krodel, "Luther's Work on the Catechism," 22.

89 See Robert Kolb, "'That I May Be His Own': The Anthropological Dimensions of Luther's Explanation to the Creed," *Concordia Journal* 21 (January 1995): 28–41.

90 Robert Kolb, *Teaching God's Children His Teaching* (Hutchinson, Minn.: Crown Publishing, 1992), 1–12.

91 See Eric W. Gritsch, "Luther's Catechisms of 1529: Whetstones of the Church," *Lutheran Theological Seminary Bulletin* 60 (1980): 3–14.

4

INTERPRETING LIFE
THROUGH THE CATECHISM

While Luther appropriated the inherited texts of the catechism, he rearranged them in such a way that the Ten Commandments preceded the Creed. To this day, the structure of Luther's Small Catechism remains one of its most distinctive features, a feature noted by Lutheran and non-Lutheran alike.[1] Luther's reordering thus raises several questions. Does the arrangement of the chief parts contribute to the overall message of the Catechism so that each chief part is in turn interpreted in light of that overall message? Likewise, if they are rearranged would the new order undermine the theme and focus of the catechism as a whole?[2] Or are the chief parts more or less independent and autonomous blocks of texts? Debate on this issue has swirled for years.[3] An evaluation of Luther's ordering must address two questions. First, it needs to be asked whether or not the classical order appropriated by Luther had an underlying rationale, and second, whether Luther intentionally altered the order, and if so, was it for theological reasons?

THE CLASSICAL STRUCTURE OF THE CATECHISM

Whatever else might be said, Luther's ordering was new and distinctive. A few others before him might have adopted a similar arrangement, but did not supply an explicit rationale. The question that arises then is whether or not the church prior to the Reformation not only had used a particular arrangement of the chief parts, but did so consciously in order to reflect its theological priorities. To be sure, most confessional manuals and devotional books did not provide a stated explanation (for that matter, neither does the Small Catechism). Moreover, in the Middle Ages, it is evident that confessional-catechetical manuals arranged the materials in a variety of ways. But a few catechetical writings prior to Luther's did have a rationale, and when they did, they showed that this arrangement reflected a theological framework that went to the heart of defining the Gospel and Christianity.

THE EARLY CHURCH

To speak of an arrangement or ordering of the chief parts in the Middle Ages, one must begin with Augustine who stood as a transitional figure between the early church and the medieval church. On the one hand Augustine brought the catechetical thinking of the early church to a close, and on the other hand he directly or indirectly influenced the catechetical tradition in the Middle Ages up until the time of Luther.

AUGUSTINE

Augustine wrote two major catechetical works applicable to this issue. The first, *Catechizing the Uninstructed*, provided a guide for catechists. It dealt with matters for introducing and preparing a new catechumen to the catechumenal process and its goal. The second, an *Enchiridion on Faith, Hope, and Love*, deals more specifically with the content of Augustine's instruction and catechesis. In these two works, Augustine outlines a sequence for the chief parts of the catechism and rationale for his arrangement that remained relatively constant and unchanged throughout the Middle Ages and well into the sixteenth century, when it was picked up by Canisius and the Roman Catechism that resulted from the Council of Trent.[4]

The classic text in which Augustine first lays out his understanding of the Christian life is his *De Catechizandis Rudibus* (Catechizing the Uninstructed).[5] In it, Augustine finds his matrix for understanding the Christian life in the Pauline triad of virtues, "faith, hope, and love" (1 Corinthians 13:13). Augustine then correlates faith, hope, and love to the three texts of the catechism, the Creed, Lord's Prayer, and Law (Ten Commandments) respectively. Faith corresponds to the Creed and deals with the narrative of past events. Hope corresponds with the Lord's Prayer, which looks to the future and our final deliverance. Love corresponds to the Law and the Ten Commandments, which deal with our present life. It may be schematized as follows:

CREED	LORD'S PRAYER	COMMANDMENTS[6]
Faith	Hope	Love
History	Resurrection	Law
Past	Future	Present

Not only did Augustine correlate the Pauline triad to the texts of the catechism, he correlated them to its order as well. Robert Bradley explains the logic of its flow or sequence, "This is the life of the Christian in its simplest statement: it flows from *faith* founded on a reality from the *past* [*narratio*], it is sustained by *hope* moving toward a *future* good [*resurrectio*], and it lives in the *present* by *love* [*lex*]."[7]

Within this matrix love emerges as the essence and goal of the Christian life for Augustine. He himself explains, "This love should be your purpose in view of which you direct all that you say. Whatever you recount as history you should so recount that he, to whom you speak, on hearing will believe, on believing will hope, on hoping will love."[8] The important place given to love as the defining characteristic of the Christian's life is developed more fully twenty years later in his *Enchiridion on Faith, Hope, and Love.*

> Now charity is, as the Apostle says (1 Corinthians 13:13), greater than faith and hope in whatever thing it is found, in the same degree that it is a better thing in itself. For what determines the goodness of a person is not what that person believes or what he hopes for, but what he loves. The one who loves rightly necessarily believes and hopes rightly. The one who does not love believes pointlessly, even if what he believes is true; and he hopes pointlessly, even if what he hopes for was taught him as leading to true happiness. This believing and this hoping have value only because they enable him to love.[9]

So within this sequence, faith and hope are nothing without love. Once again, the importance of love as the central religious concept comes through as the power which activates all other areas of the Christian life.

Augustine's theology becomes extremely important for the Middle Ages.[10] In a nascent way, it sows the seeds for the order of salvation that would eventually come to full bloom in the *Via Antiqua* and *Via Moderna*. Steven Ozment has pointed out that for the medieval theologian the central religious concept was accordingly "*caritas*—love—not faith." This was based upon the premise that like attracts like. Since God is love, if we wish to be saved or united with God we must become like God, that is, we must be shaped by love. The way of salvation in the Middle Ages was often characterized with the expression, *fides caritate formata*, faith activated and perfected by acts of love. Faith alone, by contrast, was only an initial intellectual assent to the data of revelation made by one who was still far from pure and godly. "*Sola fides*, all agreed, was a *fides informis*, even a *fides mortua*—an unformed, dead faith which even the demons could have.... Love, not faith, was the religious glue" that held the entire system together.[11]

MIDDLE AGES TO THE COUNCIL OF TRENT

In general, most medieval confessional manuals and devotional writings followed Augustine's ordering, but within the context of the penitential system that had become the focal point of the Christian life and piety. Thus the catechetical work of the church at the eve of the Reformation was dominated by private confession. Within this context, knowledge of, and obedience to, the Lord's Prayer (and other prayers), the Creed, and the Ten Commandments was tested within a system of works-righteousness.

MARTIN OF AMBERG

Martin of Amberg's "Mirror of the Conscience" (1385) appears to be a combination of a *Beichtbüchlein* and a catechism. Following the preface, Martin divides the work into five parts with a sixth part providing the conclusion. In Part I he gives the Creed together with a fairly Christ-centered commentary. Part II includes various prayers, namely, the Lord's Prayer, the Hail Mary, Hail Queen of Heaven. Part III contains the Ten Commandments and speaks about their fulfillment and transgressions. Part IV lists other traditional materials such as the seven deadly sins, the seven gifts of the Spirit, the seven works of mercy, various holy days, and the days of fasting etc. Part V deals with Christian living.

Several observations might be made about the overall work. First, the sequence follows Creed—Lord's Prayer—Ten Commandments—other matters. Second, whether intentional or not, the Ten Commandments stand at the center of the entire work.[12] In the final section Martin gives a brief rationale for his arrangement that appears to anticipate Surgant.

JOHANNES SURGANT

One of the clearest rationales for the arrangement of the catechetical materials in the late Middle Ages is supplied by Johannes Surgant (1450–1503) in his popular *Manuale curatorum*. This work shares in common with the tradition that both the Creed and Lord's Prayer precede the Ten Commandments. It should be noted, however, that it diverges slightly from the traditional sequence of Creed—Lord's Prayer—Ten Commandments in that Surgant begins with the Lord's Prayer, proceeds to the Creed, and concludes with the Ten Commandments. The *Manuale curatorum* follows this sequence:

> 1) Surgant begins by citing the German text of the Lord's Prayer and the German text of the Hail Mary. He then adds the following comment: "Since prayer [Lord's Prayer and Hail Mary] that is not

prayed in true faith is without power (for without faith no one pleases God), recite the Creed."

2) Surgant then quotes the German text of the Creed. He follows it with the comment: "Since faith without works is totally without any power and dead and comes to be alive only through obedience to the Ten Commandments, therefore obey the Ten Commandments and learn them."[13]

3) Surgant concludes by listing the Ten Commandments.

The sequence in the *Manuale Curatorum* reveals a gradation in the importance of the catechetical materials that might be described as follows: Prayer without faith is useless, that is, without knowledge of the Creed. At the same time, faith as knowledge of the Creed is lifeless apart from obedience to the commandments. Conversely, "knowledge of, and obedience to, the Decalogue shows that one has faith, and this faith, demonstrated in obedience to the commandments and verbally expressed in the Creed, guarantees the effectiveness of prayer."[14]

DIETRICH KOLDE

In Dietrich Kolde's *A Fruitful Mirror or Small Handbook for Christians*,[15] the Christian life was seen primarily as a movement "from a state of sin to a state of grace."[16] Faith or belief (creed) made possible the appropriation of grace (cult), the purpose of which is the way of life prescribed in the Law (code).[17] It opens with the words, "This is the beginning of a beautiful mirror for good Christians, which they should carry with them at all times as a handbook, since it contains everything that is necessary for the well-being and salvation of the soul."[18] It is divided into three parts, the first of which describes what must be believed (leading to contrition and confession), the second how one must live (doing the works of satisfaction), and the third, how one should die. The first two are important for consideration.

Part I addresses the Creed in chapters 1–4 and the Commandments in chapters 5–11. Both are expounded with a view toward recognizing one's failure to believe the former and fulfill the latter. Then chapters 12–19 focus on sins and how to find forgiveness, while chapters 20–22 deal with contrition, confession and satisfaction respectively. The Creed came first for two reasons. First, "because medieval theology held that one could in a state of sin through the exercise of the free will muster up an 'acquired faith' [*fides acquisita* or *informata*] that is, an acknowledgement that the church's teachings were true."[19] Second, only in a state of grace following the Creed could the Christian fulfill the Law according to God's intention (vs. according to the substance of the act).

Part II aims to assist with the life of satisfaction or penance. The first version introduced the twenty-first article with "How One Can Attain True Penance and Forgiveness of Sins." It ends with an instruction to strive for "perfect penitence as they pass from this life to the next." On the deathbed, one should pray, "Take my good will for the works [I lack]"—the layman is haunted to his last breath by a short supply of good works![20] Kolde focuses on the "how" of faith, reducing it to biblical legalism and to obedience to the Decalogue and Canon Law, and the Creed is placed into this system of works-righteousness and strict obedience to the church's practices.

PETER CANISIUS

The pattern for arranging the catechetical texts evident in Augustine, Martin of Amberg, Surgant, and Kolde continued in Roman Catholic works into the sixteenth century. For example, the catechisms produced by Peter Canisius (in deliberate contrast with Luther's) became the most widely used catechisms in the Catholic world in the late sixteenth and early seventeenth centuries. He organized his catechism into two sections. He labeled the first section, "Wisdom." It contained the traditional fourfold contents of the catechism: Creed, prayer, Decalogue, and sacraments. In the preface to 1560 German edition, he explains his rationale in terms strikingly reminiscent of Augustine:

> Everything depends on faith, hope, love, sacraments and justice, if we wish always to be God's children and to reach heaven. Without faith we do not know God; without hope we despair of God's grace; without love neither faith nor hope nor trust is of any use to us. Rather, we then remain in darkness—yes, even in death, as the holy Apostles tell us in Scripture. Without the sacraments, on the other hand, and their correct Catholic usage, the grace of the Holy Spirit is neither given nor held.[21]

Canisius labeled the second section "Justice." Here he assembled various medieval formularies—capital sins, cardinal virtues, the gifts of the Holy Spirit, Beatitudes, works of mercy, and the last things. In the above quote he added the following sentence to explain the place of these components: "And, finally, without justice there is nothing that is Christ's; rather, it is but the kingdom of the devil." Robert Bradley states, approvingly, that it is one thing to have catechetical statements that offer a word-for-word riposte of another church's or theologian's teaching, it is another to have a catechism that offers a way of life. And specifying that way of life or that purpose of life—"more than may be immediately appreciated—is *structure*" (*sic*).[22]

LUTHER'S ADAPTATION
OF THE CLASSICAL STRUCTURE

Luther's reformation insights into the essence of the Christian life yielded a different arrangement of the catechetical materials than those just examined. While he gladly adopted the classical materials that he had inherited, he adapted them into an evangelical framework that rested on a clear theological foundation. The theological rationale for his arrangement of the chief parts is not only spelled out consistently throughout Luther's writings for nearly the entire decade of the 1520s, but is repeated in Lutheran catechetical preaching throughout much of the sixteenth century.[23]

In order to unpack Luther's arrangement, it will be necessary to read his writings from two perspectives. First, we will examine those statements in which Luther makes explicit his understanding as to why and how the chief parts are sequenced together within the total picture. Second, we will examine the underlying theological substructure of the catechism that underscores and supports his stated rationale.

LUTHER'S THEOLOGICAL RATIONALE

Luther's arrangement, Ten Commandments—Creed—Lord's Prayer, is unique in that he is perhaps the first theologian to adopt the principle of beginning with the commandments for theological reasons. "At least he appears to be the first catechist who explicates the reasons for which he adopts this order."[24] Luther's rationale for the juxtaposition of the chief parts suggests that a holistic or synchronic reading of the catechism is in order, that is, each text of the catechism must be read and interpreted in light of the other texts of the catechism.[25] Luther explains his rationale for ordering the chief parts on several occasions from 1520 through 1529. By and large the rationale remains the same, although certain emphases shift due to the historical *Sitz im Leben* of the particular writing. In the earlier writings, the Ten Commandments functions primarily as a diagnostic tool for arriving at a true knowledge and understanding of oneself and, only secondarily as a teaching tool for arriving at a correct knowledge and understanding of God's will. This second function would become more pronounced in Luther's catechismal sermons and writings from 1528 onward.

Catechetical Writings from 1520 to 1525

Luther's rationale in his earlier writings must be understood within the context of the debate over the sacrament of penance from 1517 to 1520. During that period, Luther launched an all out assault on the confessional and the sacrament of penance with a flurry of tracts, sermons, and treatises.[26] In these writings he overthrows the tribunal of the confessional and criticizes it for slaughtering souls by demanding a contrition that no one could achieve and which left the penitent in doubt and despair about forgiveness. At the same time, Luther needed to provide instruction for a genuinely evangelical practice of confession. So as Luther begins to arrange the catechetical materials for an evangelical confessional manual, he consciously rejects the medieval penitential focus that increased a person's uncertainty and replaces it with an evangelical one in which a confidence in God's promised mercy alleviates the anxiety-laden quest for perfect confession as seen, for example, in Kolde's manual.

Luther first explains his arrangement of the catechetical materials in his *Brief Explanation of the Ten Commandments, Creed, and Lord's Prayer* (1520), which he prepared as a confessional aid. It establishes the order and sequence of the Ten Commandments, Creed, and Lord's Prayer within the rhythm of the Christian life:

> In order for a man to be saved, it is necessary for him to know three things. First, he must know what he ought to do and what he ought not to do. Second, when he sees that he has no power to do what he ought to do or to keep from doing what he ought not to do, he needs to know where to look, find, and receive the power that will enable him to live as he knows he ought to. Third, he needs to know how to look for this power and appropriate it for himself.
>
> In this respect, he is like a sick man. A man who is sick needs first to know what his illness is and what he can and cannot do. Then he needs to know where the medicine is that can help him live the life of a well man. Third, he must desire this medicine and look for it until he finds it or have it brought to him.
>
> Thus the commandments teach a man to recognize his sickness so that he may know and understand what he can and cannot do, what he ought to do and ought not to do. In this way he comes to recognize that he is an evil and sinful man. After this, the creed shows and teaches him where he can find the medicine or the remedy that he needs, that is, the grace which will help him become a righteous man so that he may keep the commandments and which shows him God

and the righteousness which he reveals and offers to us in Christ. Thirdly, the Lord's Prayer teaches him how he should desire, get, and appropriate this grace for himself, namely through regular, humble, consoling prayer. This is the way in which he is given the grace and thus is saved through fulfilling the commandments of God. These are the three chief things in all the Scriptures.[27]

This rationale is repeated verbatim two years later in the *Little Prayer Book* (1522). It is worth noting that the anonymously published *A Booklet for Laypeople and Children* (1525) also repeats verbatim a portion (it does not include the analogy of a sick person) of this very same rationale.[28]

In 1523, Wittenberg established the custom of regular catechetical preaching four times a year, a custom in which Luther himself participated. In his sermon from March of 1523, Luther introduces the Creed with a brief explanation of its location in relation to the Ten Commandments and Lord's Prayer.

In the first part we heard what a person needs to know, namely the Ten Commandments. From these he is taught how he ought to live before God and the world. At a time when he comes to recognize himself inwardly and he knows that it is not possible for him to obey even the letter of the Law [much less the spirit of the Law], then it should be revealed to him, how and in what manner he is filled with sickness. Through the Ten Commandments we discover that we are idolaters, and are full of envy, greed, etc. Even when we do nothing, we are still sinful. Therefore he ought to seek the medicine he needs. This text [the Creed] teaches the faith, which we preach to him before the Lord's Prayer.[29]

This quarterly preaching on the catechism appears to have followed Luther's ordering and shows that this was an intentional and deliberate decision on the part of the Wittenberg reformers.[30]

Luther's arrangement provides several departures from the medieval tradition with regard to the role played by the various catechetical texts upon the individual in relationship to one another. For Surgant and Wolff, obedience to the Decalogue is a result of knowing the Ten Commandments and putting that knowledge to work (after all, why would God give us the Ten Commandments if we could not keep them?). Moreover, summarized in terms of love, obedience makes us more like God. Thus obedience to the Ten Commandments validates the faith and makes prayer effective.[31]

For Luther, the Ten Commandments do not provide the power or ability to keep them. Instead, he makes it clear at the end of the exposition of the Decalogue that they are set on too high a plane for us. The Ten Commandments "show us how few persons live this good life. Now that we recognize this, we must find out where to get the [medicinal] herbs to enable us to live a good life and fulfil the commandments" (*LW* 43:24). Obedience to the Decalogue is the result of the Gospel: work of Christ's resurrection and the life-renewing work of the Holy Spirit. In the Second Article Luther stated, "I believe that he was resurrected from the dead on the third day to give a new life to me and all believers, thus awakening us with him by his grace and spirit to sin no more [Gal. 6:4; Gal. 2:20] but to serve him only with every grace and virtue, thus *fulfilling God's commandments*" [italics added] (*LW* 43:27).[32]

Clearly, Luther's explanation of his arrangement of the catechism's texts reflects his theology on the importance of the distinction between Law and Gospel. In one sense, the rationale for Luther's ordering in these earlier writings reflects the existential character of his theology. Luther's own experience as a "monk had taught him that the Christian life begins with the awareness of one's own sinfulness and inability to fulfill the divine commands."[33] In another sense, the ordering reflected the heart of Luther's theology of the cross, namely, that God kills in order to make alive. Theology begins with the recognition that humankind stands under the evaluating eye of God. The *cantus firmus* of these chief parts is the situation of man under sin *coram deo* followed by the conditions under which he can find relief from sin.[34] Thus Luther's sequence is Law (Ten Commandments)—Gospel (Creed, Lord's Prayer).

Catechism Sermons of 1528–1529

The pattern of Ten Commandments—Creed—Lord's Prayer, together with its rationale carried over into Luther's catechetical sermons of 1528–1529, but some of the emphases and nuances shift. Unlike the earlier writings, which were written with a view toward helping a person in confession and relieving people of the burden of sin, the catechism writings in the latter part of the decade have a more distinctly catechetical or pedagogical goal in view arising from "the demand for materials that reliably instructed people in the essentials of the evangelical faith."[35] Thus in the Small Catechism, catalogues with examples of fulfilling and transgressing the commandments fall away as does the analogy of the sick person in his discussion of the relation between the three chief parts. In addition, a positive interpretation of the Ten Commandments as a description of the Christian's new life becomes more prominent. In this the concluding statement of Luther's earlier rationale, "This is the way in which he is given the grace and thus is saved through fulfilling the commandments of God," moves to the foreground. Thus where the sequence of Law (Ten Commandments)—Gospel (Creed, Lord's Prayer) continues to be stressed in these writings, the sequence of Gospel—new life receives a stronger emphasis. Three events in particular proved significant for broadening the catechism's purpose.

First, the visitations of the churches begun in 1527 made a profound and lasting impact on Luther in two areas. The first dealt with the knowledge of Christians regarding the basic teachings of Christianity. This brief experience led him to remark in the Small Catechism:

> The deplorable, wretched deprivation that I recently encountered while I was a visitor has constrained and compelled me to prepare this catechism, or Christian instruction, in such a brief, plain, and simple version. [2] Dear God, what misery I beheld! The ordinary person, especially in the villages, knows absolutely nothing about the Christian faith, …they do not know the Lord's Prayer, the Creed, or the Ten Commandments! As a result they live like simple cattle or irrational pigs.[36]

The second event dealt with the abuse of Christian liberty evident among the people. Where in his earlier writings Luther focused on relieving people from the burden of the Law, particularly the medieval laws governing religious life, he here discovers that the laity had fallen off on the other side of the log into libertinism. "A one-sided and deficient understanding of the Reformation message had frequently created a disdain for the Law [and] a relaxation of religious morals and discipline."[37] In the *Instructions to the Visitors*, Melanchthon cites a number of examples. Some people felt that they were free from government and the paying of taxes. Others interpreted Christian freedom to mean that they could eat meat, refrain from confession and fasting, and the like (*LW* 40:302–3). Many were not attending church or supporting their pastors. Not only had people been relieved of the burden of sin, but they had relieved themselves of the Law altogether and knew little to nothing of it. This explains in part why Luther devotes nearly one half of the Large Catechism to the Ten Commandments.

Second, the first Antinomian controversy, precipitated by Agricola's rejection of the Law for the Christian life, required a response from Luther. By the time that Luther preached his Second Catechism Series, September of 1528, Agricola had reportedly affirmed that faith could exist without good works. Luther counters this with several strong statements about the Ten Commandments in the life of the Christian. He introduces the Creed with a transition that relates the Creed to the Ten Commandments:

We have heard about the Ten Commandments by which we are taught what must be done by us. Secondly, follows the Creed, which has been given in order that we might be able to do what we ought. For the Ten Commandments are impossible to do now by our own powers. Accordingly, we are taught where we should receive the strength to fulfill them. For if by our own strength we could do what the commandments require, we would have no need for the Creed or the Lord's Prayer.… (WA 30:I, 43, 27–44, 1)

Therefore the Creed is set forth which proclaims that I should believe in the Father, Son, and Holy Spirit, because I am too weak to keep the Ten Commandments.… The Creed is a power given from heaven so that we might keep the *Ten Commandments* [italics added]. (WA 30:I, 44, 25f)[38]

We believe that three persons are one God, Father, Son, and Holy Spirit, and that these three persons … have given themselves entirely to us in order to help and strengthen us *that we might keep the Ten Commandments* [italics added]: the Father by his might, the Son by his works, and Spirit by his gifts. (WA 30:I, 44, 28–31)

Luther proceeds to show how each article of the Creed contributes to the fulfillment of the Ten Commandments. In the First Article, the Father creates all the creatures in order to serve us (WA 30:I, 44, 32ff), and we then in turn serve God in their use (WA 30:I 87, 15ff).[39] In the Second Article, the Father gives us Christ "in order to acquire grace for us through his death so that we might fulfill the Ten Commandments" (WA 30:I, 45, 1–4). After speaking of the Spirit's gifts, Luther concludes the Creed with the words: "The triune God, in creation, redemption, and sanctification, gives himself to us so that we may fulfill his will as laid down for us in the commandments" (WA 30:I, 46, 5).

The sentiments of Luther's three 1528 catechism sermon series carry over into the Large Catechism. In the Large Catechism he continues with his earlier emphasis that the Ten Commandments set too high a bar for any person to keep. But then, as in the September 1528 sermons, the Large Catechism both opens and concludes its explanation of the Creed with a backward glance to the Ten Commandments. The Creed is "given in order to help us do what the Ten Commandments require of us. For, as we said above, they are set on so high a plane that all human ability is far too feeble and weak to keep them. Therefore it is necessary to learn this part as it is the other so that we may know where and how to obtain strength for this task" (LC II, 2). Conversely, if we could keep the Ten Commandments as they ought to be kept, "we would need neither the Creed nor the Lord's

Prayer" (LC II, 3). Luther concludes his exposition of the Creed by observing that through it *"we come to love and delight in all the command-ments of God* [italics added] because we see that God gives himself com-pletely to us, with all his gifts and power, *to help us keep the Ten Command-ments* [italics added], the Father gives us all creation, Christ all his works, the Holy Spirit all his gifts" (LC II, 69). Similarly, the Lord's Prayer also opens its explanation with a reference back to the Ten Commandments. "Nothing is so necessary as to call upon God incessantly and drum into his ears our prayer *that he may give, preserve, and increase in us faith and obe-dience to the Ten Commandments* [italics added] and remove all that stands in our way and hinders us from fulfilling them" (LC III, 2).

What is striking about Luther's stated rationale in the 1528–29 writings is the way in which he sets forth the Creed and the Lord's Prayer as helps for the fulfilling of the Ten Commandments. Oswald Bayer remarks that "the Creed [and also the Lord's Prayer] had never as clearly and as decisively been taken into account in its relation to the Decalogue."[40] Bornkamm also makes the observation, "By means of repeatedly referring the several main parts back to the First Commandment, Luther gave the catechism a whole-ness that combines commandment and promise, Law and Gospel, and sets such diverse components [including, to be sure, the sacraments] into a firm unity."[41] At the same time, the way in which Luther gives the catechism a "wholeness" is not what one might expect. Critics may argue that Luther's arrangement gives the impression that the primacy of the Creed has been superseded by the primacy of the Ten Commandments in the catechisms.[42] There are several ways of understanding this.

First, Luther reverses the rationale of the Middle Ages. Instead of the Ten Commandments giving value to the Creed and Lord's Prayer, the Creed and Lord's Prayer provide the resources for living according to the Ten Commandments. Second, Luther makes it clear that the Christian life does not abandon the Ten Commandments but leads us back into them as setting forth the shape of the Christian life. This especially addressed the question of libertinism among the peasants and the antinomianism of Agri-cola. Third, the Ten Commandments are dealt with in the context of voca-tion. By leading the Christian back into the Ten Commandments, Luther affirms that the Gospel sends the Christian back into the world to live out one's vocation in contradistinction to the Carthusian monks and their humanly devised religious works. Luther never tires of reiterating that the Ten Commandments outline the best of all works that we can do, even though they may not appear to be particularly exciting or glorious. Finally,

Luther's understanding of the Ten Commandments comes into play. He regards the Ten Commandments as summarized by the First Commandment's demand for faith. By referring the Creed and Lord's Prayer back to the Ten Commandments, he is referring to their help for the kindling and strengthening of the faith that the First Commandment requires.

CREEDAL FRAMEWORK OF THE CATECHISM

Luther's statements about the relation of the chief parts of the catechism to one another make it clear that his sequence was deliberate and that it establishes a Law and Gospel rhythm for the Christian life. In addition to Luther's explicit statements on the subject, there exists a second, underlying relationship between the chief texts that may be uncovered in the way Luther expounds each of the chief parts—a sequence that supports Luther's stated rationale. This relationship further unfolds the theological interdependence of the chief parts of the catechism and shows that any rearrangement of the texts would do violence to Luther's explanations themselves. This relationship is uncovered through Luther's explanations of the chief parts.

Albrecht Peters has shown that Luther expounds the catechism around three major theological centers. The first center includes the Ten Commandments and First Article of the Creed. The Second Article of the Creed stands as the second major center and serves as the link between the First Article (time and creation) and the Third Article (fulfillment and eternity). The third center embraces the Third Article and the Lord's Prayer.[43]

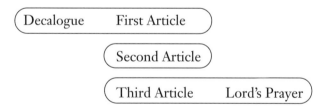

By tying the Ten Commandments to the First Article and the Third Article to the Lord's Prayer, Luther has brought the three chief parts into a thoroughly Creedal and Trinitarian framework. In doing so, he has provided a way for Christians to make sense of their lives with God in light of the Baptismal Creed and the triune salvific work in creation and history. Luther organized the three chief texts of the catechism as the sequences of the action of God for humankind and humankind's reaction to that work.[44] From God's side it proceeds from his work as Creator—Redeemer—Sanctifier. From the human side it proceeds from our experience of God's work as Law—Gospel—New Life.

Ten Commandments and First Article

By linking the Ten Commandments to the First Article, Luther interprets the Ten Commandments within the horizon of creation. That is to say, the Commandments are intended more as a response to the First Article than the Third Article. They function as an "instruction guide" for the proper use of the creaturely world. The First Article in turn provides the foundation and basis for the Ten Commandments and gives them their purpose and direction.[45] Together the First Article and the Ten Commandments provide the immediate context and framework for understanding the Second and Third articles of the Creed by supplying the setting in which redemption and sanctification take place. The positive view of creation in particular lays a foundation for the Incarnation and the means of grace. The interpretation of Ten Commandments in light of First Article is evident from a number of considerations.

First, Luther interprets the Ten Commandments as part of God's creation within the context of natural Law. They are, so to say, built into the very structure or woven into the fabric of creation itself. To use Luther's words, the Decalogue "is inscribed and engraved in the hearts of all men from the foundation of the world" (LC II, 67, 82).[46] For Luther, Moses fitted the Law of creation "nicely into his Laws in a more orderly and excellent manner than could have been done by anyone else" (*LW* 47:90; WA 50:331).[47]

As James Nestingen points out, "That the Ten Commandments were given to Moses, that they are in the Bible, that they are understood in the Old Testament as Torah—all of this is incidental to their explication of the ineradicable minimums of creatureliness."[48] For Luther, the Law permeates our daily life so that a person is generally not a *tabula rasa* when it comes to knowledge of the Law. In this way the Decalogue provides a natural contact with non-Christians by addressing people where they live and in connection with the concerns of their daily lives. The Ten Commandments describe the setting into which the Gospel breaks in with its liberating message.

Second, the Ten Commandments deal with matters that pertain to the every day affairs of people. They have "a secular or worldly hue about them" and so they do not provide a list of distinctively "religious works" to be done. This stands in sharp contrast with the Carthusian monks whom Luther criticizes for going beyond God's Law.[49] Hence the Ten Commandments speak of Christians' relations with God, neighbors, and possessions in the context of their various vocations. In this connection, when Luther expounds the close of the commandments, the threats and promises entail predominantly earthly punishments and blessings and provide the basis for obedience.[50]

By interpreting the commandments in the horizon of the First Article, Luther makes clear that the Decalogue may not be regarded as a heteronomous imposition of a set of rules and regulations. They do not apply simply because "God says so." Instead they describe who we are and how we were created to be. They delineate the shape of life as God created it.[51] Life begins, is lived, and ends under the force of the Law, under the objective moral order. In this connection, Luther also draws upon a number of sources, not the least of which include the real life experiences of every day people and the corroborating evidence of nature and history in addition to the word of God.[52] In other words, there is a "see for yourself how this works" quality to his explanations. Expressing the Law of creation, the Commandments describe the obligations and responsibilities of our creaturely life from birth to death.

Luther not only interprets the Decalogue in light of creation, he also deals with the First Article as the basis for the Ten Commandments (especially the First Commandment) and at the same time the fulfillment of the Ten Commandments.

The First Article lays the foundation for the Ten Commandments by setting forth the distinction between the Creator and his creation, as well as the relationship between them, namely the dependence of the latter upon the former. In the Small Catechism, this becomes evident with Luther's use of the inclusive particle "all." Nine times in the First Article, Luther emphasizes that God has given us "all creatures," "all my members," "all my senses," "all that I have," "all that I need," and defends me from "all danger" and "all evil." He does "all this" out of fatherly goodness and mercy. That God created everything that exists establishes an absolute difference between the Creator and creation. It thus provides the basis for the First Commandment which commands "no other gods" and which Luther explains as trusting in God above "all things" (again, note the exclusive particles). The First Article concludes on the note, "for all of which it is my duty to thank and praise, serve and obey...." In the Large Catechism Luther adds the words, "according to the Ten Commandments" (LC II, 19).

At the same time the First Article is a response to the Ten Commandments, that is, it provides what the First Commandment requires—faith in God's creaturely care. This "nexus between the First Commandment and the knowledge of the Creator was so important for Luther that the recognition of the interrelationship between the Creator and his creature must be defined as the existential fulfillment of the First Commandment which is made possible by faith in Christ."[53] In the Large Catechism he looks back to the First Commandment.

For example, the Ten Commandments explained that we are to have no other gods than the one true God. Now it may be asked: "What kind of being is God? What does he do? How can we praise or portray or describe him in such a way as to make him known?" Luther points out, "The answer is taught here [in the First Article] and in the following articles." Thus the Creed is nothing else than a response and a confession of Christians based on the First Commandment. So if you were to ask a young child, "My boy, what kind of God have you? What do you know about him?" he could say, "First, my God is the Father, who made heaven and earth. Apart from him alone I have no other God, for there is no one else who could create heaven and earth" (LC I, 10–11).

This connection between the First Commandment and the First Article of the Creed reaches back to Luther's Short Form (1520) and his *Little Prayer Book* (1522), in which Luther's explanation of the First Article echoes the First Commandment. Negatively, the believer confesses, "I renounce the evil spirit, all idolatry, all sorcery, and all false belief.... I put my trust in no creature, whether in heaven or on earth" (*LW* 43:24–25). Positively, the Christian places his or her faith entirely and totally in God alone and trusts that God will use all of creation to serve our best interests (WA 11:50, 5ff).

Second Article

The Second Article stands at the center and apex of not only the Creed, but the first three chief parts of the catechism.[54] Similarly, in his Short Form and *Little Prayer Book* the Second Article lay at the heart of Luther's rationale as the medicine that heals. In the Short Form, Luther simply gives the Second Article the title, "Jesus," which he places in the center of the page. Several years later, in his *Smalcald Articles*, Luther would call this article the chief article of the Christian faith. In the context of the catechisms, it lies between "the two poles of creation and fulfillment, between time and eternity."[55] The First Article deals with our personal creation, and the Third Article with our re-creation. The Second Article on redemption provides the transition from the First to the Third Articles and holds them together.

This transition reflects a shift that takes place in parallel with the one that occurs within the Bible from the Old Testament to the New Testament. In the realm of creation, the first center, Luther weaves the threats and promises of God throughout his treatment of the Decalogue in both catechisms and into the First Article in the Large Catechism. Within their daily lives, human creatures live between God and idol and under God's unmerited promises or his terrible threats. In the Second Article, Christ brings to a close the tyranny of sin and death by removing the wrath of God. At the same time, the Second Article shows that a new conflict is opened, this time, not between God and man, but between the believer and Satan, between faith and unbelief.

The connecting links, verbal or literary, are not as evident between the First and Second Articles as they are between the Second and Third Articles (for example, the Third Article makes an explicit reference back to the Second Article). This observation has prompted Peters to suggest that Luther interprets the first center (Ten Commandments and First Article) somewhat more distantly from the second and third centers of the catechism. This should not suggest, however, that there are no connections. If the linguistic and literary clues are lacking, the theological clues are not. There is a sense that where the First Article concludes with "for which it is my duty," the "ought" of the First Article is transformed into the "may" of the Second Article.[56]

There is a closer relationship between the Second and Third Articles. Both open by noting our helplessness: the Second Article from the standpoint of our objective captivity to Satan from which Christ frees us; the Third Article from the standpoint of our subjective captivity ("I cannot believe in Jesus Christ my Lord") from which the Spirit frees us. As the Large Catechism puts it, prior to the Spirit's work, "we knew nothing of God or Christ" (LC III, 52); we were the devil's very own people." And so, the Third Article "exposes the complete bondage of man, his enslavement to a power alien and hostile to God."[57] While the title of the Third Article, "Sanctification," addresses the work of the Holy Spirit, it quickly becomes apparent that the real focus of the article is the same as that of the Second Article, namely, the lordship of Christ but from a different perspective.[58] The Second Article deals with the work of Christ independent of our appropriation of it; the Third Article deals with the work of the Spirit who brings Christ's lordship to us. Both also close on the same theme. The Second Article ends on the note of serving Christ in everlasting innocence and blessedness on the basis of Christ's resurrection. The Third Article closes on the same eschatological note, as the believer looks forward to eternal life through the resurrection of the body.

Third Article and Lord's Prayer

Luther's explanation of the Lord's Prayer has been criticized for not bringing out more clearly and starkly its foundation in the work of Christ on account of which the Christian prays. Likewise, it appears not to emphasize the Spirit's role in prayer such as the sequence that Paul has in Galatians, namely, that the Spirit of adoption goes into our hearts crying "Abba, Father." But these criticisms fail to consider the Lord's Prayer in relation to the entire catechism. Taken in connection with the Second and Third Articles of the Creed, that criticism is immediately blunted. We pray to the Father (First Article) through the combined work of Christ and the Spirit. Christ gives us the right to pray, and the Spirit gives us the faith to pray. And so, in the introduction to the Lord's Prayer, God "tenderly invites us to believe that he is truly our Father so that we may ask him as beloved children *ask* their beloved Father."

The Lord's Prayer picks up the central theme of the Third Article itself, namely, faith. It does so, however, in the context of the struggle for faith. Once God's wrath is turned aside and we enter the kingdom of Christ, Satan becomes active in trying to recapture us. Thus, the Lord's Prayer becomes a deepening repetition of the Decalogue. "In the Decalogue, he [Luther] accents the willing obedience of the Christian toward the Fatherly Creator as the Giver of blessing; in the Our Father, he drastically depicts our struggling with the powers of chaos and herein shows us our sanctification as a constantly apprehending anew justification."[59] Put succinctly, the Christian lives in this world between the cross and eternity. In this life, he lives under constant threat and constant attack, even as he prays, "Deliver us from evil."

CONCLUSION

When the catechist or pastor devotes several months at a time to the study of one particular portion of the catechism, it may become easy to lose sight of the forest on account of the trees. The Small Catechism is designed so that its entire contents can be heard or read in a relatively brief amount of time. The Large Catechism supplies the links between the chief parts so that we can see how they fit together into a whole. In these ways, the structure of the first three parts is held in view and together they instill into the Christian a Law-Gospel, Trinitarian view of life in this world.

NOTES

1   For Roman Catholic observations, see Robert I. Bradley, *The Roman Catechism in the Catechetical Tradition of the Church: The Structure of the Roman Catechism as Illustrative of the "Classic Catechesis"* (Lanham, Md.: University Press of America, 1990), 92–93; and Berard L. Marthaler, *The Catechism Yesterday and Today: The Evolution of a Genre* (Collegeville, Minn.: Liturgical, 1995), 23–24.

2   These questions go to the heart of ones understanding of the Law, its place within life and faith, and its relation to the Gospel. Does the Law serve the Gospel or does the Gospel serve the Law? "Decalogue comes first in the hidden discipline. Whatever may be a good means on a mission to a non-Christian culture, our own culture has been promised so much, has been so overcomforted, overgraced, that we must begin with the demand and judgment of God in order to participate in the joy of Gospel," Martin E. Marty, *Hidden Discipline* (St. Louis: Concordia, 1962), xvi; or do we place the Law later, as a norm of the Christian life, which might suggest that "being a Chrsitian is defined in terms of keeping the Law," Robert C. Schultz, "The Theological Significance of the Order of the Chief Parts in Luther's Catechism," in *Teaching the Faith: Luther's Catechisms in Perspective* (ed. Carl Volz; River Forest, Ill.: Lutheran Educational Association, 1967), 52.

3   There has been considerable debate over the years on this very subject. In the nineteenth century, Gerhard von Zezschwitz and Theodosius Harnack argued for an "inner progression of thought" in the structure of the Catechism. It proceeds from Moses-Christ-Spirit and expresses the divinely appointed way of salvation: "from Law to salvation in Christ, from Christ's salvation to a new communion of love in the Spirit" Albrecht Peters, "*Die Theologie der Katechismen Luthers anhand der Zuordnung ihrer Hauptstücke*," in *Lutherjahrbuch* (Göttingen: Vandenhoeck & Ruprecht, 1976), 2. A counterpoint is provided by Johannes Gottschick, Kurt Froer, and Johann Michael Reu who argued that the chief parts were not constructed by Luther with a view toward building an interrelated system of instruction. Instead, they lay alongside one another as relatively independent blocks of material that arose out of a pedagogical necessity in a specific historical setting. The sequential ordering of the chief parts provide a most methodological link of each chief part to the center—the grace of God revealed in Christ (Peters I:39). Here it will be argued that the chief parts are not simply set alongside each other as independent and disconnected blocks of material, nor do they come together in a systematic *ordo salutis* as was frequently seen in the nineteenth century. Instead the ordering of the chief parts does provide a theological matrix for the Christian life and thus is important for understanding the overall coherence of the catechism.

4   Some variations with regard to the Ten Commandments and Lord's Prayer did occur. The one constant, however, was the location of the Creed. The *Catechismus Romanus*, the Council of Trent's official answer to Protestantism, adopted this rationale (although the sequence shifted slightly to Creed, Sacraments, Ten Commandments, Lord's Prayer, a pattern used by the *Catechism of the Catholic Church* [Mahwah, N.J.: Paulist Press, 1994]).

5   In this work Augustine deals with introductory matters for introducing a catechumen (*rudibus* = inquirers) to the catechumenate itself.

6   Although his *Enchiridion* is devoted specifically to the Creed (faith) and Lord's Prayer (hope), Augustine relates love explicitly to the Ten Commandments. See St. Augustine: *Faith, Hope and Charity* (translated and annotated by Louis A. Arand; Westminster, Md.: Newman, 1952), 111–12.

7   Bradley, *The Roman Catechism*, 27.

8   Quoted in Bradley, *The Roman Catechism*, 26.

9   Bradley, *The Roman Catechism*, 29.

10 See Bradley, *The Roman Catechism*, 37–45, for the use and development of this Augustinian structure in the theology and writings of Thomas Aquinas.

11 Ozment, *Age of Reform*, 242.

12   See Krodel, "Luther's Work on the Catechism," 390, fn 46.

13   Krodel, "Luther's Work on the Catechism," 396, fn 77. See WA 30:I, 448, fn. 1. Geffcken II: No. XXIII provides the context of these sentences. "First the German text of the Lord's Prayer is quoted, together with the German text of the Hail Mary. Both prayers conclude with a brief stentence. Then follows in German the first sentence quoted above. Next is quoted the German text of the Creed, with a concluding sentence to the effect that these are the twelve articles of the twelve Apostles. Then follows a second quoted sentence, which is followed at once by a version of the Ten Commandments with very brief explanatory statements."

14   Krodel, "Luther's Work on the Catechism," 370.

15   Three versions were published in all. The first was for simple people and children (1470) and provided a comprehensive popular summary for the laity of catholic teaching on faith, sacraments, commandments, and prayer in 24 articles. The second (cited here) was the most popular with 29 editions between 1480 and 1520. It incorporated the twenty-four articles of the first into its fifty-three articles (divided into two parts). The final version, "The Mirror of Christian Faith," was expanded to 122 articles intended for the clergy, Ozment, *Reformation in the Cities*, 29.

16   Cf. Timothy J. Wengert, " 'Fear and Love' in the Ten Commandments" *Concordia Journal* 21(January 1995): 17. See also Johannes Meyer, *Historischer Kommentar zu Luthers Kleinem Katechismus* (Gütersloh: C. Bertelsmann, 1929), 70–107; Peters I:38–49.

17   Janz, *Three Reformation Catechisms*, 17.

18   Janz, *Three Reformation Catechisms*, 31.

19   Wengert, "Forming the Faith," 28.

20   Quoted in Ozment, *Reformation in the Cities*, 32. The second version devotes chapters 23 (prayer upon rising in the morning) through 33 (prayer upon going to bed) to prayers. Chapters 33–44 are devoted to instructions on living the Christian life including a chapter on the five signs of a good Christian. Chapters 44 to the end then deal with the art of dying.

21   Quoted in Bradley, *The Roman Catechism*, 97.

22   Bradley, *The Roman Catechism*, 98.

23   Mary Jane Haemig has an excellent chapter on just this point in her dissertation, "The Living Voice of the Catechism: German Lutheran Catechetical Preaching, 1530–1580," Harvard, 1996.

24   Schulz, "The Theological Significance of the Order of the Chief Parts in Luther's Catechism," 48.

25   Although Reu rejects a holistic reading of the catechism, he does concede that these rationales are given by Luther. See "Principles for the Preparation of an Expounded Catechism" in Paul I. Johnston, *An Assessment of the Educational Philosophy of Johann Michael Reu Using the Hermeneutic Paradigms of J. F. Hebart and of J. C. K. von Hofmann and the Erlangen School* (Urbana, IL: University of Illinois, 1989), 3:517–19.

26   Between 1519 and 1521 fourteen editions of his *Sermon on the Sacrament of Penance* (*LW* 35:9–22) had been printed.

27   "Brief Explanation of the Ten Commandments, the Creed, and the Lord's Prayer, 1520," *Works of Martin Luther* (Philadelphia: A. J. Holman, 1915), II:354–55. "The grace which will help him become a righteous man." Here Luther refers to the Creed as Gospel. This Gospel bestows the righteousness of Christ on us.

Thus in speaking about "becoming righteous," Luther has in mind the passive righteousness of the Gospel.

28   Cohrs, Ferdinand, *Die Evangelische Katechismusversuche vor Luthers Enchiridion I: Die evangelischen Katechismusversuche aus den Jahren 1522–1526* (Berlin: A. Hofmann, 1900; Hildesheim: Georg Olms Verlag, 1978), 206. In order for a man to be saved, it is necessary for him to know three things. First, he must know what he ought to do and what he ought not to do. The Ten Commandments teach him this. Second, when he sees that he has no power to do what he ought to do or to keep from doing what he ought not to do, he needs to know where to look, find and receive the power that will enable him to live as he knows he ought to. The Creed teaches him this. Third, he needs to know how to look for this power and appropriate it for himself. The Our Father teaches him this.

29   *Primam partem audivimus: quid homo scire debet, nempe 10 praecepta, ex quibus homo discit, quid debeat coram deo et mundo. Quando cognoscit se intus a. et scit se non posse servare vel literam legis, oportet ut illi ostendatur, quomodo impleat, ut est cum infirmo a. Per 10 praecepta invenimus, quod simus idolatrae, pleni invidia, avaricia quamquam opera non facimus, tamen adfectus a. oportet ergo ut medicum a. Hoc docet fides, quare praedicabimus illud, antequam pater noster.* WA 11:48, 17–23.

30   I am indebted to Timothy Wengert for this. Cf. Timothy J. Wengert, "Wittenberg's Earliest Catechism," *Lutheran Quarterly*, n.s., 7 (Autumn, 1993): 256.

31   Krodel, "Luther's Work on the Catechism," 369–70.

32   As Krodel points out, "fulfillment of the commandments" is derived from the healing medicine given to the sick [*sic*] man in the history of salvation (as this history is verbally expressed in the Creed), or it is the result of the presence of Christ and his work in the sick man, i.e., of the new life. Therefore "fulfillment of the commandments" is for Luther the daily to be made concrete *Gestalt* (Reinhard Hütter) of the healed man. Krodel, note 153. See Reinhard Hütter, "The Twofold Center of Lutheran Ethics: Christian Freedom and God's Commandments," in Karen L. Bloomquist and John R. Stumme, eds., *The Promise of Lutheran Ethics* (Minneapolis: Fortress, 1998), 31–54.

33   Catechism, *Highlight and Commentary*, 6.

34   Eilert Herms, *Luthers Auslegung des Dritten Artikels* (Tübingen: J.C.B. Mohr, 1987), 6.

35   Timothy J. Wengert, "Wittenberg's Earliest Catechism," 250.

36   *A Contemporary Translation of Luther's Small Catechism* (trans. by Timothy J. Wengert; Minneapolis: Augsburg Fortress, 1995), 73–74.

37   Brecht *Luther* II, 264

38   See also Large Catechism, BSLK, 646, 15ff.

39   Eilert Herms, *Luthers Auslegung des Dritten Artikels* (Tübingen: J. C. B. Mohr, 1987), 13.

40   Bayer, Oswald, "I Believe that God has Created Me with All that Exists. An Example of Catechetical-Systematics," Lutheran Quarterly, n.s. 7 (Summer 1994): 131.

41   Bornkamm, Heinrich, *Luther in Mid-Career, 1521–1530* (tr. E. Theodore Bachmann; Philadelphia: Fortress Press, 1983), 599.

42   Bradley, *The Roman Catechism*, 92.

43   Albrecht Peters, "*Die Bedeutung der Katechismen Luthers innerhalb der Bekenntnisschriften. Eine Thesenreihe,*" *Luther: Zeitschrift der Luther-Gesellschaft* 50 (1979): 28. Albrecht Peters gives a detailed argument for this in "*Die Theologie der Katechismen Luthers anhand der Zuordnung ihrer Hauptstücke,*" *Lutherjahrbuch* 43 (1976): 15–17.

44 Krodel, "Luther's Work on the Catechism," 17.

45 So is there nothing distinctively Christian about the Ten Commandments? No. Not in terms of their content. But if faith is God's proper and appropriate solution to human rebellion, the Gospel does suggest that God intended man to live in dependence and trust upon God in every sphere of life. But faith does not destroy creation or the ontological, it receives and restores it, which allows him to extol and praise it. It is in this context that a Christian understanding must be considered. And so, Luther interprets each chief part in the light of faith. Even the commandments are embraced by it. Faith defines man both as a *homo religiosus* and *homo peccator*. Understood ontologically and existentially, Luther interprets the Law and life in light of faith.

46 This conviction remained constant throughout Luther's thought. In his lectures on Exodus in 1525 he asserted that what Moses had written in the Ten Commandments "we feel naturally in our conscience" (WA 16:431, 28–29). "I keep the commandments which Moses has given, not because Moses gave the commandments, but because they have been implanted in me by nature, and Moses agrees exactly with nature" (*LW* 35:168; WA 16:380). Toward the end of his life, in his *Second Disputation against the Antinomians*, Luther again reiterated that the Decalogue "does not come from Moses; he is not the author but the interpreter and illustrator of the biblical commandments in the minds of all men" (WA 39 I:454, 3, 15).

47 "The natural Laws were never so orderly and well written as by Moses," *Against the Heavenly Prophets*, 1525 in *LW* 40:98; WA 18:81. Cf. *Against Sabbatarians— Letter to a Good Friend*, 1538, in *LW* 47:57–98; WA 50:312–37, and *How Christians Should Regard Moses*, 1525 in *LW* 35:155–74; WA 16:363–93 "U". Cf. Ronald M. Hals, "Luther and the First Commandment: You Belong to Me," in *Interpreting Luther's Legacy. Essays in Honor of Edward C. Fendt* (ed. Fred W. Meuser and Stanley D. Schneider; Minneapolis: Augsburg, 1969), 3. Cf. Siirala, Aarne, *Gottes Gebot bei Martin Luther: Eine Untersuchung der Theologie Luthers unter besonderer Berücksichtigung des ersten Hauptstückes im Grossen Katechismus* (Helsinki, 1956). Schriften der Luther-Agricola-Gesellschaft 11, 42–43.

48 James Arne Nestingen, "Preaching the Catechism," *Word and World* 10:1 (Winter 1990): 37.

49 In the Large Catechism, Luther continually contrasts the seemingly unexciting and unglamorous works of the Ten Commandments with those undertaken by the Carthusian monks. He seems to have regarded them as the quintessential representatives of a rigorous monasticism. See Dennis Marten, "Carthusians," *The Oxford Encyclopedia of the Reformation*, I (ed. Hans J. Hillerbrand; New York: Oxford University Press, 1996), 266–69.

50 See Charles P. Arand, "Luther on the God behind the First Commandment," *Lutheran Quarterly* 8 (Winter 1994): 397–424.

51 And so there is a reason why slandering our neighbor does not result in a peaceable relationship with him and why adultery reduces the likelihood of having a long and happy marriage.

52 Thomas M. McDonough, *The Law and the Gospel in Luther: A Study of Martin Luther's Confessional Writings* (Oxford: Oxford University Press, 1963), 84–86.

53 Michael Beintker, "Das Schöpfercredo in Luthers Kleinem Katechismus," *Neue Zeitschrift für Systematische Theologie und Relgionsphilosophie* 31 (1989): 17.

54 Peters, II: 47.

55 Friedemann Hebart, "Introductory Essay," *Luther's Large Catechism: Anniversary Translation* (Adelaide: Lutheran Publishing House, 1983), xxxiii.

56 James Arne Nestingen, "The Catechism's *Simul*," *Word and World* 3 (Fall 1983): 366–67.

57 Herbert Girgensohn, *Teaching Luther's Catechism* (Philadelphia: Muhlenberg, 1959), 181.

58 It should be noted that we frequently work with two definitions of sanctification. At times, it refers to what we do as a result of the Holy Spirit's work in us. At other times, it refers to the Spirit's work itself. Luther stresses the latter in his catechisms.

59 Albrecht Peters, "Die Theologie der Katechismen Luthers anhand der Zuordnung ihrer Hauptstücke," 25.

5

The Art of Living by Faith

The Catechisms' Theme and Narrative

In answering the pastoral and spiritual needs of the Reformation, the Small Catechism marked a watershed in the history of Christian catechesis. Although Luther gladly received and made use of the rich catechetical tradition that he inherited, he appropriated and transformed that heritage so as to make it capable of carrying the evangelical message of the Reformation to the laity.[1] As a result, the classic texts of catechesis within the Small Catechism became the bridge by which the message of the Reformation moved out from the university and castle church and into the parishes and homes of average people. Its structure and message helped replace old patterns of thought with new patterns, old values with new values, and legalistic forms of piety with evangelical forms of piety.[2]

Luther knew that the task of writing a catechism required him to set forth what, in the final analysis, is vital for all Christians to know.[3] Thus the challenge that faced Luther when he wrote the Small Catechism was to lift "out of the multiplicity of that which the church has to offer in its message the essential and determinative."[4] The genius of the Small Catechism lies in the way that it pulls together the chief parts of the catechism so as to concentrate their focus on a singular biblical theme woven through the entire Scriptures. In this way, the catechism became a cipher for the central doctrinal contents of the Christian faith.[5] That is to say, the catechism provides the access code or password that unlocks the various dimensions of Christian existence. It simplifies the complex without being simplistic and makes sense of the whole without overwhelming with quantity. In a sense, then, "all catechismal teaching is hermeneutical."[6]

To be sure, Luther was more an *ad hoc* theologian than a systematic theologian with the result that the catechism does not present a systematic theology as commonly understood. That does not mean, however, that

Luther's thinking lacked coherence. In the Small and Large Catechisms, Luther comes as close as anywhere[7] to providing a unified exposition of the faith. In many ways, this catechetical material lay at the center of Luther's theological interest. Having preached and written on the parts of the catechism regularly over a period of thirteen years, he was arguably better prepared to write the catechisms than any other writing.

To say that the Small Catechism possesses an inner coherence is to say that it finds its center in its message, which holds the whole together. This emerges in two ways. First, Luther expounds those texts in such a way that they concentrate our attention on the center of the Christian's faith and life to which and from which everything flows. Second, he utilizes those texts to interpret the various areas of the Christian life such as a Christian world view, the shape of the church's worship life, and the piety of daily life.

FAITH AS THE CATECHISM'S CENTRAL THEME

The whole content, sum, and substance of Luther's catechisms comes to expression in the classic words of Luther's explanation to the Second Article in the Small Catechism, "That I may be his own and live under him in his kingdom." With these words the Christian confesses that Christ has secured his or her future against the anti-faith forces of sin, death, and the devil. With the future no longer in doubt (even as Christ is risen from the dead), the Christian can now live confidently in this world (in spite of the ongoing presence of sin), in the here and now in this "between time" of Christ's first coming and his second coming. This means that the Christian learns how to live from the benefits of Christ. In the catechism Luther seeks to arouse and strengthen a confidence and trust that places all of life into God's hands. In the process, the Reformation emphasis of *sola fide*—in all its fullness—finds its catechetical expression.

LUTHER'S UNDERSTANDING OF FAITH

Luther's focus on faith signaled a paradigm[8] shift for the Christian view of life. The Middle Ages regarded faith as an important component of the Christian life, but would never have placed it into the center. At best, faith was seen as a knowledge of history and its events. Faith alone was only an initial intellectual assent to the data of revelation made by one who was still far from pure and godly. "*Sola fides*, all agreed, was a *fides informis*, even a *fides mortua*—an unformed, dead faith which even the demons could have.... Love, not faith, was the religious glue."[9] Faith as historical knowledge could not provide a confidence of salvation.

Dietrich Kolde's catechism provides an excellent example of the uncertainty that had been considered essential. In the conclusion of his *Mirror of a Christian Man*, Kolde writes, "There are three things I know to be true that frequently make my heart heavy. The first troubles my spirit, because I have to die. The second troubles my heart more, because I do not know when. The third troubles me above all. *I do not know where I will go* [italics added]."[10]

The reason for this uncertainty was that life was conceived as a journey from earth to heaven whose outcome was anything but certain. Fellowship with God could only happen when the sinner becomes "like God" since God cannot have fellowship with unrighteousness. This was based on the premise that like attracts like. Since God is love, human beings must become like God, that is, love. Ozment has pointed out that for the medieval theologian the central religious concept was "*caritas*—love—not faith." The way of salvation was *fides caritate formata*, faith was brought to life and perfected by acts of love. But for this to happen, the heart must be purified through love,[11] and this could only take place through the habitual practice of love. And so salvation was a process that took place "*within* us as we perfect ourselves."[12] Thus the answer given to the uncertainty expressed by Kolde was "When in doubt, try harder!" Ironically, though, that answer was at the same time the cause of such anxiety, because it raises the question, "Have I done my best?"

Luther makes faith the theme of the catechism because he identifies it as the locus of our relationship with God. This is due to his radically different understanding of faith from the way in which the Middle Ages understood it. Faith is no longer conceived merely in terms of an intellectual knowledge. Faith is instead defined as the reception of God's gifts.

Luther announces this new definition of faith in his Short Form of 1520. In his introduction to the Creed, he distinguishes between believing something *about* God and believing in God. He calls the former a *Wissenschaft* (cognition, knowledge, scholarship) or *Merkung* (observation, taking notice of something, maybe even memorizing). The latter by contrast involves not only believing that what the Creed says about God is true, but it means to trust and "without any doubt believe God will be to me … as it is being said" he will be. In other words, faith trusts that God is my Father and acts toward me as a father acts. It means to trust that God is our Father regardless of the external circumstances in which I may find myself—regardless whether I live or die.

INTEGRATING FAITH INTO THE CATECHISM

Luther takes his new understanding of faith and weaves it through every part of the catechism until it becomes the theme of the entire work.[13]

Just as a theme defines a musical composition, so the theme of faith in the catechism shapes and is shaped by the exposition of its various portions in such a way that the different chief parts become variations on the theme.

As Luther integrates the theme of faith into the various components of the catechism, he deals with it in light of the distinctive features that characterize the particular section under consideration. The first section (Ten Commandments—Creed—Lord's Prayer) charts out a Christian view of life as it is lived from faith. The second section (Baptism—Absolution—Lord's Supper) focuses on the sacramental life of the church that provides the foci of worship and nourishes the life of faith. The final section (Daily Prayers and Table of Callings) erects a framework for daily living wherein Christians exercise and live out their faith. When taken together they provide the Christian "with an organic grasp of the universe, with a sequential, though by no means rigid and strait-jacketing, view of life."[14] And so the catechism is given as a way of life to guide the Christian this side of eternity[15] and by which the Christian learns the art of living by faith.

COMMANDMENTS—CREED—LORD'S PRAYER

In the first section, "the heritage of Christendom," Luther uses the theme of faith to form an *inclusio* or parenthesis around each chief part. For example, it appears both at the beginning of the Ten Commandments, "We should fear, love and trust," and again at the end, "God promises grace and every blessing; therefore we should love and trust in him...." The theme of faith also frames the three articles of the Creed. Each article opens with the words "I believe." Each in turn concludes with the exclamation, "This is most certainly true!" The theme of faith continues with Luther's introduction to the Lord's Prayer: "With these words our Heavenly Father tenderly invites us to believe that he truly is our Father and that we truly are his children." He concludes the Lord's Prayer on the same note. "Amen" means "that I should be assured that such petitions are acceptable to our heavenly Father and are heard by him. 'Amen, amen' means 'Yes, yes, it shall be so.'"

Not only does the topic of faith frame each of these first three chief parts, but it is woven through each individual commandment, article, and petition so as to unite them all around the theme. In the Decalogue, the First Commandment (we should fear and love God)[16] is repeated in each of Luther's explanations for the other commandments. In the Creed, the Christian learns to speak the vocabulary and grammar of faith. As Luther put it, one learns "to speak faith talk" (WA 30:I, 43–44). Here the *pro me* character of faith emerges in the frequent and repeated use of the first singular personal pronoun. While "I" am the subject of the confessing, Luther takes that "I" and turns it into the object ("me") of God's activity. In the Lord's Prayer, Luther organizes each petition in such a way that everything for which we pray has already been promised to us by God, but we pray that they may be received by us.[17]

BAPTISM—ABSOLUTION—LORD'S SUPPER

The theme of faith continues throughout the second three parts of the Small Catechism which deal with the biblical texts regarding the church's sacraments. These provided the most direct contacts with the Word for most of the people. In connection with them, Luther brings out the theme of faith most strongly when discussing their benefits and the way in which they are received.

Thus in the third question on Baptism, he writes, "It is not the water in fact that does them, but the Word of God which is in and with the water, and faith, which trusts such Word of God in the water." In his brief liturgical form for confessing sins to the pastor, he has the pastor ask, "Do you believe that my words are God's words?" He then exhorts the Christian to receive forgiveness from the pastor as from God himself, and as he puts it, in "no way doubt, but firmly believe, that through it [absolution] our sins are forgiven before God in heaven." Finally, the Lord's Supper brings out this theme as well, in the answer to the fourth question. Here, worthiness is no longer defined by a series of penitential acts of purification, but as believing. "They are truly worthy and well prepared who have faith in these words, 'Given and shed for you for the forgiveness of sins' … for the words 'for you' require all hearts to believe."

PRAYERS—TABLE OF DUTIES—LITURGICAL ORDERS

The theme of faith appears throughout the final section of the catechism where Luther focuses on the exercise of faith in daily life. In the morning and evening prayers, Luther encourages a person to make the sign of the cross and then say, "Under the care of the Father, Son, and Holy Spirit."[18] Both prayers open on a note of thanks (in view of God's goodness) and conclude with the words, "into your hands I commend my body and soul and all things." These prayers also have two effects. Morning prayer sends us forth to work with joy. Evening prayer sends us to bed in peace. This confidence was also part of Luther's own praying.[19]

Contrast Luther's morning prayer with that of Kolde's. One should pray proceeds as follows upon waking.

O dear God, how I waste my precious time! I waste my precious time! How timid and slow I am! How I must burn [in purgatory] for my sloth! During the night all spiritual souls have sung God's praise [the vigils of the religious] and I have overslept! There has been great joy in heaven, and I have given it no thought. There has been great lamentation in purgatory, and I have not prayed [for those who there groan]. Many have died during the night, yet God has spared me.[20]

Appearing in Article Seven, "Prescription for a Good Life," Kolde has provided exercises for a lay person to do once or twice a day until they become habitual. Before the meal, the head of the family should recall the words of the Psalmist (Psalm 145:15, 16) which acknowledges the completeness of God's provision. In the meal prayers, both thanks is given and a blessing is asked.

Luther also included a "Table of Duties, literally, a "*Haustafel*," which he calls "The household chart of some bible passages for all kinds of holy orders and estates, through which they may be admonished, as through lessons particularly pertinent to their office and duty."[21] It was probably less a poster than a listing of Bible passages that dealt with different callings in life. This section strikingly illustrates the breakdown of the distinction between clergy and laity as a result of faith. Luther has taken the word "holy orders" once used to designate monks and nuns, "and applied it instead to the walks of life, or estates, of the ordinary Christian: government, church, but especially the household."[22] As a result, Luther's holy orders and stations are not limited to special religious groups. Instead, they include the following: bishops, pastors, and preachers (here magistrates are dealt with!); husbands, wives, and parents; children; servants, maids, day-laborers, workers; masters and mistresses of households; youths; widows; and the community (*Gemeine*) as a whole. For Luther, "religious duties are not modeled on clerical ideals but are tailored to the particular profession involved; each is instructed in fear and love of God, to be the best of whatever he or she is."[23] Luther's view of the two kinds of righteousness also freed one to serve with the focus on our neighbor and not on ourselves.

THE NARRATIVE OF FAITH:
THE ART OF LIVING BY FAITH

By means of his arrangement and exposition of the individual chief parts, Luther constructs a narrative by which he could "lead those people, who had been given into his care, from their daily life into an eschatological way of faith of a mature Christian person."[24]

The first three chief parts of the Small Catechism provide a framework for Luther to describe the overarching narrative of the Christian life. As the narrative unfolds in the first section, the Ten Commandments emphasize "the need for faith," the Creed "the gift of faith," and the Lord's Prayer "the cry of faith." The narrative begins with an assessment of daily life that emphasizes the reality of the obligations (Ten Commandments) that confront us and in which the demand for faith is the presupposition for blessed living. The narrative proceeds to the proclamation of the Gospel (Creed) which speaks of all the gifts that frame our entire life, beginning with our birth and culminating in our resurrection. This narrative culminates in prayer (Lord's Prayer) as the battle cry of the Christian life in its struggle with Satan as the power of unbelief. Together these three chief parts exercise the Christian's faith in the daily battle with death. "Everyone must fight the battle with the devil alone ... so everyone must know and be armed with the chief things that concern a Christian" (*LW* 51:70; WA 10 III:1.7–2.2, 1522).

THE NEED FOR FAITH AS THE STARTING POINT FOR THE ART OF LIVING

Although the catechism addresses Christians, Luther does not open with a discussion of Baptism, but with a presentation of the Ten Commandments which he then interprets within the horizons of the First and Second Articles. Within the context of the First Article, the Ten Commandments address human beings as creatures and delineate the contours of creaturely life. Thus the catechism begins not with the creation of the Christian life, but with the creation of life itself. It emphasizes that our first relationship to God does not begin at Baptism but begins at birth.[25] It is one of creature to Creator. Thus the catechism focuses on the structure of that relationship to God as expressed toward world and neighbor. Here, the Law (natural Law) must be regarded as good and beneficial even as creation is good and beneficial for life. Within the context of the Second Article, the Ten Commandments address human creatures as sinners. Here, the Law is experienced negatively, that is, as judgment. It is within this structure that we can also encounter the Law as restriction, limitation, burden, and accusation. Its tie to the First Article also makes clear that the accusations of the Law do not strike out of the "clear blue sky." Instead, they arise from within the setting of daily life and the obligations that humans encounter in daily life. Thus, the catechism focuses on how our new relationship with God begins with a recognition of sin. In doing so, Luther maintains a paradox about the Law. The Commandments function both descriptively and prescriptively, with the former always passing over into the latter.

THE HUMAN BEING AS RELIGIOUS CREATURE
(*Homo Religiosus*)

Within the horizon of the First Article, the obligations of the Ten Commandments encounter the human being from within creation itself (for example, natural Law, conscience, and the structures of life) and not only as an external command.[26] In other words, the Commandments are valid not because God had written them onto tables of stone for Moses, but because God "had written them into the warp and woof of human existence."[27] As a written text, the Decalogue describes "a collage of readily recognizable perspectives and parameters for the human living of human life."[28] For this reason, Luther expounds the Commandments as a description of life "from the bottom up." That is to say, he expounds the Law as we encounter and experience it throughout the various network of relationships and created structures in which we find ourselves. In particular, these include a triad of interdependent relationships between the human being, creation, and neighbor. Within these relationships, the Ten Commandments speak of "the ineradicable minimums of creatureliness."[29]

As a creature of God, a human being is by definition a dependent being. At the most basic level, every person is dependent upon creation (air, water, food, and so forth) for life itself. People are also dependent upon neighbors (parents, spouse, employer, society, and so forth) for community and the sustenance of life. In addition to these needs, human beings ultimately need a foundation for security, meaning, identity, and a framework for making sense of life. All of this is to say that life cannot be lived without faith. Human beings need to put their trust in something or something outside themselves. This creaturely need explains Luther's strongly anthropocentric orientation to the First Commandment in the Large Catechism when he says that faith makes both true God and false idol in our hearts (LC I, 2). Thus, Luther does not see the core of the commandment as requiring faith so much as it already presupposes that everyone already has faith (and hence a god) by virtue of their need for meaning, security, or identity.[30] This demand for faith manifests itself at the level of the human heart, which needs a point that transcends the temporal and to which it can anchor its trust. Therefore, the heart asks about (and seeks after) God.[31] It seeks a dependable foundation.

Because faith defines the most fundamental characteristic of human beings, the First Commandment goes to the heart of human existence. And so it does not address the issue of whether or not one should have faith. It is not an issue of theism versus atheism. The question centers on true faith or false faith. Where the object of faith is the true God, there one's faith is true. And their faith will find the support it needs.

At this point Luther helps Christians understand the process by which their wandering minds construct figments of their imagination in the quest to find security. "Many a person thinks that he has God and everything when he has money and property."[32] Conversely, he who has nothing doubts and despairs as if he never heard of God. The evidence of idolatry occurs when things are taken away and depression overwhelms the idolater. Thus the First Commandment calls upon the human creature to distinguish between God and the world: the former is the Creator; the latter is creation. This is the most basic ontological distinction that can be made. It emerges in the words "no other gods" and "above all things." This distinction becomes the presupposition for everything else that the catechism has to say about God and life in God's world. Life is found with God alone, for he alone creates, defines, and preserves life. The demand to seek life from God requires that we follow his lead and gratefully accept the world as it comes as God's will for us. Only in this way does the heart come "to terms with and accepts whatever God sends."[33]

Luther knew that it was not easy to trust God in this way. And so he underscores the First Commandment in both catechisms by referring to the threat and promise of Exodus 5:6 at this point in the Large Catechism.[34] God's threats warn us against the danger of following other gods, for they cannot deliver on the promises that we imagine they can. The promises emphasize God's insistence and desire to be our God and provide us with all that we need. As he does with the commandments, Luther interprets the threats and promises "from the bottom up." That is to say, God's wrath is manifested in part by destroying our idols through his curse on creation. When God's gifts are used other than God intended (i.e., idols), they break, because creation cannot bear the weight of our faith. Only when our idols disappoint, do we "learn to distinguish between the illusory world of idolatry that people create for themselves (and which God destroys) and the real world established by God. Conversely, the promise leads us to perceive the hidden hand of God within creation. In this way, "trust passes through the world and clings to the God who is not of this world."[35] That is to say, he stands behind all these creaturely gifts as the good Giver. They do not contain him; he holds them in his hands.[36]

Although Luther followed the tradition of formally dividing the commandments into two tables, his real division was between the First Commandment and the remaining nine. In the Second through the Tenth Commandments, Luther took the distinction that the First Commandment made in theory and applied it to our experience in this world.[37] The need for faith manifests itself in the midst all the manifold demands that press in upon us day in and day out within the God-given fourfold shape of life: home, occupation, society and church. Commandments Two through Ten instruct us on actions appropriate in those four situations.[38] Each commandment opens by echoing the First Commandment. Only by distinguishing between God and the world can we deal with the world properly, i.e., according to the purpose for which it was given (LC I, 47). In other words, only by relying on God can one use possessions properly—as gifts to be used to help one's neighbor rather than turning them into idols to which we must cling for fear of losing life itself. Our neighbor is to be seen as both an instrument of God for blessing us and as an individual whose need serves as God's summons for us to be his instrument in helping others.

The Second and Third Commandments describe the ramifications of the First Commandment and continue to focus on the human being's vertical relationship with God. The trust required in the First Commandment is practiced through the use of God's name.[39] The Second Commandment teaches us to use God's name in order to oppose evil and as the source of good. Only by using God's name in faith can it become an instrument of blessing. To do that, however, we need to be trained in the use of God's Word that expounds the name. We can only believe through the activity of the Word, and so we never finish learning the catechism or the Scriptures. This becomes the theme of Luther's explanation for the Third Commandment. The proper way to rest in observance of the holy day is to devote the day to God's Word.[40] In the end we do not make the day holy as much as the Word makes both the day and us holy.

The Fourth Commandment functions as a transition from the vertical relationship with God to the horizontal relationships with neighbor and in the world. As such, it belongs to both tables. In dealing with parents as God's representatives, our relationship with them is analogous to our relationship with God. There is a "givenness" to that relationship with them that we did not choose or create. "Our parents, through whom we have received life and whom we have neither chosen nor shaped, have generated us and raised us. They are typical of the fact that all of life is a given."[41] We are dependent on life as it is given to us. From parents, Luther unfolds an understanding of all temporal authority in the three (sometimes four) situations of life as representatives of God for the purpose of preserving peace and order in the horizontal realm. As we receive from them, we find ourselves in a reciprocal responsibility of receiving their gifts and not hindering them through disobedience, but instead using them for our neighbor.

Luther sees the Fifth through the Tenth Commandments as proceeding outward in a sequence of priorities from the neighbor's being. Each commandment speaks of one of God's creaturely goods, and obedience consists first in receiving these as gifts from God and dealing with them as God intended. The Fifth Commandment deals with the life of those in the human community, specifically, with the preservation and quality of life itself.[42] It deals with the inviolability of one's neighbor as a person like oneself. The Sixth Commandment protects our closest neighbor, namely, our spouse who is also our highest good. It deals with sexuality as one of the most vital elements of our being and personalities. The Seventh focuses on the next set of relations involving the neighbor's temporal goods as semi-detached parts of our being and important for our well-being.[43] Stealing threatens to destroy the community by depriving our neighbors of their property. The Eighth Commandment addresses the set of relations having to do with our neighbor's temporal integrity and reputation. This forms the basis for much of our interaction with others. The last two, the Ninth and Tenth, "underline the evil in our natures and the perils of unlimited desire for sensual satisfaction and for material things, which begin with the neighbor's property and end with his wife and household and livestock."[44]

Within the horizon of creation, and in the realm of our horizontal relationships, the Ten Commandments possess an authority to bring about what they demand. They derive this authority in part from their ability to describe accurately life as we encounter it. As a result, there is a strong "try it for yourself and see if it isn't true" character to them. For example, "see if coveting leads to contentment or discontentment?" Or "see for yourself whether cherishing your spouse leads to a happier or unhappier marriage." Thus the Law's warnings can deter destruction of the community and rewards can encourage its maintenance. Through the needs of our neighbors the commandments exert a pressure to act in their behalf. Here on the horizontal plane the first use of the Law is not concerned with motivations as it is with actions. It has in view the maintenance of creation and society. Thus Luther makes a special point to show how each of the commandments refers to and protects a particular gift of our neighbor. The commandments presuppose that while we cannot create life, we are capable of destroying it. Therefore, God steps in like a kind Father with his commandments to protect it. This curbing function is positive and serves God's work in the preservation of creation. They do not make people godly, but they do make society a better place to live.

Hᴜᴍᴀɴ Bᴇɪɴɢ ᴀꜱ ᴀ Fᴀʟʟᴇɴ Cʀᴇᴀᴛᴜʀᴇ (*Homo Peccator*)

While the Ten Commandments address us as creatures within the horizon of the First Article, they immediately pass over to address us as sinners within the horizons of the Second and Third Articles. The Commandments, which were previously descriptive and positive, now become prescriptive and negative. Within creation the Law describes the structure and framework of life and sets forth how God intended it to function. For that reason, it also calls attention to the disorder that occurs within our lives when creation does not function according to God's ordering of it. This disorder occurs in all the relationships of the human creature, the vertical with God and the horizontal with neighbor and non-human creation. In calling attention to this disorder it accuses us of irresponsible living that results from failing to use creation as God intended it and using it for some other purpose (i.e., idolatry).

The Ten Commandments reveal that in the end, to live as a fallen creature within the world is to live with the nonnegotiable conditions of creaturely existence that continually confront us with the limits and consequences that they impose. The fallen creature who lives "under the commandments inevitably lives with disappointment."[45] The First Commandment ultimately provides the key for diagnosing dysfunctional lives, for it goes to the heart of the matter while the other nine commandments assess only the symptoms.[46]

Although the First Commandment requires a person to distinguish between God and the world, the heart often clings to creaturely things that it equates with life (thereby deifying them) such as possessions, power, and pleasure.[47] Inevitably, these idols prove to be more illusions than solutions to problems. The heart eventually encounters disappointment when such creatures cannot bear the weight of faith and cannot ultimately provide that which the heart seeks or needs. Self-chosen gods, be they youthfulness, money, or popularity, invariably disappoint, and lead to yet more exhausting searches for new ones to take their place.

Unfortunately, when people find a single god insufficient, they then create a pantheon of little or larger sources of identity. The First Commandment lays bare the illusion of their promise. It confronts us with our doubts and desire to have other gods. More specifically, it shows us that human beings are irreversably committed to the quest of finding something to which they can attach their hearts other than God. "Here the Lutheran paradigm hits its stride by attacking all mythologies of fulfillment, self-transcendence through self-actualization, creating a new world through product relationships—the secular pieties and all their religious counterparts—by telling the truth about the limits and impingements of creaturely life."[48]

The same applies to the second table of the Law. As people live within the network of relationships within the four estates of family, work, society, and church, and as they carry out the responsibilities entailed by those relationships, they eventually encounter the limitations of both themselves and others. As we seek to meet the demands of daily life placed upon us by our roles and responsibilities, we come face-to-face with our inadequacies, inabilities, and our limitations both as creatures (we are not the Creator) and as sinners (because we attempt to take matters into our own hands). It may come in the form of "you're not a good mother or father," or, "you're not living up to expectations." It may also result from the attempt to find acceptance by others. This may happen in the endeavor to preserve and protect our name and reputation, or to enhance ourselves with a view toward acceptance by others—even if it happens at someone else's expense.

By interpreting the Law simultaneously within the contexts of the First and Second Articles, Luther shows that its accusations do not come at us out of the "clear blue sky." This means that the Ten Commandments are not prescriptions to be leveled by someone who, armed with the Law, seeks to induce guilt or need where there was none. The Ten Commandments recognize that people already realize something is wrong. Life is not working the way it should. Hearts are restless. People know of a pressure that makes them dissatisfied with life. They have plenty of evidence that something is wrong but need a way to process it and diagnose it.[49]

The Ten Commandments interpret and explain how people experience the Law in daily life. Thus by keying the Decalogue to daily experience, Luther shows that because human beings do not experience authentic creaturely life, then they will instead experience "the Law as entrapment, containment, and fright over their mortality."[50] It may be experienced as high blood pressure, weariness, or stress. This is true whether or not they have ever heard the verbal articulation of the Law's accusations. The proclamation or criticism leveled by the Ten Commandments then sharpens that criticism by confronting us with our denial that anything is wrong!

GOD'S GIFTS SUSTAIN
THE ART OF LIVING BY FAITH

If the Ten Commandments unveil the restlessness of human hearts, the Creed leads its hearers to find rest in God.[51] By explaining the Creed against the backdrop of the Ten Commandments Luther shows that God is not a detached and distant God, nor is his work irrelevant to the human creature. Instead, God incarnates himself and becomes deeply involved within human life. His gifts enter into the reality of everyday life, replete with its demands and limitations. In this, Luther shows that "Gospel preaching that does not recognize or deal with the firstness of the Ten Commandments loses contact with the realities of daily life."[52] The Creed, then, shows a God who breaks into our situation with his gifts in order to awaken in us the faith that distinguishes between God and his world. In the process, the Creed establishes the foundation for the First Commandment's claim by showing that God is the giver of all gifts. The First Article shows how God creates and sustains us as creatures. The Second and Third Article gifts show how God rescues sinners. And so the Creed teaches us to see that no aspect of our existence remains untouched by God's giving of himself through his gifts. This should not, however, be taken as a sequence of God's actions. All three articles apply to Christians simultaneously so that they represent three aspects of the triune God's work.

FIRST ARTICLE: FAITH IN THE CREATOR'S CARE

Where Luther opened the First Commandment with our creaturely need to have a god, he opens the First Article with the confession that "God has made me." I am a creature. That is where I begin. This means that we belong not to ourselves, and so also the course of our lives belongs not to ourselves.[53] In his letter to Peter the Barber, Luther writes, "You are God's creation, his handiwork, his workmanship.... But what you are, know, can do, and can achieve is God's creation.... God has created everything out of nothing. Here is the soul's garden of pleasure, along whose paths we enjoy the works of God" (*LW* 43:210). Luther develops this point by showing that "nothing that is came from anywhere else than his creative hand and breath."[54] He shows God to be the exclusive giver of our lives and the whole context of created reality through the frequent use of the word "all" (nine times) in the Small Catechism. In doing so, he picks up the *creatio ex nihilo* of the church's faith and affirms that there is no more fundamental distinction than that of Creator and creation. For this reason God's creating depends upon no external force or internal compulsion. Thus, when God creates, it too, is an act of sheer generosity ("without any worthiness in me"). If God has created everything that gives me life, then I should seek everything from him and not from creation.

The First Article also highlights the role and place of the creaturely. Although the First Commandment requires us to cling to the Creator and not the creation, this does not mean that the creaturely is evil. In the First Article, Luther confesses that creatures function as God's instruments and hands for bestowing his blessings. In a way, they are his coworkers or the masks behind which he smiles (note the "together with all creatures"). Thus "when you see the tree bearing fruit, you are seeing God the Creator" (WA 30:II, 87, 6–9; 88, 5–6, 10–11)! But the Creator is not in (panentheism) the creature or equated with the creation (pantheism). "He stands instead behind all these gifts of his, as the Good Giver. They do not contain him; he holds them in his hands."[55] In this way Luther not only seeks to arouse the Christian's faith in God's creaturely and providential care, but to help faith seek God's gifts in, with, and under the creaturely. The latter function as the instrument(s) through which God conveys his goodness.

In this way, the First Article lays an important foundation for the Second and Third Articles. It demonstrates that in all three articles, God works through creaturely means in order to accomplish his work. It also means that we are not to look outside the creaturely for his presence and work.

SECOND ARTICLE: JESUS CHRIST ... IS MY LORD

Here we arrive at, arguably, the most beloved section of the entire catechism—made the more so by its simplicity. Where the First Article centered our attention on the Father as our Creator, the Second Article focuses our entire attention on the statement: "Jesus Christ … is my Lord."[56] With this the Christian confesses his identity and ours. Luther then proceeds to tell the story of how it came about that I needed a Lord and how Christ became my Lord. Thus it begins with a different starting point than the First Article.[57]

The Second Article opens not with a discussion of my needs as a dependent creature, but of my needs as a fallen, trapped, and tyrannized sinner, as expressed by the confession that I am a "lost and condemned creature." Such need entails bondage to both the power of sin and the guilt of sin ("as a lost and condemned creature"). It addresses the fallen creature, the one who has failed to distinguish between the Creator and creation and now finds himself under the dominion and tyranny of idols and Satan. God is no longer God in my life. And so Luther begins the discussion of Jesus' Lordship at the point where I need a Lord. As he put it, "Before Christ came, I had no lord and king" (LC II, 27). Where in the First Article God created something out of nothing, here we see that he recreates something new out of sin. This he accomplishes by means of the Son's incarnation (true God ... true man) and with his work (his precious blood and his innocent suffering and death). In death he achieves victory. In "Christ, God has come to reclaim creature and creation for himself and so sets us free to live in the very good for which we were created."[58]

Jesus became my Lord in order that I might be his own and live under his care. More specifically, the lordship of God proves itself in the lordship of Christ over all anti-God powers. Christ brings us to the Father by overcoming sin, death, and the devil, which would keep us from living under the care of the Father.[59] Through his life, suffering, death, and resurrection, Christ overcomes everything that would keep us from coming to the Father. In a sense, he has put me back on the Father's lap (WA 30:I, 89, 16–17).[60] The Second Article describes the new situation in which I find myself. In other words, "that I may be his own" "describes the new reality which has been created as the result of action completed by someone else in the past."[61]

Christ died in order to make me his, in order to create a new reality in which I will be his, live under him in his kingdom, and actually serve him. To this theological dimension, there corresponds an anthropological dimension. If the heart and conscience are freed from the accusation of the Law and from God's wrath which breaks in with it, then we are freed to struggle against the satanic demons. They have lost their power because God's wrath no longer stands behind them.

This last point paves the way for the struggle of faith picked up and pursued by the Third Article and the Lord's Prayer. Hence we look forward to the final separation that culminates in the Third Article ("give eternal life to me and all believers") as well as the Seventh Petition ("Deliver us from the Evil One").

THIRD ARTICLE: THE SPIRIT BRINGS US TO FAITH

The Third Article continues the theme of Christ's lordship, but with a focus on the implementation of his lordship in my life here and now. It answers the question, "How does Christ become my Lord, and how do I become his possession and come to live under his care?" Whereas in the Second Article Christ establishes his lordship over all the evil forces that would hinder it, the Third Article concentrates on the entrance of Christ into our lives. In the Second Article, Christ *established himself* as my *Lord*. In the Third Article he takes personal possession of me as *my Lord*. To live under Christ is to live as the beneficiaries of his victory and the recipients of his gifts.

The Third Article thus deals with my incorporation into this kingdom by awakening the faith that binds us to him. The Spirit brings the Lordship of Jesus to bear upon our lives so that the liberation won by Christ becomes a reality for us. "Faith is our first and foremost concern because in faith the Spirit makes the Christ of Calvary in the past as well as the new Adam of the future present to us now."[62]

In the second half of the article, Luther stresses that the Holy Spirit does not take possession of me in isolation from other Christians. He simultaneously gathers me into the church, kindles faith, thereby creating and extending the church. The Spirit keeps us together in Jesus Christ in the one true faith. Thus the Small Catechism describes the work of the Spirit in the believer and within the church in parallel statements (call, enlighten, sanctify, and keep). It links them together through the adverb *gleich wie* (even as). As the Spirit creates faith in individuals he simultaneously gathers them into the church and keeps them in Jesus Christ! The Large Catechism stresses that the same word that creates faith within the individual also creates the church. "Where Christ is not preached, there is no Holy Spirit to create, call and gather the Christian Church."[63] "Again, where he does not cause the Word to be preached and does not awaken understanding in the heart, all is lost." This church lives from, is centered in, and aims at the forgiveness of sins (in which Christian church)…. This is another way of saying (by way of hendiadys) that the one Gospel creates the one church.

THE TRINITY

When the Ten Commandments and Creed are considered together, we see how Luther juxtaposes and unites the two. In the Ten Commandments he takes the "the universal basis of the quest for God in the human heart" and juxtaposes it "with the exclusiveness of the answer given by the God of the Bible and the Father of Jesus Christ."[64] The First Commandment identifies God only from our side as the object of fear, love, and trust, by saying that we are to avoid all other gods.

The First Commandment, however, does not reveal the identity of the true God. It only tells us to forsake substituting anything in creation for the true God. Similarly, to believe that God blesses us and does good things is not necessarily a Christian distinctive. It belongs to reason's definition of God. The created world teaches us as much. The critical question centers on the identity of God. If the First Commandment determines the goal of the Creed, the Creed in turn informs our understanding of the First Commandment as a requirement for faith in the triune God, Father, Son, and Holy Spirit. The God who issued the command to forsake all other gods reveals himself in the Creed as the triune God. And so in the end the First Commandment cannot be fulfilled apart from faith in the *Triune* God, whose work the Creed makes known to us. In the Large Catechism, it is not until after Luther deals with the three articles of the Creed individually that he then addresses the question of the unity of the Trinity. In the end, he approaches the theme from the standpoint of the economic Trinity, that is, the manifestation of the Father, Son, and Spirit within the history of salvation. Thus he begins with the three persons and asks how these three are one (see LC II, 63ff).

THE LORD'S PRAYER: THE BATTLE CRY OF FAITH

Like the Creed, Luther sees the Lord's Prayer as helping the Christian keep the Ten Commandments. This means two things. First, the Creed and Lord's Prayer do not remove the Christian from the world as did monasticism. Instead, they send the Christian back into the world, into his or her vocation, there to live under Christ's dominion and protection. Second, within daily life one needs faith and here prayer emerges as the fulfillment of the First Commandment and the gift of the Creed. In some ways, prayer becomes both the evidence and test of faith. If a person expects God to help, then that person will pray. If a person does not expect anything from God, then that person will not pray. Luther brings this out well in his beautiful introduction to the Lord's Prayer where he states that God invites us to believe so that we may ask! Prayer as petition highlights the receptive character of faith itself. This comes through strongly in Luther's explanations of the petitions. Thus rather than being seen as a means of grace, prayer emerges instead as a means of faith!

At the same time that the Christian is sent back into the world, the implementation of Christ's reign has several ramifications for the Christian life. Having been brought under the lordship of Christ to live in faith by receiving his gracious gifts, the Christian finds himself or herself embroiled in a spiritual warfare and struggle for faith.[65] For Luther, prayer becomes most decidedly the struggle of faith itself in the ongoing life of the Christian.

It is an old insight of Luther that the work of the triune God among men will be brought to completion in the eschaton. In the meantime, it is realized only in a beginning way on earth. Therefore, no person fulfills the Ten Commandments perfectly—and indeed, expressly not those who believe and begin to become godly through faith. Prayer is rooted in this situation of the now and the not yet polarity.[66]

In the present situation the Christian life emerges as a life under the cross. The struggle for faith does not take place prior to conversion as in much of non-Lutheran Protestantism, it commences with the kindling of faith.[67] And so, in the Lord's Prayer, we pray for faith against unfaith. In this way the Lord's Prayer has a way of bringing a deep comfort to people battling with an abiding sense of their own unbelief.[68] In the Lord's Prayer, the Christian prays for faith to receive the blessings enumerated in the Creed and prays against Satan who would undermine faith by depriving the Christian of Christ's blessings.

As Luther proceeds through each petition, he strikes the note that we pray to appropriate the promised gifts of God as our very own. This is evident from several considerations. First, in nearly every petition in the Small Catechism Luther answers the question, "What does this mean?" by admitting that those things for which we pray will come to pass whether or not we pray.[69] According to Luther's exposition of the Lord's Prayer in the catechisms, prayer does not, in the first instance, create the holiness of God's name. Our prayers do not effect the coming of his kingdom or bring about the fulfillment of his will, etc. Instead, prayer seeks to receive as gifts all that God gives even without our asking. God would have us pray for faith to receive his gifts. This is clearly the case in the second half of Luther's answer to the question, "What does this mean?"

In prayer faith seeks to have God and his gifts as our own, *pro nobis*. For example, the Fourth Petition is not primarily a prayer for food, since God has already done all that is necessary for the provision of food. Luther answers that God bids us instead to pray "in order to have us acknowledge and confess that he is already bestowing many blessings upon us and that he can and will give us still more" (*LW* 21:144).[70]

At the same time, we pray against unbelief. Unbelief and the old Adam are aroused to opposition through faith and prayer. As a result, life here is "lived under the cross, under the assault of Satan and his temptations."[71] The Christian is constantly subject to attacks, trials, and temptations. Christian prayer always expresses this conflict. But the Christian prays in spite of this opposition. "In spite of" are the key words. For whenever a good Christian prays, "Dear Father, Thy will be done," God replies from on high, "Yes, dear child, it shall indeed be done in spite of the devil and all the world," and we might add, in spite of all appearances. Satan cannot stand the Word of God that works faith which then seeks everything in God (*LW* 43:232). The devil wants to be god in Christ's place. "He wants to make us believe lies rather than thy Word" (*LW* 43:232). The Christian lives in this struggle between faith and unbelief, between God and Satan. As a result, the din of battle dominates as the theme of Luther's exposition of the Lord's Prayer in the Large Catechism almost from the very beginning (LC III, 2).[72]

And so each of the explanations of the Lord's Prayer acknowledges the conflict while looking for help from God. The first two pray for God's Word and faith in that Word. These two themes were already announced in the introduction ("with *these words* God tenderly *invites* us to believe" [italics added] and are summarized in the Third Petition. The Fourth Petition prays for daily life. The Fifth and Sixth Petitions have in view our sin, both the forgiveness of it and the protection from the ambushes and attacks by sin, our flesh, and Satan which would lead us into despair or unbelief. Where the Third Petition focuses on external threats from the devil, the world, and our sinful nature, the Sixth has in view the internal threats that often are not seen and thus catch us unawares.

Although the theme of struggle is evident in all the petitions, it reaches a climactic conclusion in the last petition. Here, prayer for protection against the devil emerges its explicit theme. It is the condition without which (*conditio sine qua non*) there is no fulfillment of all the others. It is the devil who frustrates and attacks us. Hence, for Luther, the prayer against the devil is the decisive one; he is the one who can cause us to fall back into unbelief (LC III, 105) and prevent us from appropriating God's gifts as our own. The last petition thus compresses the thoughts of all the previous petitions into the idea that the sum total of all our prayers should be aimed at this enemy of ours. This petition is directed against all misfortune—every evil that befalls us in the devil's kingdom and every tragic misery and heartache. There is "nothing for us to do on earth but to pray constantly against this arch-enemy" (LC III, 116). And so the Lord's Prayer goes to the heart of our deepest need.

THE NOURISHMENT OF FAITH: THE CHURCH'S SACRAMENTAL LIFE

In the Third Article the Holy Spirit calls people to faith by the Gospel and keeps Christians safe in Jesus Christ. Here Baptism, Absolution, and the Lord's Supper show themselves to be the very Gospel itself, but in three different forms. The inclusion of these elements in the catechism provided for a juxtaposition of Word (Ten Commandments, Creed, Lord's Prayer) and Sacrament (Baptism, Lord's Supper) that is vital for understanding Luther's own work.[73]

Lutheran sacramental theology makes two points: First, the Word of God is a dynamic power through which God works in a variety of forms (contra the Anabaptists). The Word is not merely information that somehow requires a decision for action on our part. Second, only as the Word of God is maintained as the work of God, does faith retain the character of receptivity or reception of those gifts. Where the first three chief parts encompassed the entire life of an individual from the beginning of creaturely life to the resurrection, the sacraments encompass the total life of the Christian from the new birth to the resurrection of the dead. Indeed, they do more than encompass it, they bring it about. Interestingly, Luther does not begin with a definition of what constitutes a sacrament. He does note what they have in common and the gifts that they deliver. Instead, Luther deals with them one at a time in order to focus on their *proprium*, that is, the distinctive character and features of each. This in turn brings out the value of each for the Christian life.

While faith is brought out in these last three chief parts, the real focus of Luther is in dealing with those who have divorced faith from its object, namely, the promises of God. As a result, he focuses on the importance of the external Word without which faith cannot exist. This section, Baptism, Absolution, and the Lord's Supper, is vital for the theology of the entire catechism and especially for sharpening the Lutheran understanding of both Word and faith. In the early 1520s, Luther dealt with Rome which stressed the objective efficacy of the sacraments with its teaching of the *ex opere operato* character of the sacraments, but did not stress the need for faith to receive the sacraments' blessings. In the late 1520s the sacramentarians emphasized the need for faith, but let go of the objective efficacy of the sacraments with the end result that faith had nothing to which it could cling. Both cases revealed a misunderstanding of faith. Thus over and against Rome, Luther stressed the necessity of faith for receiving and appropriating the blessings of the sacraments. In the case of the sacramentarians, Luther emphasized God's presence and work in selected elements from the created order.

BAPTISM

The importance of the Word in Baptism appears in the opening words of Luther's explanation in the Small Catechism. Baptism is not plain water by itself. Instead, it is water enclosed by God's command and word. Here, Luther extends Augustine's dictum—that word and element come together to make a sacrament—to include three elements: water, word, and command. The command (institution) expresses God's will and the word expresses the promise as the instrument of God's work. The command serves a similar role to that which it played in Luther's account of the Decalogue. That is to say, it illumines the glory of what God establishes over and against those practices devised and instituted by human beings (especially those of the Carthusians). The command, in other words, gives something ordinary (like water) its glory. What God commands cannot be useless (LC IV, 7). Second, the Word is an instrument of God's work, which again renders Baptism incomparably greater than any human work (LC IV, 11–14). Luther's stress on the command and word thus directs faith to fasten its grasp upon the water as encompassing God's promise and gifts in spite of its rather ordinary appearance.

More than anything else, Baptism is the missionary sacrament or evangelistic sacrament by which a person is transferred from one lordship to another. Baptism incorporates the Christian into Christ himself. Thus in the Small Catechism, Luther uses the same language to speak of Baptism as he did to speak of Christ in the Second Article. In other words, Christ and Baptism do the same thing. Christ rescued (erlösen) us from sin, death, and the power of the devil. Similarly, Baptism also rescues (erlösen) us from sin, death, and the power of the devil. In Baptism God links our destiny to the destiny of Jesus Christ.[74] The gifts that Christ acquired in the Second Article are here delivered in Baptism. In this way, Baptism becomes the gateway to all of God's blessings: "the forgiveness of sins, life, and salvation." Luther is able to bring out the point that since it is the Word which makes Baptism the conveyor of Christ's gifts, faith's task is to receive those gifts. Those gifts are there whether faith receives them immediately or at some point in the future.

For Luther, then, Baptism was the sacrament of justification par excellence. In the same way that justification implies that "God is no respecter of persons," so Baptism as the sacrament of justification "becomes the great equalizer of Christians. Even age no longer divides them."[75] Wengert points out that Baptism provided Luther with some of his first criticisms of monasticism and that out of it grew his unique understanding of the Christian life in terms of vocation, including the vocation of children (see the Table of Christian Responsibilities!). This stands in contrast with the views both of Roman theologians who argued that the mortal sins willed by adults destroyed baptismal grace and of Anabaptists who reserved Baptism for those old enough to decide.[76] In a medieval system that divided Christians into spiritual and carnal Christians, children, parents, and workers came off as second-class Christians, compared to those who were called to the monastic life and who performed special works that ordinary Christians could not. Now, even children had a vocation and were a holy order on account of Baptism.

Baptism thus gives Christians a foundation for their entire life. It is a miniature and complete picture of the Christian life. It involves the believer's birth, discipleship, conflict with Satan, death, and resurrection. Luther especially brings this out in his fourth question to Baptism, where he links the Christian to the death and resurrection of Christ. Elsewhere, Luther stresses that this brings about a real death and resurrection for the Christian. "This death and resurrection we call the new creation, regeneration, and spiritual birth. This should not be understood only allegorically as the death of sin and the life of grace, as many understand it, but as actual death and resurrection" (*LW* 36:68). The definitive act of dying and rising with Christ becomes the pattern for the life of the Christian as Luther indicates in his appropriation of Romans 6.

CONFESSION—ABSOLUTION

Luther's discussion of confession, along with the shape of his liturgical rite, shows how he redefines its essence and practice so that it ceases to be a burden and instead becomes an instrument by which the Gospel is conveyed personally to an individual.

First, the pastor no longer functions as examiner, judge, and executioner over the Christian's conscience. Instead, he exists for one purpose and one purpose only—to offer the forgiveness of sins.[77] In 1524 with his Palm Sunday sermon, which entered the *Little Prayer Book*, Luther maintained that when going to the priest, a person should go to hear absolution and not to be so concerned with confession. The advantage of private confession is its personal dimension. It is an opportunity to receive the Gospel personally. Thus confession becomes a place of promise where sin and guilt are overcome with God's promises. It is for this reason more than any other that Luther treasured private confession and continued to practice it all his life.[78]

Second, Luther simplifies the process of confession for the laity, thereby relieving some of the anxiety associated with the sacrament.[79] In the Large Catechism he rejects the coercion to confess and the requirement to enumerate all sins in order to purify oneself. He dispensed with the extensive and complicated set of distinctions between sins and the circumstances in which sins were committed. More importantly, he drew the distinction between sins against God's commandments and violations of humanly devised laws of the church. Most importantly, one goes to confession to receive God's mercy through trust in the promise.

Unlike in the Middle Ages when confession had become the plank to which a person clung after making shipwreck of the ark of Baptism, Luther sees it as the continuation of Baptism. Indeed, it continues the pattern of dying and rising, exhaling and inhaling, the rhythm of the Christian life. Private absolution brought out the personal application of the Gospel to the penitent. The doctrine of faith returned this sacrament to a Gospel sacrament. With no need for an inquisitor who must determine the proper amount of recompense, the pastor becomes a "forgiveness-person" into whose mouth has been placed the Word of God. In absolution we become what we are—baptized.

With regard to its location in the Small Catechism, Luther placed the discussion of confession between Baptism and the Lord's Supper. This location suggests a dual character which ties it back to Baptism on the one hand and to the Lord's Supper on the other. In the Large Catechism Luther appends a "brief exhortation to confession" to his discussion on the Lord's Supper. By tying it to the Lord's Supper he reaffirmed the connection between confession and the Lord's Supper that Pope Innocent III established at the Fourth Lateran Council (1215), but from the perspective of a Lutheran understanding of repentance and faith.[80] In the course of defending the inclusion of this topic within the catechism three years later, Luther explained the connection between the two sacraments. In his "Open Letter to those in Frankfurt on the Main," he wrote, "because it is Christ's body and blood that are given out in the Sacrament, we will not and cannot give such a Sacrament to anyone unless he is first examined regarding what he has learned from the Catechism and whether he intends to forsake the sins which he has again committed."[81] In this connection, the practice of confession provides a catechetical opportunity for instruction on the sacrament.

LORD'S SUPPER

The Lord's Supper provides the food for the daily life of the Christian (LC V, 23–25). As daily food, the Lord's Supper sustains the Christian's faith in the struggle of the church militant and bears witness to the eschatological banquet of the church. In pursuing a life of faith, the catechism seeks to awaken a hunger and thirst within the believer for the means of grace, through which the catechumen personally lays hold of Christ and through which Christ lays hold of the catechumen. Faith makes use of this meal and strengthens itself thereby, while the Christian awaits the time when he or she will eat at the eschatological banquet with Christ himself.

Luther's task of catechizing people on the Lord's Supper faced a formidable challenge on several fronts. On the one hand, Rome agreed with Luther that Christ's body and blood were truly present but denied that its benefits were to be received by faith. On the other hand, Zwingli insisted that faith was the goal and effect of the sacrament but denied the true presence of the body and blood. Of these two, Luther regarded the latter as the worse of the two evils, for the Sacramentarians took away "the Sacrament totally, where the papists only took half."[82] Luther addresses these errors in his Holy Week Sermons of 1529 (the contents of which find their way into the Large Catechism), including on receiving both kinds, the real presence, not turning the sacrament into a work, receiving it by faith in the Word, and exhortation to receive the Lord's Supper.

For Luther, both sides went wrong in their denigration of the words and promises of Christ. As Wengert, points out, the Lord's Supper, in its "late-medieval incarnation as the mass, had become a feast for the eyes. The words of institution were whispered *sotto voce* by a richly attired, distant priest. The worshipers were often fenced off from the officiant by means of ornately carved wood screens."[83] The buildings contained imposing tabernacles to house the consecrated host. Chronicles from this era even "recorded Sunday-morning stampedes from one church to another, as the faithful rushed to catch a glimpse of the central act of elevation, when the priest's offering was consummated."[84] To those who had made the sacrament into a sacrifice effective by its mere performance, Luther "hammered away at the promise, 'Given for you … shed for you for the forgiveness of sins,' and the faith that the promise engenders." "To those who denied that Christ was present in and with the bread and wine, he pointed to Christ's simple words, 'This is my body.'"[85]

In four brief questions, Luther provides a single, yet full summary of these debates. Questions 1 and 3 appear to have in view the Sacramentarians. Questions 2 and 4 appear to be aimed more at the Roman Catholic Church inasmuch as these questions deal with the benefits of the Lord's Supper and the worthiness of those who receive it. In the first question of the Small Catechism, Luther stresses the words as defining the essence of the sacrament, "This is my body.… This is my blood.…" The second question stresses the treasure and benefits of the sacrament that faith receives and by which faith is strengthened. "These words, 'Given and shed for you for the forgiveness of sins,' show us that in the Sacrament forgiveness of sins, life, and salvation are given through these words." The third question, regarding the power and benefits of the sacrament, emphasizes that the eating and drinking by themselves do not create the benefits, but the words, "Given and shed for you for the forgiveness of sins" (see LC V, 33). He goes on to stress that they, along with the bodily eating and drinking, are the main thing in the Sacrament. "Since this treasure is fully offered in the words, it can be grasped and appropriated only by the heart" (LC V, 36). Finally, regarding worthiness, only faith in the words makes one worthy because the words bring what they say, the forgiveness of sins.

THE EXERCISE OF FAITH IN THE DAILY LIFE OF THE HOUSEHOLD

Whereas the previous section focused on the nourishment of faith within the Christian community through sacraments and selected orders of creation, this next section deals with the exercise of faith within the wider human community, beginning in the household.

Luther provides a section on prayers to frame the daily life of the Christian and a section on orders for living life in the various callings and relationships in life. Together, they embrace the many activities and situations of the Christian's life outside of the divine worship. As seen in chapter one, these sections expressed the catechisms' catholicity as having arisen from the tradition of the church. Here their evangelical character will be explored. Although often overlooked, these texts are integral parts of the catechism as they constitute a Lutheran piety that reflects a new evangelical understanding of the Christian life.

In each instance these parts show how the Gospel reshaped Christian piety after overthrowing the bifurcation of life between the religious life of monks and nuns and the secular life of the laity. "Monasticism, like claims of pietism or spirituality in later generations, implied a division of Christians into the truly spiritual (or *perfecti*) and carnal Christians."[86] Children, parents, outcasts, and the real poor were regarded as second-class Christians, able only in a state of grace to fulfill the Ten Commandments, compared to the "converted" (as the monks were called) and their oblates, whose very vows, Thomas Aquinas had argued, "fulfilled not only the commands but also the counsels of the New Testament."[87] Becoming a monk or nun provided "a holy escape from the drudgery and sinfulness of ordinary" daily life and offered increased opportunities for salvation.

When Luther overthrew the two-fold tier of medieval spiritual life with his teaching on the Gospel, he created a crisis. What would replace the former pattern of piety? And yet, the elimination of this distinction also opened the way for a resacralizing of lay life. Carrying out one's responsibilities in the different walks of life became the most God-pleasing way to serve God. Next to his recovery of the Gospel, this proved to be one of Luther's greatest contributions and most important accomplishments.

DAILY PRAYERS

Luther recognized that people's lives need an order and pattern in which the life of faith can grow, and so he made provision for cultivating a Christian or evangelical piety of daily prayer. He knew that a "formal discipline of prayer provides a "how," a "when," and a "where" for prayer that can cultivate "a habit of mind which will keep our lives turned to God throughout the day, through a lifetime."[88] Luther himself had experienced the value of developing a discipline of daily prayer. He had grown up in a school system that provided such a daily structure. After becoming a monk, the extensive medieval monastic system of prayer shaped his life day in and day out.

The monastic prayer system structured itself according to the *horarum*. These monastic hours split the day into a series of celebrations from Lauds (midnight) through Matins, Prime, Terce, Sext, Nones, Vespers, and Compline. The purpose of these hours was to praise God and meditate on his Word throughout the entire day. As a rule, the laity in the Middle Ages patterned their prayer life on the devotional pattern of these monastic exercises. Generally, they could each participate in their own way. For example, when the bells rang in order to announce the hours, this would make people aware of their recital and allow them to commemorate the hour in some way such as saying the Lord's Prayer.[89] Confessional manuals and prayer books likewise promoted a laicized monastic routine. In doing so, they transferred the ascetic piety of monasticism into the secular world and in doing so promoted a *contemptus mundi* (contempt of the world) through a rigorous introspection and discipline such as one would find in the monastic routine. In other words, in the late Middle Ages, the ideal piety, even for the lay person, was a "clericalized" piety that promoted an introspective conscience.

When the doctrine of faith overthrew the bifurcation of the Christian life into the religious sphere and the secular sphere, the old forms of prayer and piety, modeled as they were on the monastic life, needed to be replaced. In this context, Luther recognized the urgency of cultivating an evangelical discipline of daily prayer among the people in which every day life was once again valued highly. Consequently, the suggestions for prayer, along with the prayers themselves that are provided by Luther are keyed not to the rhythms of life within the monastery, but to the rhythms of everyday life within the household. They are tied to the activities of waking up, eating, and going to bed. These activities provide the structure and setting for habits of meditation on God's Word and praying to take hold. To be sure, the prayers he offers here are not to be considered the only prayers that a Christian speaks. But in a sense they provide the iron rations for a Christian's prayer life to see him or her through the most difficult times of life[90] by being stamped on the Christian's heart through repeated praying.[91] In the process, they can also stimulate the Christian to further praying by keeping the Christian's mind turned to God throughout the day (Second Commandment).

In its full form Luther's house prayers provide something of a liturgy for the home as a "house church." In this "liturgy," he brings the prayers of the Scriptures and its customs of the church's communal worship life into the home itself. From the Scriptures, he incorporates selections from the Psalms as well as the Lord's Prayer and the Creed into all four times of prayer. From the church's liturgy, he incorporates certain practices and customs. For example, the morning and evening prayers open with the Trinitarian invocation and with the Christian making the sign of the cross, thereby recalling Baptism as the basis for prayer. The morning and evening prayers then may be spoken while either kneeling or standing. For the dinner prayers, the members of the household are to "go to the table reverently" and "fold their hands."

The content of the prayers then reflect the different contexts in which they are spoken. It is worth noting that the prayers reflect their respective settings. The morning and evening prayers are spoken in the singular, "I," presupposing the individual praying in the privacy of his or her bedroom. The before- and after-dinner prayers, on the other hand, are spoken in the plural "we." For it is assumed that they are spoken within the context of the family sitting together at the table.

MORNING AND EVENING PRAYERS

Luther's morning and evening prayers bear a striking similarity to one another, particularly in their pattern, their openings, and their conclusions. The central section of each then differs by praying for the particularities appropriate for that time of day. The middle portions are expressed in chiastic form.

> "I thank you my heavenly Father, through Jesus Christ, Your dear Son, that you have
>
> [morning:] kept me this night from all harm and danger; and I pray that you would keep me this day also from sin and every evil, that all my doings and life may please you.
>
> [evening:] graciously kept me this day; and I pray that you would forgive me all my sins where I have done wrong, and graciously keep me this night.
>
> For into your hands I commend myself, my body and soul, and all things. Let your holy angel be with me, that the evil Foe may have no power over me."

The morning prayer proceeds from "kept this night" to "keep me this day"; the evening prayer reverses the order and proceeds from "kept me this day" to "keep me this night." In both cases they cast an eye toward evil and sin, one praying for protection and the other praying for forgiveness. The concluding statements are drawn from the Psalms.[92]

The opening of both prayers expresses confidence in approaching God on the basis of Christ's work. This is apparent already in the invocation in which the Christian says, "under the care of" the Father, Son and Holy Spirit. The central section of each prayer reflects Luther's conviction that prayer places the Christian on the front line in our battle with sin and Satan. This was also reflected in the *Booklet for Laity and Children* (1525), where after reciting the Creed and Lord's Prayer, it recommended that one read something from the Bible and Psalms "that may be used to strengthen your faith against all errors, sins, and assaults." These prayers thus focus on the central concerns of the Christian's life. In addition, neither of these prayers leave a person uncertain or in doubt about God's goodness. They look to God throughout the rest of the day or night.

These prayers had two effects upon the Christian. Morning prayer sends the believer forth to work with joy. Luther recommends saying or singing a hymn on the Ten Commandments which guide Christians in their various relationships during the day. Evening prayer sends the Christian to bed in peace. In other words, don't toss and turn worrying about tomorrow. The *Booklet for Laity and Children* further recommended that one "must get accustomed to recalling whatever one heard or learned during the day from the Holy Scriptures and fall asleep thinking about it."[93] This "confidence was also part of Luther's own praying."[94]

DINNER PRAYERS

The prayer Luther uses prior to asking the blessing before eating confesses the creaturely provision of God. The actual prayer follows the recitation of a passage from Psalm 145:15–16 and Psalm 136:1, 25; 147:9–11. The prayer for blessing and thanksgiving are thus spoken in response to the psalm verses. This approach highlights the Lutheran doctrine of prayer, which must always be regarded as centered on the Word. In other words, prayer arises from the Word, centers on the Word, and is shaped by the Word of God. Into the context of the morning and evening prayers, Luther also integrates the text of the catechism so that the Christian not only implores God's aid and blessing but also give him thanks and meditate upon his Word—in the form of its summary, the catechism.

Luther's dinner prayers emphasize two important facets. First, they stress God's provision and our creaturely need. They thus emphasize that God gives and we receive. Both psalms highlight God's complete provision for our lives. The psalms used for the thanksgiving highlight not only that God gives food to every creature, but that he detests the proud and takes delight in those who fear him and put their hope in him. Second, these texts stress the goodness of God's creation.

Schulz sees one distinctive peculiarity in Luther's blessing. Where the traditional text read, "Bless us and your gifts," Luther renders it as "Bless us and *these* your gifts."[95] In these words one has a blessing not only on the person, but also on the food. Perhaps it ties in with 1 Timothy 4:4–5, "For everything God created is good, and nothing is to be rejected if it is received with thanksgiving, because it is consecrated by the word of God and prayer." This does not mean that the creaturely gifts are given a different character than they had previously, it shows that they become tools in the hands of God to bless us.

TABLE OF CHRISTIAN CALLINGS

With the table of Christian callings or responsibilities, Luther provides an evangelical alternative to medieval piety that was based on ascribing holiness of living to certain structures and not to others. Luther's teaching on faith placed everyone on an equal footing and opened the door for a revaluation of daily life.

In this section he deals with the matter of how Christians live their lives within the human community. In a sense, it fits in very well with the section on prayers. Following the Morning Prayer, Luther exhorts people to go about their work singing a hymn on the Ten Commandments or something along those lines. Now Luther deals with the human community in various situations wherein we work, play, and worship. Together with the section of prayers, it encompasses the totality of a Christian's daily life within the world.

Just as in the previous section where the doctrine of faith erased all distinctions between the prayers of monks and ordinary Christians, so in this section the doctrine of faith overthrows the distinction between the works of the religious orders and the tasks of secular walks of life. Already, Luther signals this shift in the introductory sentence: "A Chart of Some Bible Passages for the Household: Through these verses all kinds of *holy orders* and estates may be admonished, as through lessons particularly pertinent to their office and duty."[96]

Here, Luther has taken the technical term "holy orders," used in the Middle Ages to designate the work of monks and nuns, and applied it to the walks of life or estates of the ordinary Christian, namely, government, church, and especially the household.[97] Thus with the language of "holy orders," Luther fashions a deliberate polemic against medieval theology's view that this applied only to the religious ways of life. Luther's teaching on the two-fold righteousness provides the framework within which he considers the different walks of life. He stresses that being saved and being holy are two entirely different matters. "We are saved through Christ alone; but we become holy both through this faith and through these foundations and orders" (*LW* 37:365). As a result, Luther's holy orders and stations no longer include special religious groups. The passages deal with the duties or obligations of people in their different walks of life. Kolb prefers the term "Responsibilities" to "Duties," which he defines simply as "God's structure for human living." Carrying out those responsibilities is called "obedience."[98] For that reason, this section could be called a "Household Chart of Christian Callings."

In the Table of Christian Callings, Luther shows that God so designed human life that we meet one another through various structures (or estates or orders). As Christians live their lives in the day-to-day world, they find themselves in a world divided between household and work, society and government, church and school.[99] This division was common in medieval thinking (those who fight, those who pray, and those who work). Often, medieval thought valued the sacred (clergy) over the secular (commoners and nobles). Rather than placing the three estates within a hierarchy of sacred-secular, Luther places it into framework of two governments. Kolb notes that where "household" included family and economic activities in Luther's day, we, as heirs of the industrial revolution, must speak of four situations: home, occupation, society, and congregation. "Society" may be further subdivided into 1) formal societal structures that include the political arenas of life, and 2) informal societal structures that include the relationships in neighborhood and friendships. In the Large Catechism, Luther identified the home as the most basic of life's structures from which the other two arise. In his Table of Christian Callings, Luther begins with the church, proceeds to the earthly authorities, and concludes with the household—to which he devotes the most space and gives the greatest treatment.

The Christian's responsibilities within these structures are determined by virtue of his or her relationship to others. The structure proceeds from ecclesiastical authorities to earthly authorities to family (which includes the economic order). Within these three estates, Luther discusses eleven groups of people, nine of which are related to the household. Luther's order proceeded: "To Bishops, Pastors, and Preachers," "On Worldly Authority [magistrates]," "To Husbands," To Wives," "To Parents," "To Children," "To Workers of All Kinds [maids, day laborers]," "To Employers and Supervisors [masters and mistresses of households]," "To Youth," "To Widows," "To Everyone [the community as a whole (*Gemeine*)]."[100] The third and central compilation of texts addresses the individual stations within the family and economic order. Luther takes the various responsibilities and people involved in these three estates from five "tables" or "listings" that he finds in the New Testament itself: Col 3:18–4:1; Eph 5:22–6:9; 1 Tim 2:3–15; 6:1–2; Titus 2:1–10; 1 Peter 2:13–3:7.[101] Peters concludes that Luther's "deliberately intentional and cautiously worked out structure ... forms from the biblical material an 'original portion of a Catechism with a genuine Lutheran stamp.' "[102]

Finally, Luther refers to a "fourth" estate or situation that encompasses all the others and transcends them, namely the "common order of Christian love." It serves the neighbor not only within the three orders, "but also serves every needy person in general with all kinds of benevolent deeds, such as feeding the hungry, giving drink to the thirsty, forgiving enemies, praying for all men on earth, suffering all kinds of evil on earth, etc." (*LW* 37:365). Peters notes that the relation between the all-absorbing order of Christian love and the three specific divine stations, or between our proper Christian station and the distant offices and station parallels the relationship of the two tables, that is, the First Commandment and all the other commandments. Just as the First Commandment runs through all the other commandments and holds them together, so also Christian love permeates and penetrates all of the other orders and holds them together. Luther concludes, "Let each his lesson learn with care, and all the household well shall fare."

The Table of Duties forms a companion piece to the Decalogue, especially to the Fourth and Sixth Commandments. The Fourth and Sixth Commandments emphasize the work of marriage and the family and then picked up the personal responsibility of these within the three orders. Instead of presenting general commands for human living, the Table of Christian Callings "describes and prescribes actions appropriate for God's horizontal government of our lives" within "God's scheme or form for human life."[103] It brings us full circle back to the Ten Commandments. "Thus the Table of Duties refers to the Decalogue after the Creed and the Our Father and thereby unifies the Catechism. It develops the lived-out love of the Christian faith and moves the created community to live in the light of the "practical use of the Gospel."[104]

MARRIAGE AND BAPTISMAL BOOKLETS

Like the previous two sections, these two services have a direct bearing on the household. In a sense, these two services "defined the house church itself." The one was created by God's "left hand through marriage" and the other by God's "right hand through Holy Baptism."[105] The *Marriage Booklet* looks forward to the establishment of the household. Thus its service deals with the household in relation to God's creation. The *Baptism Booklet* anticipates the reception of individual members of the household into the household of faith. As in the others, Luther stresses their value over and against the humanly devised vows of monasticism.

MARRIAGE BOOKLET

Luther and the other reformers of the sixteenth century transferred "the accolades Christian tradition had since antiquity heaped on the religious in monasteries and nunneries to marriage and the home."[106] In the preface to the *Marriage Booklet*, Luther contrasts the marriage estate with the monastic estate:

Because up to now people have made such a big display at the consecration of monks and nuns (even though their estate and existence is an ungodly, human invention without any basis in the Bible) how much more should we honor this godly estate of marriage and bless it, pray for it, and adorn it in an even more glorious manner. For, although it is a worldly estate, nevertheless it has God's Word on its side and is not a human invention or institution, like the estate of monks and nuns. Therefore it should easily be reckoned a hundred times more spiritual than the monastic estate, which certainly ought to be considered the most worldly and fleshly of all, because it was invented and instituted by flesh and blood and completely out of worldly understanding and reason.[107]

On account of the Word, Luther speaks of marriage as a blessed estate created by God (LC I, 208–9). Elsewhere, he praises it as a godly and blessed, honorable and necessary estate, pleasant and blessed before God. For Luther, marriage was the best forum for exercising faith.

This is not to say that marriage is a purely Christian institution. In the introduction of the *Marriage Booklet*, Luther indicates that although the church ought to bless it when asked to do so, it is in its origin a secular or "worldly matter." In his writing, "About Marital Matters," he calls it an outward worldly thing … just as clothing and food, house and homestead. For Luther, marriage belonged in the First Article as God's creation. The worldly character of marriage is taken into account by Luther in the opening lines of his Marriage Booklet when he exhorts pastors to avoid issuing directives concerning it. Instead, they should allow each city and territory to follow the customs that they already have in place. With regard to changes in these customs, Luther again advises that pastors should leave it to the princes and town councils to arrange things as they wish.

Those couples who desired the prayers and blessing of the church "indicate thereby—whether or not they say so expressly—to what danger and need they were exposing themselves.[108] They show thereby how much they need God's blessing and the church's prayers since the devil daily causes so much unhappiness in marriage through unfaithfulness, adultery, and discord. Luther's rite for these couples was divided into three distinct but related actions. First came the publication of the banns from the pulpit with the request that should anyone object they speak up. Second, the actual act of matrimony, vows, the exchange of rings, and the pronouncement of marriage took place outside the doors of the church in line with the ancient custom. It witnessed to the worldly nature of marriage. Third, they move inside the church and, standing before the altar, the pastor reads several pertinent Bible passages about marriage and the roles of husband and wife in marriage. Finally, the pastor lays his hands upon the newly-married couple and prays for God's blessing on them.

BAPTISMAL BOOKLET

Baptism had been a relatively neglected sacrament in late medieval theology, having been overshadowed by the sacrament of penance. Luther restored Baptism to a central position by linking it to Christ's death and resurrection. As a result, Baptism came to be viewed by Luther as the sacrament of justification *par excellence*. It also became the great equalizer of Christians so that even "age no longer divides them."[109] This also eliminated the distinction among different groups of Christians and provided Luther with an important critique of monasticism.

In his sermon on Baptism (1519), Luther denied that the vows of chastity, of the priesthood, or of the clergy were more significant or higher than Baptism. Baptism thus became the basis for Luther's teaching on vocation. "For in Baptism we all make one and the same vow: to slay sin and to become holy through the work and grace of God, to whom we yield and offer ourselves, as clay to the potter. In this no one is better than another" (*LW* 35:41). These themes occur in strong colors in the Baptismal booklet.

Of some interest are the benefits of Baptism that Luther highlights in the *Taufbüchlein*. He emphasizes the reception of a person into the life of the church as an enlistment into a lifelong battle against Satan.

> For here in the words of these prayers you hear how plaintively and earnestly the Christian church brings the infant to God, confesses before him with such unchanging, undoubting words that the infant is possessed by the devil and a child of sin and wrath and so diligently asks for help and grace through Baptism, that the infant may become a child of God.

> Therefore, you need to consider that it is no joke at all to take action against the devil and not only drive him away from the little child but also hang around its neck such a mighty, lifelong enemy. Thus it is extremely necessary to stand by the poor child with all your heart and with a strong faith and to be pleased with great devotion that God, in accordance with these prayers, would not only free the child from the devil's power but also strengthen the child, so that the child might resist him like a fighter in life and in death. I fear that people turn out so badly after Baptism because we have dealt with them in such a cold and casual way and have prayed for them at their Baptism without any zeal at all.

> He himself calls it a "new birth," through which we, being freed from the devil's tyranny and loosed from sin, death, and hell, become children of life, heirs of all God's possessions, God's own children, and brothers and sisters of Christ.

> Ah, dear Christians, let us not value and treat this unspeakable gift so half-heartedly. For Baptism is our only comfort and doorway to all of God's possessions and to the communion of all the saints. To this end may God help us. Amen.[110]

While Luther received and used the Roman rite of Baptism, he revised it and removed all that obscured the true glory of Baptism, namely, death and resurrection, that is, full and complete justification. "This, for Luther, was the 'glory of Baptism' which careless authors had obscured in the Medieval Liturgy."[111] His concern was to give "liturgical expression to the theology of Baptism as the sacrament of salvation. His criterion was theology, or the Word of God. The 1523 version initially made few changes. It involved: 1) Luther retained features that added nothing to Baptism or were of no importance to Baptism[112] in order to avoid offending sensitive consciences. 2) He emphasized those features that were an integral part of the Baptismal liturgy such as the vows, and Creed, immersion in the water for dying and rising, and the Trinitarian formula conveying the forgiveness of sins. 3) Finally, he omitted or changed certain features to make clear the glory of Baptism. These included the exorcism of salt, the blessing of water,[113] and making a distinction between male and female children. He also substituted the "Flood Prayer" for the prayer "God of our Fathers." The 1526 version was revised more significantly. Its most striking feature lies in "the omission of most of the ceremonies which 'men have added to embellish Baptism.' "[114]

CONCLUSION

The simplicity of the Small Catechism's language and the brevity of its words may initially conceal from the catechumen the profound world of thought that lies within. Like a small inlet of water that leads to the ocean, so Luther's catechism opens up an entire world of biblical thought. The doctrine of faith, far from being an isolated teaching limited to the article on salvation, provides the key for centering the Christian life upon all the gifts of God in every sphere of human life. In doing so, it becomes the narrative theme of Christian existence and living.

NOTES

1   Luther pointedly notes, however, that this heritage had rarely been taught and treated correctly (LC Short Preface, 6).

2   See debate over the success and nature of Lutheran catechizing begun with Gerald Strauss' *Luther's House of Learning: Indoctrination of the Young in the German Reformation* (Baltimore: John Hopkins University Press, 1978). For responses see James M. Kittelson, "Success and Failures in the German Reformation: The Report from Strasbourg," *Archiv für Reformationsgeschichte* 73 (1982): 153–74, and Scott H. Hendrix, "Luther's Impact on the Sixteenth Century," *The Sixteenth Century Journal* 16 (1985): 3–14.

3   Janz, *Three Reformation Catechisms*, 4.

4   Herbert Girgensohn, *Teaching Luther's Catechism*, Vol. 1 (Philadelphia: Muhlen-berg, 1959), 1.

5   Peters I, 16–17.

6   Martin Marty, "Future of Catechism," *Currents in Theology and Mission*, 1994, 330–31.

7   One could make an argument for *Luther's Great Confession* (1528), the *Smalcald Articles* (1537), or *Exposition of the Three Creeds* (1538). See William R. Russell, *The Schmalkald Articles: Luther's Theological Testament* (Minneapolis: Fortress, 1994).

8   A paradigm is the conceptual framework, presuppositions, or underlying pillars of a person's view of the world so firmly in place that a person doesn't have to think about it. The catechism is an excellent summary of the paradigm shift that took place in the Reformation.

9   Ozment, *Age of Reform*, 242.

10 Janz, *Three Reformation Catechisms*, 127.

11 Ozment notes that Luther was criticized for permitting "a foul and dirty bride to enter spiritual matrimony with Christ. When faith and trust alone are the agents of union, righteousness and iniquity intermingle and embrace. The man who is still *peccator in re* becomes one with Christ." Steven E. Ozment, "*Homo Viator*: Luther and Late Medieval Theology," in *The Reformation in Medieval Perspective* (ed. with introduction by Steven E. Ozment; Chicago: Quadrangle Books, 1971), 151.

12 Carter Lindberg, *The European Reformations* (Cambridge, Mass.: Blackwell Publishers, 1996), 63.

13 Friedemann Hebart, "Introduction," *Luther's Large Catechism: Anniversary Translation and Introductory Essay* (Adelaide: Lutheran Publishing House, 1983).

14 Martin Marty, *The Hidden Discipline* (St. Louis: Concordia, 1962), xv.

15 Hebart, "Introduction," xxiv.

16 In his Third Sermon Series (1528) Luther weaves the two words, "fear and trust" through each explanation of the commandments.

17 Luther's explanations in the Lord's Prayer do not seem entirely original to him. The Weißenberg Catechism uses similar language and bear an uncanny resemblance to Luther's explanation.

18 Luther here does not use the words "*Im Namen…*" but "*Das walte Gott Vater, Sohn und Heiliger Geist, Amen*" See Wengert's, *A Contemporary Translation*, 51–53.

19 Brecht, II, 177.

20 Quoted in Ozment, *Reformation in the Cities*, 30.

21 Wengert, *A Contemporary Translation*, 57.

22 Wengert, *A Contemporary Translation*, 42. It is generally seen here that Luther took his cue from John Gerson's *Tractus de modo vivendi omnium fidelium* ("Tract on the way of living for all the faithful") or at least he had precedent for including such a piece.

23 Ozment, *Reformation in the Cities*, 156.

24 Albrecht Peters, *Kommentar zu Luthers Katechismen: Band 1: Die Zehn Gebote* (Göttingen: Vandehoeck & Ruprecht, 1990), 8.

25 See Gustav Wingren's classic discussion of the relationship between an ontological versus an epistemological approach to theology as determined by whether or not one begins with the First Article or the Second Article of the Creed, *Creation and Law* (tr. Ross Mackenzie; Edinburgh: Oliver and Boyd, 1961).

26 See Luther's treatment of the Ten Commandments as natural Law in *Against the Heavenly Prophets* and *How Christians Should Regard Moses*.

27 Robert A. Kolb, *Teaching God's Children His Teaching: A Guide for the Study of Luther's Catechism* (Hutchinson, Minn.: Crown Publishing, 1992), 3–1.

28 Paul Lehmann, "The Commandments and the Common Life," *Interpretation* 34 (1980): 343.

29 James Arne Nestingen, "Preaching the Catechism," *Word and World* 10, 1 (Winter 1990): 36.

30 Kolb, *Teaching God's Children His Teaching*, 2–2, 2–3.

31 This recalls Augustine's famous statement, in his Confessions, "Thou has made us for thyself, and our hearts are restless until they find rest in thee, O Lord." This need not be read so much as a synergistic statement as simply a description of the core of our humanity as created by God.

32 Kolb, *Teaching God's Children His Teaching*, 2–3.

33 Mildenberger, *Theology of the Lutheran Confessions* (tr. Erwin L. Lueker; Philadelphia: Fortress, 1986), 144.

34 See Charles P. Arand, "Luther on the God behind the First Commandment," *Lutheran Quarterly* 8 (Winter 1994): 397–424.

35 Mildenberger, *Theology of the Lutheran Confessions*, 144.

36 Robert Kolb, " 'That I May Be His Own': The Anthropology of Luther's Explanation to the Creed," *Concordia Journal* 21 (January 1995): 28–41.

37 Commandments Two through Nine are in a sense nine commentaries on the First Commandment.

38 Kolb, *Teaching God's Children His Teaching*, 3–1.

39 Friedrich Mildenberg, *Theology of the Lutheran Confessions*, 144.

40 Large Catechism I, 91, 99.

41 Mildenberg, *Theology of the Lutheran Confessions*, 146.

42 Kolb, *Teaching God's Children His Teaching*, 3–2.

43 Kolb, *Teaching God's Children His Teaching*, 3–2.

44 Lehmann, "The Commandments and the Common Life," 355.

45 Nestingen, "Preaching the Catechism," 36.

46 Kolb, *Teaching God's Children His Teaching*, 2–10.

47 Mildenberger, *Theology of the Lutheran Confessions*, 143.

48 Nestingen, "Preaching the Catechism," 41.

49 Kolb, " 'That I May Be His Own': The Anthropology of Luther's Explanation of the Creed," *Concordia Journal* 21 (January 1995): 29.

50 Nestingen, "Preaching the Catechism," 41.

51 Kolb, " 'That I May Be His Own': The Anthropology of Luther's Explanation to the Creed," 29.

52 Nestingen, "Preaching the Catechism," 41.

53 Michael Beintker, "Das Schöpfercredo in Luthers Kleinem Katechismus," *Neue Zeitschrift für Religionsphilosophie* 31 (January 1989): 16.

54 Beintker, "Das Schöpfercredo in Luthers Kleinem Katechismus," 6.

55 Kolb, "'That I May Be His Own': The Anthropology of Luther's Explanation to the Creed," 32.

56 Large Catechism II 26, 27, 31.

57 In general, Luther discussed the matter of sin more in connection with the Second Article than with the First Article. For example, See his *Great Confession of 1528*. While he makes reference to God protecting us from all danger in the First Article and thus alludes to evil, it focuses more on external intrusions that can deprive us what God has given than on personal guilt or sin.

58 Nestingen, "Preaching the Catechism," 41.

59 Reiner Jansen, *Studien zu Luthers Trinitätslehre* (Frankfurt/M.: Peter Lang, 1976), 16.

60 Kolb, "'That I May Be His Own': The Anthropology of Luther's Explanation to the Creed," 36.

61 Nestingen, "The Catechism's *Simul*," *Word and World* 3 (Fall 1983): 366.

62 Ted Peters, *God—The World's Future* (Minneapolis: Fortress, 1992), 230.

63 Jonathan D. Trigg, *Baptism in the Theology of Martin Luther* (Leiden: E. J. Brill, 1994), 177.

64 Heinrich Bornkamm, *Luther in Mid-Career, 1521–1530* (tr. E. Theodore Bachmann; Philadelphia: Fortress Press, 1983), 599.

65 Charles P. Arand, "The Lord's Prayer in Luther's Catechisms: The Battle Cry of Faith," *Concordia Journal* 21 (January 1995): 42–65.

66 Eilert Herms, *Luthers Auslegung des Dritten Artikels*, 14.

67 C. S. Lewis has captured this well in his *Screwtape Letters*.

68 Nestingen, "Preaching the Catechism," 40.

69 "God's name is certainly holy in itself; the kingdom of God certainly comes by itself without our prayer; the good and gracious will of God is done even without our prayer; and God certainly gives daily bread to everyone without our prayers, even to all evil people...." In the Large Catechism, Luther continues this theme into the fifth petition, "Not that God does not forgive sin even without and before our prayer; he gave us the Gospel, in which there is nothing but forgiveness, before we prayed or even thought of it" (LC III, 89). These blessings are not dependent upon our prayers.

70 So we pray that God's name may be kept holy among us; that the kingdom of God may come to us also; that his will be done among us also; and most importantly and clearly, "that God would lead us to realize this and to receive our daily bread with thanksgiving."

71 Kolb, *Teaching God's Children His Teaching*, 5–4.

72 Albrecht Peters, "Die Vaterunser—Auslegung in Luthers Katechismen," *Lutherische Theologie und Kirche* 3 (1979): 76–78. See *Anfechtung*. See also Large Catechism III, 30.

73 Wengert, *A Contemporary Translation*, 34.

74   Timothy J. Wengert, "Luther on Children: Baptism and the Fourth Commandment," *Dialog* 37 (Summer 1998): 186.

75   Wengert, "Luther on Children," 186.

76   Wengert, "Luther on Children," 186–87.

77   "The priest, bishop, [and] pope are only servants who hold out to you Christ's word on which you should rely with a solid faith, as if on a solid rock. … For this reason, too, the word is not to be honored on account of the priest, bishop, [or] pope but rather the priest, bishop, [or] pope [is to be honored] on account of the word, as those who bring you the word and tidings of your God that you are freed from sins" (St. Louis edition, 1:249).

78   Brecht, II, 19–20.

79   Edwards, *Printing, Propaganda, and Martin Luther*, 188, note 48.

80   Nevertheless, confession remained a necessary precondition for communion in Lutheran churches and in fact virtually never took place without the Eucharist following. The two were closely intertwined, no confession without communion and no communion without confession. On the Saturday before communion, the pastor would ask about knowledge of the catechism and then confession. Myers, *Poor, Sinning Folk*, 67.

81   Martin Luther, "An Open Letter to Those in Frankfurt on the Main, 1533," tr. Jon D. Vieker, *Concordia Journal* (October 1990): 343.

82   Martin Luther, "The Lord's Supper: On the Real Presence," *The 1529 Holy Week and Easter Sermons of Dr. Martin Luther* (St. Louis: Concordia, 1997), 46.

83   Timothy J. Wengert, "Luther's Catechisms and the Lord's Supper," *Word and World* 17 (Winter 1997):54–55

84   Wengert, "Luther's Catechisms and the Lord's Supper," 55.

85   Wengert, "Luther's Catechisms and the Lord's Supper," 55.

86   Timothy J. Wengert, "Luther on Children: Baptism and the Fourth Commandment," *Dialog* 37 (Summer 1998): 187.

87   Wengert, "Luther on Children: Baptism and the Fourth Commandment," 187.

88   Kolb, *Teaching God's Children His Teaching*, 7–3.

89   See R. N. Swanson, *Religion and Devotion in Europe, c. 1215–c. 1515* (Cambridge, England: Cambridge University Press, 1995), 93.

90   Peters, III, 204.

91   Peters, III, 191. In the superscription, Luther's exhortation to the head of the household shows that the house prayers should serve as stamped and repeated texts for training in daily prayer.

92   For example, "Into your hands I commend myself, my body and soul and all things," could be taken directly from the Psalms, particularly, Ps 31:6 "Into your hands I commit my spirit"; Ps 91:11, "For he will command his angels concerning you to guard you in all your ways"; and Ps. 34:8, "blessed is the man who takes refuge in him." While the Psalms do not speak directly of an old evil foe, Mt 13:28ff would be good place to start.

93   See forthcoming Source Book for the *Book of Concord* from Fortress.

94   Brecht, II, 177.

95   As quoted in Peters, V, 202.

96 Wengert, *A Contemporary Translation*, 57.

97 Wengert, *A Contemporary Translation*, 42. It is generally seen here that Luther took his cue from John Gerson's *Tractus de modo vivendi omnium fidelium* ("Tract on the way of living for all the faithful") or at least he had precedent for including such a piece.

98 Kolb, *Teaching God's Children His Teaching*, 8–4.

99 Wengert, "Luther on Children: Baptism and the Fourth Commandment," 187.

100 Two other groupings, "That which Christians should responsibly do for their teachers and pastors" and "That which the subjects owe to the authorities," were not originally included. They are distinguished from the others in 1) their lengthy title; 2) the haphazard collection of Bible passages. They also interrupt the flow. They ascribe unmarried women to the domestic sphere.

101 This was not the first time that Luther worked on such a such a Table of Responsibilities. Already in his prayer booklet of 1522 he had begun such a project. There he pointed his readers toward Paul's Letter to Titus in order "to give instruction for living a Christian life." In the "first chapter he found guidelines for 'what kind of a person a bishop or pastor should be,' in the second for 'persons in all situations of life—the young and the old, women and men, masters and servants,' in the third for conduct toward governmental authorities.'" More immediately, he had addressed the issue again in his *Great Confession* of 1528.

102 Peters, V, 104.

103 Kolb, *Teaching God's Children His Teaching*, 8–2.

104 Peters, V, 98.

105 Wengert, *A Contemporary Translation*, 44.

106 Ozment, *Protestants*, 153.

107 Wengert, *A Contemporary Translation*, 62. Already in 1519 in his sermon on marriage Luther insisted that people could do no better for themselves or Christendom than raise their children well (Edwards, 47). "There is nothing in pilgrimages to Rome, to Jerusalem, or to Saint James [Compostela], nothing in building churches, endowing masses, or whatever works might be named compared to this one work, [namely] that those who are married bring up their children [well]. That is their straightest road to heaven. Indeed, heaven could not be nearer or better achieved than through this work" (WA 2:169–70).

108 See Brecht, II, 258.

109 Wengert, "Luther on Children: Baptism and the Fourth Commandment," 186.

110 Wengert, *A Contemporary Translation*, 68.

111 Spinks, Brian, "Luther's Taufbüchlein," *Liturgical Review* (May 1996): 14.

112 For example, breathing under the eyes, signing with the cross, placing salt in the mouth, putting spittle and clay on the ears and nose, anointing with oil, vesting in the christening robe, giving a burning candle into the hand, etc.

113 In a Sermon at the Baptism of Berhard von Anhalt, 1540, Luther dismissed the idea of blessing the water: "For example, the magicians, witches, and weather prophets also employ a sign or creature, such as a root or herb, and speak over it the Lord's Prayer or some other holy word and name of God. This they say is not an evil thing but rather both: a creation of God and precious words and holy names; therefore it should possess power and accomplish what it is used for; just as the Pope also juggles and conjures with his chrism, holy water, and salt.… Do

you too have a word and command of God which says you should consecrate salt or water and speak such words over them?" Quoted in Spinks, "Luther's *Taufbüchlein*" (May 1996): 16.

114 Spinks lists among other items the exsufflation and the first of the two opening prayers, the giving of salt, the first of two exorcisms, the prayer after the exorcism, the Effeta, the two anointings before and after Baptism on the placing of a lighted candle into the child's hand." Spinks, "Luther's *Taufbüchlein*," 20. See "Baptismal Booklet," par. 5 in *The Book of Concord*, ed. Kolb-Wengert.

APPENDIX A

TEXTS AND EDITIONS
OF THE SMALL CATECHISM

The following provides a brief overview of the changes that the Small Catechism underwent in the months and years immediately following its initial publication. New additions to each printing following the chart edition of January and March in 1529 are highlighted in italics.

1529, JANUARY AND MARCH
CHART EDITION

Luther's catechism work first appeared in January 1529. Each section was printed on large sheets of paper, to be sold like newspapers and hung up in churches, schools, and homes.[1] During the first week of 1529 these catechetical charts contained the three chief parts with explanations. The other parts appeared shortly thereafter (WA 30:I, 243ff.).

- Ten Commandments
- Creed
- Lord's Prayer
- Baptism
- Lord's Supper
- Morning and Evening Prayers
- Benedicte and Gratias

1529, MAY 16

Following is Luther's High German Wittenberg Book Edition, the original of which is lost. Title: *Der Kleine Catechismus für die gemeyne Pfarherr und Prediger.*[2]

- *Preface to Pastors and Teachers*
- Ten Commandments
- Creed

- Lord's Prayer
- Baptism
- Lord's Supper
- Morning and Evening Prayers
- Benedicte and Gratias
- *Table of Responsibilities*
- *Marriage Booklet*

1529, JUNE 13

On June 13, 1529, the Small Catechism was published in an enlarged and revised Wittenberg edition. It is the first high German edition. Title: *Der kleine Catechismus für die gemeine Pfarher und Prediger.*[3]

- Preface to Pastors and Teachers
- Ten Commandments
- Creed
- Lord's Prayer
- Baptism
- Lord's Supper
- Morning and Evening Prayers
- Benedicte and Gratias
- Table of Responsibilities
- Marriage Booklet
- *Baptismal Booklet*
- *Short Form of Confession*
- *German Litany with Music*
- *Three Collects*
- *20 Illustrations*

At this point, the word "Enchiridion" (or "Little Handbook") appeared on the title page. Reu suggests that this was due to the addition of several liturgical forms which meant that the little book was growing into the size of a pastoral manual. With the addition of these liturgical elements, Luther hoped to bring about an intelligent appreciation and active participation in the various services of the church. "In fact, during the sixteenth century, the Small Catechism largely served the purpose of a 'church book' that was taken along when people went to church as today they take the hymnbook."[4] At times Psalm 111 was added, which was sung at the Lord's

Supper; the Te Deum, the Magnificat, and the Prayer against the Turk ("Lord Keep Us Steadfast in Thy Word").

1531 WITTENBERG EDITION

The last edition of the Small Catechism prepared by Luther for the printer appeared in 1531 under the title: *Enchiridion: The Small Catechism for Ordinary Pastors and Preachers.* In addition to the parts of the previous two editions, it contained several new features: an introduction to the Lord's Prayer; an explanation of the "Amen" of the Lord's Prayer; three questions on confession; a form for private confession; and twenty-three woodcuts. Title: *Enchiridion. Der kleine Catechismus für die gemeine Pfarher und Prediger.*[5]

- Preface to Pastors and Teachers
- Ten Commandments
- Creed
- Lord's Prayer
- *Introduction to the Lord's Prayer with its beautiful exposition.*
- *Introduction to the "Amen." No edition had a doxology.*
- Baptism
- *Confession: Wie man die Einfaeltigen soll lehren beichten.*
  1. *What is confession;*
  2. *What sins should we confess;*
  3. *Which are these?*
  Form of Private Confession.
- Lord's Supper
- Morning and Evening Prayers
- Benedicte and Gratias
- Table of Responsibilities
- Marriage Booklet
- Baptismal Booklet
- Short Form of Confession?
- German Litany with music
- Three Collects
- *23 Woodcuts*

1546 AND LATER EDITIONS

Following Luther's death in 1546, two additional elements found their way in and settled into the Small Catechism as used by churches from the Saxon tradition. This includes the Missouri Synod. These texts are:

1) Office of the Keys. No such part exists in any of the editions during Luther's lifetime nor does it appear that the materials originated with him. It does, however, reflect his teaching in a treatise on "The Keys" (*LW* 40:321–77) that appeared in 1530.[6]

2) Christian Questions for Those Who Want to Receive the Lord's Supper. They appear for the first time in a separate Erfurt edition of 1549. In Luther's Small Catechism we find them for the first time in an undated Wittenberg edition (1551–1566). Reu believed that Dr. Lange of Erfurt (died in 1548) was their author.[7]

LATIN TRANSLATIONS AND EDITIONS

Two Latin translations appeared in 1529. The one that became *the* Latin translation in Germany was that made by Johannes Sauermann. Intended for the Latin schools. The title is changed and Luther's preface is left out. Headings are changed from addressing the head of the household to addressing the teachers.[8] The text that appeared in the *Book of Concord* of 1584 is based on Sauermann.

NOTES

1   These sheets themselves carried over from the 15th century; see John W. Constable, "Sixteenth Century Catechisms: Their Genesis and Genius," in *Teaching the Faith: Luther's Catechisms in Perspective* (ed. Carl Volz; River Forest, Ill.: Lutheran Educational Association, 1967), 21.

2   Reu, Johann Michael, *Dr. Martin Luther's Small Catechism: A History of its Origin, Its Distribution and its Use* (Chicago: Wartburg, 1929), 26–28.

3   Ten on the Decalogue; three on the Creed; and seven on the Lord's Prayer. See Reu, *Dr. Martin Luther's Small Catechism*, 28–31.

4   Reu, *Dr. Martin Luther's Small Catechism*, 30.

5   Reu, *Dr. Martin Luther's Small Catechism*, 30–33.

6   Reu, *Dr. Martin Luther's Small Catechism*, 39.

7   See Reu, *Dr. Martin Luther's Small Catechism*, 44–45.

8   Reu, *Dr. Martin Luther's Small Catechism*, 50ff.

APPENDIX B

ABBREVIATED TEXT
OF THE TEN COMMANDMENTS

Questions are often raised by children and adults alike about the text of the Ten Commandments as used by Luther in the Small Catechism. In particular they arise because Luther's text of the Ten Commandments appears to be somewhat truncated in the Small Catechism. Thus, over the years, some church bodies have often replaced Luther's text with the full text of the Ten Commandments in a modern biblical translation while others have remained with Luther's text.

In the tradition that Luther adopted, the first four commandments were usually presented in an abbreviated form. Thus he did not include with the First Commandment the prologue "I am the Lord your God who led you out of Egypt." At most, he would use the first half of the phrase, "I am the Lord your God" but not the second half "who led you out of Egypt."[1] Similarly, in the First Commandment, "You shall have no other gods before me" Luther omitted in his text the phrase "before me." Similarly, he did not include the verses from Exodus 20, which give the command not to make graven images. In the Second Commandment, he omits the phrase "the Lord" from "you shall not take not the name of *the Lord* your God in vain" (italics added). Also, Luther did not include the threat attached to the Second Commandment (Ex 20:7). The Third Commandment likewise does not include the full complement of verses (Ex 20:8–11). The same thing applies to the Fourth Commandment, in which the promise is not included (although Luther does adapt it for use in the Large Catechism).

So the question is: why did Luther not use the full biblical text of the Ten Commandments? Johannes Meyer provides an explanation: "[Luther] used the traditional abbreviated memory text of the Ten Commandments where possible because it was familiar to everyone. Luther was aware of others using the full text, but he chose not to follow the purist principle of the Bohemian Brethren, who quoted the entire biblical text of the Decalogue as 'God had spoken it to Moses'" (*LW* 43:15).[2]

Here and there, however, Luther did make slight adjustments to the biblical text over and against the tradition. For example, he went with "other gods" instead of "strange gods" in the First Commandment. He went with the word "sanctify" in the Third Commandment instead of "remember." Similarly, he rendered "Sabbath" as "day of rest" (*Feiertag*). These were usually done for well thought-out theological and hermeneutical reasons.[3]

NOTES

1 See Arand, "The God Behind the First Commandment" for a discussion of this feature.

2 See Meyer, 88.

3 See Meyer, 89ff.

APPENDIX C

NUMBERING OF THE TEN COMMANDMENTS

One of the most immediately recognizable features of Luther's catechisms (at least in a culture shaped by American Evangelicalism) and an issue that often arises among theological students has to do with the numbering of the Ten Commandments. More specifically, which numbering is correct? The problem arises because the Bible indicates that there are Ten Commandments or Words (Ex 34:28, Deut. 4:13, and Deut 10:4). Yet if one counts them in Exodus 20:2–17 or Deuteronomy 5:6–21, one will probably arrive at more than ten, at least eleven and perhaps as many as twelve commandments. This then raises the question, which Ten Commandments did Moses have in mind? Put another way, how do we get twelve into ten?

Within the history of the Christian church, there have been three main ways.[1] Relying in part on the work of Bo Reicke, James Voelz has provided a most helpful summary that can be schematized according to the following table:

MASORETIC– ROMAN CATHOLIC– LUTHERAN TRADITIONS	HELLENISTIC JUDAISM– EASTERN ORTHODOXY– REFORMED TRADITIONS	JEWISH RABBIS
Prologue	Prologue	1) Prologue
1) No other gods	1) No other gods	2) No other gods
Graven Images	2) Graven Images	Graven Images
2) God's Name	3) God's Name	3) God's Name
3) Sabbath	4) Sabbath	4) Sabbath
4) Parents	5) Parents	5) Parents
5) Killing	6) Killing	6) Killing
6) Adultery	7) Adultery	7) Adultery
7) Theft	8) Theft	8) Theft
8) Reputation	9) Reputation	9) Reputation
9) Coveting	10) Coveting	10) Coveting
10) Coveting	Coveting	Coveting

Of those three traditions, Lutheranism followed the western catholic tradition. While this was certainly in line with its conservative and catholic character, it was supported with several theological reasons.

As can be seen, The Lutheran-Catholic tradition from the time of Augustine combined the commands regarding "other gods" and "graven images" in the First Commandment. This in turn required them to distinguish between the commands regarding coveting (the Ninth and Tenth Commandments, whose order is switched in Exodus and Deuteronomy). Conversely, the Reformed-Orthodox traditions (including Hellenistic Judaism, Philo, and Josephus) from the time of Irenaeus made a distinction between the command to have no other gods and the prohibition against making graven images. Finally, the Jewish Rabbis followed their own system which essentially combined the other two systems. For them, the introduction or prologue was understood as the First Commandment and separated from the rest. The commandments against false gods and image making were combined as in the Masoritic and Western tradition to form the Second Commandment. The Tenth Commandment was taken in the tradition of Hellenistic Judaism and the East.[2] Of the three approaches, it has been the least influential in Christendom, either in the East or in the West.

The entire question on numbering really revolves around the prohibition against graven images.[3] Once it has been dealt with, everything else falls into place. It is worth noting, however, the approaches to this commandment reveal not only how the graven images command was explicated, but they also reveal an underlying approach to the entire Bible.[4]

Generally the Western tradition regarded the prohibition to make graven images as a further explanation of the command to have no other gods. In the Reformed tradition, the First Commandment deals with false gods while the prohibition against graven images latter deals with false ways to worship the *true* God. In other words, according to this approach, it pertains to the *true God* and how he is or is not to be portrayed and worshipped. This then allowed them to combine the commands against coveting. Luther's basic approach to Scripture itself differs. Among other things, it included a hermeneutic that rooted the Ten Commandments in natural law, thus making the Mosaic legislation valuable "for pedagogical purposes … because it is a clear expression of natural law."[5] Furthermore, Luther saw that the "Old Testament commandment against idol forms and likenesses has no such congruence" in the New Testament.[6]

NOTES

1 James W. Voelz , "Luther's Use of Scripture in the Small Catechism," in *Luther's Catechisms—450 Years: Essays Commemorating the Small and Large Catechisms of Dr. Martin Luther* (ed. David P. Scaer and Robert D. Preus; Fort Wayne, Ind.: Concordia Theological Seminary Press, 1979), 55–64.

2 Voelz, "Luther's Use of Scripture in the Small Catechism," 58.

3 Voelz, "Luther's Use of Scripture in the Small Catechism," 58.

4 Voelz, "Luther's Use of Scripture in the Small Catechism," 60–61.

5 Voelz, "Luther's Use of Scripture in the Small Catechism," 61.

6 Voelz, "Luther's Use of Scripture in the Small Catechism," 61.

APPENDIX D

A Woodcut Sampler

To obtain clear prints of woodcuts from the earliest editions of Luther's Small and Large Catechisms is a difficult task at best. By and large, the biblical narratives portrayed by the woodcuts, along with the contemporary settings in which they were drawn, remained the same from one edition of the catechism to the next. What changed were the details and intricacies of the drawings themselves.

Accordingly, the following woodcuts are intended to give the reader some idea of not only what the woodcuts portrayed, but how they complemented the text of the catechism itself and drew the text into the world of the sixteenth century. The following woodcuts have been compiled from several sources, most notably, *Luther's Small Catechism: A New English Translation Prepared by an Intersynodical Committee* (Philadelphia: United Lutheran Publication House, 1929). Johann Michael Reu, who served on the committee that prepared this anniversary edition, selected the prints from an edition prepared in 1533 by Hermann Guelfferich at Frankfurt on the Main. These pictures were drawn by Hans Brosammer. Those that portrayed different narratives than the woodcuts in 1531 are noted below each woodcut.

First Commandment
Israelites Dancing around the Golden Calf
Exodus 32

Second Commandment
The Blasphemy of Shelomith's Son
Leviticus 24:10–16

Third Commandment
Congregation Listens to the Preacher While Someone Gathers Wood
Numbers 15:32–36

Fourth Commandment
Drunkenness of Noah
Genesis 9:20–27

Fifth Commandment
Cain Murdering Abel
Genesis 4:1–16

Sixth Commandment
David and Bathsheba
2 Samuel 11

Seventh Commandment
Theft of Achan
Joshua 7

Eighth Commandment
Story of Susanna
Daniel 13 (Apocrypha)

Ninth Commandment
Jacob with Laban's Sheep
Genesis 30

Tenth Commandment
Joseph and Potiphar's Wife
Genesis 39

First Article
God Blessing His Creation

Second Article
Christ Dies on the Cross

Third Article
Pentecost
Acts 2

Lord's Prayer
Christ Teaching His Disciples How to Pray
Luke 11

First Petition
Matthew 5 and Luke 7
(In the 1531 edition, this was also used for the "Address.")

Second Petition
Luke 11
(The 1531 edition used the same woodcut for Acts 2
as found in the Third Article.)

Third Petition
Jesus in Gethsemane
Matthew 26
(The 1531 edition portrayed Christ falling under the cross
as he carried it. The Bible text was Matthew 27.)

Fourth Petition
John 6:1–15

Fifth Petition
Matthew 18

Sixth Petition
Matthew 4:1–11

Seventh Petition
Woman Pleading for Daughter Who Is Demon Possessed.
Matthew 15:21–28

Baptism
Matthew 3
(The 1531 edition portrayed the Baptism of an infant.)

Lord's Supper
Mark 14, Luke 22, 1 Corinthians 11

BIBLIOGRAPHY

A Contemporary Translation of Luther's Small Catechism: Study Edition. Philadelphia: Augsburg Fortress, 1994.

A Short Explanation of Dr. Martin Luther's Small Catechism: A Handbook of Christian Doctrine. St. Louis: Concordia Publishing House, 1943.

Amos, Thomas L. "Preaching and the Sermon in Carolingian World." Pages 41–60 in *De Ore Domini: Preacher and the Word in the Middle Ages*. Kalamazoo: Medieval Institute Publications, 1989.

Arand, Charles P. "Classic Catechism—1995." *Concordia Journal* 22 (January 1996): 66–75.

_____. "Does Catechesis in the LCMS Aim for the *Ars Vivendi Fide?*" *Concordia Journal* 22 (January 1996): 57–65.

_____. "Luther on the God Behind the First Commandment." *Lutheran Quarterly* 8 (Winter 1994): 397–424.

_____. "The Lord's Prayer in Luther's Catechisms: The Battle Cry of Faith." *Concordia Journal* 21 (January 1995): 42–65.

Arand, Charles P. and James W. Voelz. "Catechismal Services: A Bridge between Evangelism and Assimilation." *Concordia Journal* 3 (July 1997): 177–91.

Augustine. "Faith and Works." *Treatises on Marriage and Other Subjects*. Pages 221–82 in The Fathers of the Church. Vol. 27. Translated by Sister Marie Liguori. New York: Fathers of the Church, 1955.

_____. *First Catechetical Instruction (De Catechizandis Rudibus)*. Ancient Christian Writers. Translated by Joseph P. Christopher. Westminster, Md.: Newman Press, 1946.

_____. *Enchiridion on Faith, Hope, and Love, The*. Edited by Henry Paolucci. South Bend, Ind.: Gateway Editions, 1961.

Ayo, Nicholas, ed. and trans. *The Sermon-Conferences of St. Thomas Aquinas on the Apostles' Creed*. Notre Dame: University of Notre Dame, 1988.

Bast, Robert James. *Honor Your Fathers: Catechisms and the Emergence of a Patriarchal Ideology in Germany, 1400–1600*. Leiden: E. J. Brill, 1997.

Battenberg, F. W., ed. *Beichtbüchlein des Magisters Johannes Wolff (Lupi)*. Gießen: Verlag von Alfred Topelmann, 1907.

Beintker, Michael. "Das Schöpfercredo in Luthers Kleinem Katechismus." *Neue Zeitschrift für Religionsphilosophie* 31 (January 1989): 1–17.

Bertram, Martin H. "Introduction" to Luther's *Little Prayer Book* (*LW* 43:6). Martin Nicol's chapter, "Katechismusmeditation." Pages 150–67 in *Meditation bei Luther*. Göttingen: Vandenhoeck & Ruprecht, 1984.

Bornkamm, Heinrich. *Luther in Mid-Career, 1521–1530*. Translated by E. Theodore Bachmann. Philadelphia: Fortress Press, 1983.

Bossy, John. *Christianity in the West, 1400–1700*. Oxford: Oxford University Press, 1985.

_____. "Moral Arithmetic: Seven Sins into Ten Commandments." Page 215 in *Conscience and Casuistry in Early Modern Europe*. Edited by Edmund Leites. Cambridge: Cambridge University Press, 1988.

Bradley, Robert I. *The Roman Catechism in the Catechetical Tradition of the Church: The Structure of the Roman Catechism as Illustrative of the "Classic Catechesis.* Lanham, Md.: University Press of America, 1990.

Braune, Wilhelm and Karl Helm. *Althochdeutsches Lesebuch*. 15th ed. Edited by Ernst A. Ebbinghaus. Tübingen: Niemeyer Verlag, 1969.

Brecht, Martin U. *Doctor Luther's Bulla and Reformation: A Look at Luther the Writer*. Valparaiso, Ind.: Valparaiso University Press, 1991.

_____. *Martin Luther: Shaping and Defining the Reformation 1521–1532*. Minneapolis: Fortress Press, 1990.

Brown, Christopher B. "Singing the Gospel: Lutheran Hymns as a Source for the Popular Reception of the Reformation." Unpublished paper.

Burkhardt, C. A. H. *Geschichte der deutschen Kirchen—und Schulvisitationen im Zeitalter der Reformation*. Leipzig: Verlag von Fr. Wilh. Grunow, 1879.

Cohrs, Ferdinand. *Die Evangelische Katechismusversuche vor Luthers Enchiridion I: Die evangelischen Katechismusversuche aus den Jahren 1522–1526*. Berlin: A. Hofmann, 1900; Hildesheim: Georg Olms Verlag, 1978.

Constable, W. John. "Sixteenth Century Catechisms: Their Genesis and Genius." Pages 20–21 in *Teaching the Faith: Luther's Catechisms in Perspective*. Edited by Carl Volz. River Forest, Ill.: Lutheran Educational Association, 1967.

Cyril of Jerusalem, *The Works of St. Cyril of Jerusalem: Procatechesis and Catecheses 1–12, and Catechesis 13–18 and Mystagogical Lectures*. The Fathers of the Church, Vols. 61 and 64. Translated by Leo P. McCauley and Anthony A. Stephenson. Washington: The Catholic University of America Press, 1968.

Dickens, Arthur Geoffrey. *The German Nation and Martin Luther*. New York: Harper & Row, 1974.

Edwards, Jr., Mark U. *Printing, Propaganda, and Martin Luther*. Berkeley: University of California Press, 1994.

Enchiridion of Erasmus, The. Translated and edited by Raymond Himelick. Bloomington: Indiana University Press, 1963.

Fisher, J. D. C. *Christian Initiation: Baptism in the Medieval West*. London: Society for Promoting Christian Knowledge, 1965.

Gatch, Milton McC. "Basic Christian Education from the Decline of Catechesis to the Rise of the Catechisms." Pages 79–108 in *A Faithful Church: Issues in the History of Catechesis* by John H. Westerhoff III and O. C. Edwards, Jr. Wilton, Conn.: Morehouse-Barlow, 1981.

_____. *Preaching and Theology in Anglo-Saxon England: Aelfric and Wulfstan*. Toronto: University of Toronto, 1977.

Geffcken, Johannes. *Der Bildercatechismus des funfzehnten Jahrhunderts und die catechetischen Hauptstücke in dieser Zeit bis auf Luther*. Leipzig: T. O. Weigel, 1855.

Gerson, Jean. *Je croy en la benoiste et sainte Trinité, Oeuvres Complètes*. Pages 206–9 in Vol. VII: L'Oeuvre francaise. Edited by P. Glorieux. Paris: Desclée & Cie, 1966.

Gillhoff, Johannes. *Zur Sprache und Geschichte des kleinen Katechismus*. Leipzig: Verlag der Dürr'schen Buchhandlung, 1909.

Girgensohn, Herbert. *Teaching Luther's Catechism*. 2 Vols. Philadelphia: Muhlenberg Press, 1959.

Göbl, Peter. *Geschichte der Katechese im Abendlande vom Verfalle des Katechumenats bis zum Ende des Mittelalters*. Kempten: Verlag der Joseph Kösl'schen Buchhandlung, 1880.

Goetz, Hans-Werner. *Life in the Middle Ages from the Seventh to the Thirteenth Century*. Notre Dame: University of Notre Dame Press, 1993.

Green, Ian. *The Christian's ABC: Catechisms and Catechizing in England c. 1530–1740*. Oxford: Clarendon Press, 1996.

Gregory of Nyssa: The Lord's Prayer. Ancient Christian Writers. Translated by Hilda C. Graef. Westminster: Newman Press, 1954.

Gritsch, Eric W. "Luther's Catechisms of 1529: Whetstones of the Church." *Lutheran Theological Seminary Bulletin* 60 (1980): 3–14.

Habeck, Irwin J. "Profit and Peril in Preaching on the Catechism." *Wisconsin Lutheran Quarterly* 76 (1979): 133–45.

Haemig, Mary Jane. "Preaching the Catechism: A Transformational Enterprise." *Dialog* 36 (1997): 100–4.

_____. "The Living Voice of the Catechism: German Lutheran Catechetical Preaching, 1530–1580." Ph.D. diss., Harvard, 1996.

Hals, Ronald M. "Luther and the First Commandment: You Belong to Me." *Interpreting Luther's Legacy: Essays in Honor of Edward C. Fendt*. Edited by Fred W. Meuser and Stanley D. Schneider. Minneapolis: Augsburg, 1969.

Hamilton, Bernard. *Religion in the Medieval West*. London: Bernard Hamilton, 1986.

Harmless, William. *Augustine and the Catechumenate*. Collegeville, Minn.: The Liturgical Press, 1995.

Harran, Marilyn. *Martin Luther—Learning for Life*. St. Louis: Concordia Publishing House, 1997.

Hebart, Friedemann. "Introduction." Pages xviii-xix in *Luther's Large Catechism*: Anniversary Translation. Adelaide: Lutheran Publishing House, 1983.

Hendrix, Scott H. "Luther's Impact on the Sixteenth Century." *The Sixteenth Century Journal* 16 (1985): 3–14.

Herlihy, David. *Medieval Households*. Cambridge, Mass.: Harvard University Press, 1985.

Herms, Eilert. *Luthers Auslegung des Dritten Artikels*. Tübingen: J.C.B. Mohr, 1987.

Hütter, Reinhard. "The Twofold Center of Lutheran Ethics: Christian Freedom and God's Commandments." Pages 31–54 in *The Promise of Lutheran Ethics*. Edited by Karen L. Bloomquist and John R. Stumme. Minneapolis: Fortress, 1998.

Janz, Denis. *Three Reformation Catechisms: Catholic, Anabaptist, Lutheran*. New York: Edwin Mellen Press, 1982.

Jetter, Harmut. *Erneuerung des Katechismusunterrichts. Theologische und pädagogische Grundfragen zu Luthers Kleinem Katechismus in der Gegenwart*. Heidelberg: Quelle & Meyer, 1965.

_____. "Katechismuspredigt." *Theologische Realenzykolpädie*. Edited by Gerhard Krause and Gerhard Müller. Berlin: de Gruyter, 1988. Vol 17: 744–86.

Jordahn, Bruno. "Katechismus-Gottesdienst im Reformationsjahrhundert." *Luther: Mitteilungen der Luthergesellschaft* 30 (1959): 76–77.

Jungman, Josef Andreas. *Handing on the Faith: A Manual of Catechetics*. London: Burns & Oates, 1959.

Fraas, Hans-Jürgen, Wolfgang Grünberg, Gerhard Bellinger, and Peter Hauptmann. "Katechismus." Pages 710ff. in *Theologische Realenzyklopädie*. Vol. XVII. Edited by Gerhard Krause & Gerhard Müller. Berlin: de Gruyter, 1988.

Karant-Nunn, Susan C. *Luther's Pastors: The Reformation in the Ernestine Countryside*. Philadelphia: The American Philosophical Society, 1979.

Kelly, J. N. D. *Early Christian Creeds*. 3rd ed. London: Longman Group Limited, 1979.

Kittelson, James M. "Luther the Educational Reformer," Page 101 in *Luther and Learning: The Wittenberg University Luther Symposium*. Edited by Marilyn J. Harran. London and Toronto: Associated University Presses, 1983.

_____. *Luther the Reformer: The Story of the Man and his Career*. Minneapolis: Augsburg, 1986.

_____. "Successes and Failures in the German Reformation: The Report from Strasbourg," *Archiv für Reformationsgeschichte* 73 (1982): 152–75.

Kolb, Robert A. *Teaching God's Children His Teaching: A Guide for the Study of Luther's Catechism*. Crown Publishing, Inc.: Hutchinson, Minn., 1992.

_____. " 'That I May Be his Own': The Anthropology of Luther's Explanation to the Creed," *Concordia Journal* 21 (January 1995): 28–41.

_____. "The Layman's Bible: The Use of Luther's Catechisms in the German Late Reformation." Pages 16–26 in *Luther's Catechisms—450 Years: Essays Commemorating the Small and Large Catechisms of Dr. Martin Luther*. Edited by David Scaer and Robert D. Preus. Fort Wayne, Ind.: Concordia Theological Seminary Press, 1979.

Krodel, Gottfried. "Luther's Work on the Catechism in the Context of Late Medieval Catechetical Literature." *Concordia Journal* 25 (October 1999): 364–404.

Krych, Margaret A. "The Catechism in Christian Education." *Word and World* 10 (1990): 43–47.

Large Catechism. *The Book of Concord*. Edited by Theodore Tappert. Philadelphia: Fortress Press, 1959.

Leaver, Robin A. "Luther's Catechism Hymns: 1. "Lord Keep Us Steadfast in Your Word." *Lutheran Quarterly* XI (Winter 1997): 397–410.

_____. "Luther's Catechism Hymns: 2. "Ten Commandments." *Lutheran Quarterly* XI (Winter 1997): 410–21.

_____. "Luther's Catechism Hymns: 3. Creed." *Lutheran Quarterly* XII (Spring 1998): 79–88.

_____. "Luther's Catechism Hymns: 5. Baptism." *Lutheran Quarterly* XII (Summer 1998): 161–69.

_____. "Luther's Catechism Hymns: 6. Confession." *Lutheran Quarterly* XII (Summer 1998): 171–80.

_____. "Luther's Catechism Hymns: 8. Confessional Substance." *Lutheran Quarterly*, XII (1998): 322.

_____. "The Chorale: Transcending Time and Culture." *Concordia Theological Quarterly* 56 (1992): 123–44.

Leroux, Neil R. "Luther's *am Neujahrstage*: Style as Argument." *Rhetorica* 12 (1994): 1–42.

Lindberg, Carter. *The European Reformations*. Cambridge, Mass.: Blackwell Publishers, 1996.

Loewenich, Walter von. *Martin Luther: The Man and His Work*. Translated by Lawrence W. Denef. Minneapolis: Augsburg, 1982.

Lynch, Joseph H. *The Medieval Church: A Brief History*. London, New York: Longman, 1992.

Mahreholz, C. "Auswahl und Einordnung der Katechismuslieder in den Wittenberger Gesangbüchern seit 1529." Pages 123–32 in *Gestalt und Glaube: Festschrift für Vizepräsident Professor D. Dr. Oskar Söhngen zum 60. Geburtstag am 5. Dezember 1960*. Witten and Berlin, 1960.

Marten, Dennis. "Carthusians." Pages 266–69 in Vol. I: *The Oxford Encyclopedia of the Reformation*. Edited by Hans J. Hillerbrand. New York: Oxford University Press, 1996.

Marthaler, Berard L. *The Catechism Yesterday and Today: The Evolution of a Genre*. Collegeville, MN: The Liturgical Press, 1995.

Marty, Martin E. "The Challenge of Catechesis: The Changing Cultural Landscape." Pages 9–24 in *Formation in the Faith: Catechesis for Tomorrow*. Concordia Seminary Publications, 1997.

_____. "The Future of Catechism." *Currents in Theology and Mission* (1994): 330–31.

_____. *The Hidden Discipline*. St. Louis: Concordia Publishing House, 1962.

Maurer, Wilhelm. *Historical Commentary on the Augsburg Confession*. Translated by H. George Anderson. Philadelphia: Fortress Press, 1986.

_____. *Luthers Lehre von den drei Hierarchien und ihr mittelalterlicher Hintergrund*. München, 1970.

McDonough, Thomas M. *The Law and the Gospel in Luther: A Study of Martin Luther's Confessional Writings*. Oxford: Oxford University Press, 1963.

McKitterick, Rosamond. *The Frankish Church and the Carolingian Reforms, 789–895*. London: Royal Historical Society, 1977.

Meding, Wichmann von. "Luthers Katechismuslieder." *Kerygma und Dogma* 40 (October 1994): 250–71.

Meusel, Carl. *Kirchliches Handlexicon*. Vol. III. Leipzig: Justus Naumann, 1891.

Meyer, Johannes. *Historischer Kommentar zu Luthers Kleinem Katechismus*. Gütersloh: C. Bertelsmann, 1929.

Mildenberger, Friedrich. *Theology of the Lutheran Confessions*. Translated by Erwin L. Lueker. Philadelphia: Fortress Press, 1986.

Mitchell, Leonel L. "The Development of Catechesis in the Third and Fourth Centuries: From Hippolytus to Augustine." Pages 49–78 in *A Faithful Church: Issues in the History of Catechesis*. Edited by John H. Westerhoff III and O. C. Edwards, Jr. Wilton, Conn.: Morehouse-Barlow, 1981.

Myers, W. David. *Poor, Sinning Folk*. Ithaca, N.Y.: Cornell University Press, 1996.

Nestingen, James Arne. "Preaching the Catechism," *Word and World* 10:1 (Winter 1990): 33–42.

_____. "The Catechism's *Simul*," *Word and World* 3 (Fall 1983): 366–67.

Ong, Walter. *Orality and Literacy: The Technologizing of the Word*. London: Routledge, 1982.

Ozment, Steven E. *Age of Reform: an Intellectual and Religious History of Late Medieval and Reformation Europe.* New Haven: Yale University, 1980.

_____. *"Homo Viator:* Luther and Late Medieval Theology." Pages 142–54 in *The Reformation in Medieval Perspective.* Chicago: Quadrangle Books, 1971.

_____. *The Reformation in the Cities: The Appeal of Protestantism to Sixteenth-Century Germany and Switzerland.* New Haven: Yale University Press, 1975.

Peters, Albrecht. "Die Bedeutung der Katechismen Luthers innerhalb der Bekenntnis-schriften. Eine Thesenreihe." *Luther: Zeitschrift der Luther-Gesellschaft* 50 (1979): 28.

_____. "Die Theologie der Katechismen Luthers anhand der Zuordnung ihrer Hauptstücke." *Lutherjahrbuch.* Göttingen: Vandenhoeck & Ruprecht, 1976.

_____. *Kommentar zu Luthers Katechismen: Band 1: Die Zehn Gebote.* Edited by Gottfried Seebaß. Göttingen: Vandehoeck & Ruprecht, 1990.

Pieper, Paul. *Deutsche National-Literatur. Historisch-kritische Ausgabe.* Edited by Joseph Kürschner. Berlin and Stuttgart, 1884.

Piepkorn, Arthur Carl. "Suggested Principles for a Hermeneutics of the Lutheran Symbols." *Concordia Theological Monthly* 29 (January 1958): 1–21.

Ratzinger, Joseph Cardinal and Christoph Schönborn. *Introduction to the Catechism of the Catholic Church.* San Francisco: Ignatius Press, 1994.

Rentschka, P. *Die Dekalogkatechese des h. Augustinus: ein Beitrag zur Geschichte des Dekalogs.* Kempten, 1905.

Reu, Johann Michael. *Dr. Martin Luther's Small Catechism: A History of its Origin, Its Distribution and its Use.* Chicago: Wartburg, 1929.

_____. "Principles for the Preparation of an Expounded Catechism." Cited in Paul I. Johnston. "An Assessment of the Educational Philosophy of Johann Michael Reu Using the Hermeneutic Paradigms of J. F. Hebart and of J. C. K. von Hofmann and the Erlangen School." Urbana, Ill.: University of Illinois, 1989.

Robinson, Paul. "'For the Salvation of Simple Christian People': Preaching the Faith in the Middle Ages." Unpublished paper delivered at the Theological Symposium "Formation in the Faith: Catechesis for Tomorrow," held at Concordia Seminary, St. Louis, Missouri, May 6–7, 1997.

_____. "What is Meant by Daily Bread?": Luther's Catechisms and the Medieval Sermonic Tradition." *Lutheran Quarterly* (Winter, 1999–2000): 435–47.

Rosin, Robert. "Christians and Culture: Finding Place in Clio's Mansions." *Christ and Culture: The Church in a Post-Christian America.* Symposium papers. No. 4. St. Louis: Concordia Seminary Monograph Series, 1996.

Rupp, Gordon. "Protestant Spirituality in the First Age of the Reformation." Pages 155–70 in *Popular Belief and Practice.* Edited by G. J. Cuming and Derek Baker. Cambridge: Cambridge University Press, 1972.

Russell, William R. *The Schmalkald Articles: Luther's Theological Testament.* Minneapolis: Fortress Press, 1994.

Saint Caesarius of Arles: Sermons or Admonitions on Various Topics. Translated by Sister Mary Magadeleine Mueller. Fathers of the Church. New York: Fathers of the Church, Inc., 1956.

Saint Peter Chrysologus: Selected Sermons and Saint Valerian Homilies. Translated by George E. Ganss. Fathers of the Church. New York: Father of the Church, Inc, 1953.

Schulz, Robert C. "The Theological Significance of the Order of the Chief Parts in Luther's Catechism." *Teaching the Faith: Luther's Catechisms in Perspective*. Edited by Carl Volz. River Forest, Ill.: Lutheran Educational Association, 1967.

Scribner, R. W. *For the Sake of Simple Folk: Popular Propaganda for the German Reformation*. Oxford: Clarendon Press, 1994.

_____. "Oral Culture and the Diffusion of Reformation Ideas." Pages 49–70 in *Popular Culture and Popular Movements in Reformation Germany*. London: The Hambledon Press, 1987.

Sehling, Emil, ed. *Die Evangelischen Kirchenordnungen des XVI Jahrhunderts*. Leipzig: O. R. Reisland, 1902.

Siirala, Aarne. *Gottes Gebot bei Martin Luther: Eine Untersuchung der Theologie Luthers unter besonderer Berücksichtigung des ersten Hauptstückes im Grossen Katechismus*. Schriften der Luther-Agricola-Gesellschaft 11. Helsinki, 1956.

Slattery, Joseph Anthony. "The Catechetical Use of the Decalogue from the End of the Catechumenate through the Late Medieval Period." Ph.D. diss. Catholic University of America, 1979.

The Small Catechism. 1986 Translation. St. Louis: Concordia, 1986.

Spencer, H. Leith. *English Preaching in the Middle Ages*. Oxford: Clarendon Press, 1993.

Spinks, Bryan. *Luther's Liturgical Criteria and his Reform of the Canon of the Mass*. Notts [England]: Grove Books, 1982.

_____. "Luther's Taufbüchlein." *Liturgical Review* (November 1975): 17–20 and (May 1996): 13–21.

Spitz, Lewis W. "Further Lines of Inquiry for the Study of 'Reformation and Pedagogy.'" Pages 294–306 in *The Pursuit of Holiness in Late Medieval and Renaissance Religion*. Edited by Charles Trinkaus with Heiko A. Oberman. Leiden: E. J. Brill, 1974.

Steinmeyer, E. v. *Die kleinerer althochdeutsch Sprachdenkmaler*. Berlin, 1916.

Stiller, Günther. *Johann Sebastian Bach and Liturgical Life in Leipzig*. St. Louis: Concordia Publishing House, 1984.

Strauss, Gerald. *Luther's House of Learning: Indoctrination of the Young in the German Reformation*. Baltimore and London: The Johns Hopkins University Press, 1978.

Strayer, Joseph R., ed. *Dictionary of the Middle Ages*. New York: Charles Scribner's Sons, 1988.

Swanson, R. N. *Religion and Devotion in Europe, c. 1215-c. 1515*. Cambridge, England: Cambridge University Press, 1995.

Tentler, Thomas N. *Sin and Confession on the Eve of the Reformation*. Princeton: Princeton University Press, 1977.

Theodore of Mopsuestia. *Catechetical Homilies: Commentary of Theodore of Mopsuestia on the Lord's Prayer, and on the Sacraments of Baptism and the Eucharist*. Woodbrook Studies, Vol. VI 11–16. Cambridge: W. Heffer and Sons, Ltd., 1933.

Thompson, Virgil. "The Promise of Catechesis." *Lutheran Quarterly* 4:3 (Autumn 1990): 259–70.

Trigg, Jonathan D. *Baptism in the Theology of Martin Luther*. Leiden: E. J. Brill, 1994.

Veit, Patrice. *Das Kirchenlied in der Reformation Martin Luthers: Eine Thematische und Semantischen Untersuchung*. Wiesbaden: Steiner Verlag, 1986.

Voelz , James W. "Luther's Use of Scripture in the Small Catechism." Pages 55–64 in *Luther's Catechisms—450 Years: Essays Commemorating the Small and Large Catechisms of Dr. Martin Luther.* Edited by David P. Scaer and Robert D. Preus. Fort Wayne, Ind.: Concordia Theological Seminary Press, 1979.

Weidenhiller, P. Egino. *Untersuchungen zur deutschsprachigen katechetischen Literatur des späten Mittelalters.* München: C. H. Beck'sche Verlagsbuchhandlung, 1965.

Weinrich, William C. "Early Christian Catechetics: An Historical and Theological Construction." Pages 65–73 in *Luther's Catechisms—450 Years: Essays Commemorating the Small and Large Catechisms of Dr. Martin Luther.* Edited by David P. Scaer and Robert D. Preus. Fort Wayne, Ind.: Concordia Theological Seminary Press, 1979.

Wengert, Timothy J., ed. *A Contemporary Translation of Luther's Small Catechism: Study Edition.* Philadelphia: Augsburg Fortress, 1994.

_____. "'Fear and Love' in the Ten Commandments" *Concordia Journal* 21 (January 1995): 14–27.

_____. "Forming the Faith through Catechisms: Moving to Luther and Today." Pages 25–48 in *Formation in the Faith: Catechesis for Tomorrow.* Concordia Seminary Publications Symposium Papers. No. 7. St. Louis: Concordia Seminary, 1997.

_____. *Law and Gospel: Philip Melanchthon's Debate with John Agricola of Eisleben over Poenitentia.* Grand Rapids: Baker Books, 1998.

_____. "Luther on Children: Baptism and the Fourth Commandment." *Dialog* 37 (Summer 1998): 185–89.

_____. "Luther's Catechisms and the Lord's Supper." *Word and World* 17 (Winter 1997): 54–60.

_____. "Philip Melanchthon's 1522 Annotations on Romans and the Lutheran Origin of Rhetorical Criticism." Pages 118–40 in *Biblical Interpretation in the Era of the Reformation.* Edited by Richard A. Muller and John L. Thompson. Grand Rapids: Eerdmans, 1996.

_____. "Wittenberg's Earliest Catechism." *Lutheran Quarterly*, n.s., 7 (1993): 247–60.

Wilkinson, John, ed. *Egeria's Travels.* London: S.P.C.K., 1971.

Wills, Elbert Vaughan. "The Elementary-School Ordinance From the Württemberg Church Code of 1559." *Lutheran Church Quarterly* II (July 1929).

Winger, Thomas. "Orality and the Interpretation of Written Documents." "Orality as the Key to Understanding Apostolic Proclamation in the Epistles," Th.D. Diss. St. Louis: Concordia Seminary, 1997.

Wingren, Gustav. *Creation and Law.* Translated by Ross Mackenzie. Edinburgh: Oliver and Boyd, 1961.

Works of St. Cyril of Jerusalem: Procatechesis and Catecheses 1–12, and Catechesis 13–18 and Mystagogical Lectures, The. Translated by Leo P. McCauley and Anthony A. Stephenson. The Fathers of the Church. Vols. 61 and 64. Washington: The Catholic University of America Press, 1968.